Negotiating the Personal in Creative Writing

NEW WRITING VIEWPOINTS
Series Editor: Graeme Harper, *University of Wales, Bangor, Wales, UK*

The overall aim of this series is to publish books which will ultimately inform teaching and research, but whose primary focus is on the analysis of creative writing practice and theory. There will also be books which deal directly with aspects of creative writing knowledge, with issues of genre, form and style, with the nature and experience of creativity and with the learning of creative writing. They will all have in common a concern with excellence in application and in understanding, with creative writing practitioners and their work, and with informed analysis of creative writing as process as well as completed artefact.

Full details of all the books in this series and of all our other publications can be found on http://www.multilingual-matters.com, or by writing to Multilingual Matters, St Nicholas House, 31–34 High Street, Bristol BS1 2AW, UK.

NEW WRITING VIEWPOINTS
Series Editor: Graeme Harper

Negotiating the Personal in Creative Writing

Carl Vandermeulen

MULTILINGUAL MATTERS
Bristol • Buffalo • Toronto

Dedication

I dedicate this work to my best teachers, who took teaching personally, who respected the persons entering their classrooms and who expected us to take a personal interest in the work that brought us together: Dorothy Edwards (kindergarten), Stanley Wiersma (Calvin College), Wayne Knutson (University of South Dakota), Robert Brooke, Joy Ritchie and Kate Ronald (University of Nebraska).

Library of Congress Cataloging in Publication Data
A catalog record for this book is available from the Library of Congress.
Vandermeulen, Carl.
Negotiating the Personal in Creative Writing/Carl Vandermeulen.
New Writing Viewpoints
Includes bibliographical references.
1. Creative writing–Study and teaching. 2. Writing centers.
PE1404.V36 2011
808'.042071–dc232011028013

British Library Cataloguing in Publication Data
A catalogue entry for this book is available from the British Library.

ISBN-13: 978-1-84769-438-6 (hbk)
ISBN-13: 978-1-84769-437-9 (pbk)

Multilingual Matters
UK: St Nicholas House, 31–34 High Street, Bristol BS1 2AW, UK.
USA: UTP, 2250 Military Road, Tonawanda, NY 14150, USA.
Canada: UTP, 5201 Dufferin Street, North York, Ontario M3H 5T8, Canada.

Copyright © 2011 Carl Vandermeulen.

All rights reserved. No part of this work may be reproduced in any form or by any means without permission in writing from the publisher.

The policy of Multilingual Matters/Channel View Publications is to use papers that are natural, renewable and recyclable products, made from wood grown in sustainable forests. In the manufacturing process of our books, and to further support our policy, preference is given to printers that have FSC and PEFC Chain of Custody certification. The FSC and/or PEFC logos will appear on those books where full certification has been granted to the printer concerned.

Typeset by The Charlesworth Group

Contents

Acknowledgements vii
Introduction: Negotiating the Personal and Interpersonal ix

1 Considering Where We're Coming From 1
2 The Workshop: 'More or Less Unfortunate Misunderstandings' 22
3 Reflection and the Dialogic Self 46
4 Response in Writers' Groups 68
5 Teacher Response to Student Writing.................... 86
6 Negotiating Authority as Teachers, Models, Mentors 113
7 Problems and Crises in Relationships.................... 137
8 Resolving Dilemmas of Grading 172
9 Constructing the Practice and Identity of 'Writer' 197

References 221

Acknowledgements

That writing is a collaborative rather than an individual achievement is evident most of all to an author finishing a book. Here are some of those to whom I'm grateful:

- To Anna Roderick and Graeme Harper for their confidence in my work and for the opportunity I now have to see it in the excellent company of the other contributions to creative writing studies that make up the New Writing Viewpoints series from Multilingual Matters.
- To students in my creative writing classes at Northwestern College (Iowa) who consented to my use of their work, and especially to the students in the 2000 and 2002 classes in Reading and Writing Poetry who agreed to be interviewed in order to help me understand the mysterious interpersonal dynamics that can occur among those collaborating to become writers of the artistic genres.
- To my colleague Joonna Trapp, who sat in on my Y2K class, helped me reflect upon what was happening in it, interviewed most of the students afterwards, responded to drafts of chapters and all along offered the kind of wholehearted encouragement that has earned her the gratitude of hundreds of students and colleagues.
- To students Brina Wiuff and Susanne Stahl Kosec for studying my 2002 classes and writing conference papers with me about my courses.
- To other colleagues, especially Amy McCann, Barbara Turnwall, Kim Van Es, Joel Westerholm and Jeff and Karen Barker.
- To Northwestern College, for a $10,000 research grant that enabled me to hire a student assistant and to travel and interview fellow creative writing teachers in the Midwest.
- To Hannah Dutt Elder, my student assistant, for help with contacting teachers and for invaluable help with thinking through what they were telling us.
- To creative writing teachers who responded to my survey and follow-up email, and especially to those who welcomed me into their classes and took time from busy lives for an interview. I am

most indebted to Jim Heynen, Gina Franco, Carolyn Holbrook, Joey Horstman, Anna Leahy, Mary Swander, Jill Baumgaertner, Laura Apol, Martin Cockroft, Barbara Bogue, Jack Ridl, Andy Mozina, Nicole Mazzarella, Lisa Percy, Ryan Pendell and Eliot Khalil Wilson.
- To Cobus and Alida Du Preez and to Fred Hoffman, all of Tzaneen, Limpopo, South Africa, for offering their homes as places to live and write and for providing their good company as well as the rousing accompaniment of vervet monkeys, baboons, praying mantises, spotted owls, louries and hadedas.
- To my wife, Amy Fichter, a photographer and a professor of life drawing, for countless conversations about the art of teaching in the arts and for sharing the conviction that this teaching humanly matters.

Introduction
Negotiating the Personal and Interpersonal

> *The interaction that goes on in teaching is not just between minds and information but also between persons, even in the university setting. If our job is partly teaching, not just research, then we have to care about relationships and persons.*
>
> Peter Elbow (1990: 207)

I began this writing on sabbatical in South Africa, in a region almost as hazardous as it is fascinating. A short walk from where I lived in sub-tropical Limpopo runs the Ramadipa River, its brief meander shrouded by towering trees, its banks obscured by tangled grass. I walked through its bordering ribbon of jungle on an abandoned stretch of highway to a crumbling bridge over the river, railings on both sides stripped away. Nearby, down a just-visible two-track, a clearing set in a bend in the river held a huge picnic table and *braai* (barbecue) – a wayside abandoned along with that stretch of highway.

I walked there again and again for the mystery of the place. But I always approached with caution because my host had warned, 'Be watchful,' adding two particulars: 'Hippos sometimes come up this far, and you don't want to get caught between a hippo and his water'; and 'If you go out in the evening, wear shoes and jeans because of the snakes.' I learned that 'the snakes' include the green mamba, the black mamba, the spitting cobra and the lazy puff adder, who turns aggressive if you step on him. All are venomous, as is a tiny tree snake that mimics a branch. Out there somewhere too is the python, not venomous, also not tiny.

The personal and interpersonal wilderness of the creative writing course holds its own fascinations but also its hazards, many of them hidden. Things can go wrong and people can get hurt. One of my motives for this writing can be put in a word that also comes from South Africa. Post-Apartheid leaders Nelson Mandela and Bishop Desmond Tutu lifted up the ideal of *ubuntu*, which means that pain caused to one person is felt by all, including the one who inflicts it, just as an act of generosity to one benefits all, perhaps especially the benefactor. So in the spirit of *ubuntu*, I say that for our students to become good makers of art that does some human good, we need to provide good and humane places for their becoming, as artists and as persons. That means we also need to be watchful – and to know what to watch *for*.

Negotiating the Personal

Concern for the becoming of persons characterizes composition more than creative writing. The emergence of the field of composition several decades ago brought about a shift in emphasis from the written product to the whole process of writing, including finding material, exploring means of invention, drafting, getting response and revising. As Robert Brooke, Ruth Mirtz and Rick Evans (1994: 38) observe in *Small Groups in Writing Workshops: Invitations to a Writer's Life*, this shift changed a teacher's focus from the text to the writer and to *experiences* that help students construct the identity of writer. Wendy Bishop (1997: 43) says that teachers in composition made their courses more therapeutic in the sense that they focused on helping writers gain confidence and find their voices.

For the most part, this shift has not occurred in creative writing. The dominant full-class workshop approach, as Tom C. Hunley (2007) also observes, provides a forum for critiquing near-finished texts, but leaves too little class time for the experiences that help writers develop skills, find ideas, gain confidence and work out a process that suits the genre. I share his belief that introductory courses need to focus on fundamental – and personal – kinds of growth that enable the process of writing and of becoming a writer. That is one way I mean my title – that to really *teach* creative writing is to negotiate the personal.

It's worth adding that a concern for the growth of persons was a generative force in creative writing. According to Paul Dawson (2005: 53–56) in *Creative Writing and the New Humanities*, the Progressive Education Movement, with its emphasis on growth through personal expression, naturally turned to composing in the artistic genres. Creative writing got its start, at least in the schools, because doing artistic work was believed to be good for learners, not because of a perceived need to help outstanding writers become published authors. D.G. Myers (1996), in *The Elephants Teach*, confirms that creative writing arose as a 'discipline of education' (p. 6), a discipline that 'stood for teaching' (p. 7) rather than for the professionalization of literary study, a discipline 'founded on the humanistic argument that literature is not a genre of knowledge but a mode of aesthetic and spiritual cultivation' (p. 7).

My conviction is that the teaching of creative writing, at least in undergraduate courses and particularly in introductory courses, should retain that early emphasis. I'm pleased if a few of my best students go on to study writing in grad school and become writers, teachers of writing or both. But I'm as pleased if writers of ordinary talents gain a heightened awareness of the familiar world around them, recover a fascination for and new awareness of language, gain access to marvelous writers whose works they would not otherwise have known or been able to read – and produce work that surprises others and themselves. A good creative writing class is a dialogue that welcomes all voices, respects all persons.

Negotiating the Interpersonal

Because students become writers largely through relationships with and responses from both teachers and peers, and because the writing our students do *matters* to them, to teach creative writing is also to negotiate the *interpersonal*. Remember that most of our students have chosen our courses, often because they think of themselves as writers, so this choice places their *identity* at risk. In addition many writers view their writing as an expression of self and of what they experienced rather than as a means for a *reader* to gain significant experience. And now they have come to a *course* where writing that some like to call 'heartwork' will be analyzed and interpreted, frequently misapprehended and at some point evaluated.

Even when writers do become willing to put their work out for others to experience, the response from peers is likely to stir up a paradoxical mix of emotions: a need to be accepted; a desire to have one's writing understood; and at the same time a wish to impress – perhaps even to be the most impressive writer in the group. Part of the challenge for teachers is enabling a diverse set of writers, each torn by contradictory feelings and motives, to work together, responding to others' writing in ways that are genuinely helpful, sometimes transformative, for the writing as well as for the writer.

We may hesitate to say so, but becoming a writer often depends primarily upon the interpersonal relationship with the writer-teacher, a relationship highly complex in its distances, as well as in its attractions and resistances, and thus in the range and depth of emotions it evokes. Although some of the time we teach at a distance typical for teachers (leading discussion of published writing, giving assignments, offering advice on craft), more of the time than is true for most colleagues in language and literature we teach close-up, often one-to-one, not just talking but *listening*, and even listening for what writers want to say and haven't yet managed to say, perhaps, in addition, helping them to become aware of gaps and contradictions that hint at thoughts, fears and desires that elude their conscious awareness. You might say – and prefer not to say – that we have something like a counseling relationship with at least some of our students, coming to understand them at a depth few of their other teachers approach. Think how much it matters to be *understood*. Who cannot quickly list the names of people who have deeply understood them in ways that helped them know themselves?

Complicating this relationship, we who teach the arts are also expected to live what we teach, not only to enable us to ground our assignments and our responses in our own artistic experience, but also to let students glimpse and perhaps identify with the life of an artist. We may shrug off the mantle of Model Writer; yet recall how *we* needed teachers who so fascinated us as persons and artists that we wanted to be like them and have a life like we imagined theirs must be. So it shouldn't surprise us that some of our own students want to become the writer and person that our performance of self evokes for them. They may even suppose that we possess mysterious powers to effect their transformation.

Adding contradiction to complication is the location of creative writing within academia. To compose a play, essay, poem or story, students must submit to the materiality of language, give way to the play of words. Such play cannot be contrived or controlled. Yet in a context of assignments, deadlines and grades, students have learned to need control. Worse, creative writing students are more likely to experience their teachers as contradictory because as agents of academic institutions that sell certification, we are required to do what other coaches, counselors and models steer clear of: rate members of our classroom community on a Hot-or-Not scale. We do so, fully aware that a grade less than 'A' may wound those who cherished our understanding and admiration, but probably not realizing that those who saw us as their Artist-Hero may view such a grade as a maneuver to spurn them in order to reserve for ourselves the place of greatest distinction in the classroom. Such suspicion of betrayal will cool close relationships – and may even spiral into a rivalry that is mystifying to both sides. Ironically, such a turnabout is more likely to occur where it is least expected – with teachers who think of themselves as listeners, encouragers or collaborators and who thus fail to see that these ways of taking students *personally* actually raise the stakes, making some students want so desperately to write well that they shut down, unable to write a word for fear of the response. Teachers close to them can make the most unkindest cut of all.

Mapping the Terrain of Our Classrooms

One teacher in comparing her criticism class with her creative writing workshop acknowledged that 'the prep time on a workshop is much less' but that 'the emotions around teaching a workshop are 20 times as high. Each one is different. I never know what it is going to be like when I go into them' (Spahr, 2004). Vividly confirming her experience is a little story in Sandra Desjardins's (2004) syllabus for 'Creative Writing' under the heading 'That thing called insecurity':

> Every semester, almost every member of our group comes to my office at some time or another and tells me that everyone else in the class is so accomplished and brilliant and that he/she feels so unaccomplished and unbrilliant. At this point, the person usually cries, freezes up, yells at me, rips up writing, and/or emits various foul condemnations of writing. Exhausting as this is for me, I have come to accept this as part of the frustration of writing, and the anxiety of going down into the psyche; and it is a natural part of the process that you might be going through as a developing writer during the semester. The point is this: you don't know how truly good your own writing is and how insecure everyone else is. Remember that.

I could hardly ask for stronger confirmation that to teach creative writing is to negotiate the personal.

But *negotiation* includes questioning our own practice along with the assumptions behind it. So I would value a conversation with Desjardins about whether such extreme responses are necessarily 'part of the frustration of *writing*'. Perhaps they reveal frustration with the *means* by which students are learning to write – such as too-early reliance on the full-class workshop or on critique as the expected mode of response. I'd also ask her why she thinks that 'the anxiety of going down into the psyche' is connected to students' concern that the others are better writers. Does taking risks of self-exposure also heighten doubts about capability?

Such questions illustrate that our teaching calls for a thoughtful analysis, aided by conversations with teachers who face similar problems, and informed by studies that help us name and know our experience. Most of us have dedicated years of time and attention, much of it in formal education, to becoming readers and writers; but few of us got as much help with constructing the identity and composing the practice of *teacher*. One way our field differs from composition is that more teachers there have engaged seriously with pedagogy, by which I mean not techniques for teaching so much as theoretical and critical perspectives that can ground our reflections about students' learning, about what it is to teach, even about our personae as teachers.

When pedagogy is understood this way, nobody needs it more than creative writing teachers, not only because our students' learning depends as much upon emotion as upon intellect, but also because our highly personal and interpersonal teaching occurs within institutions that resist or exclude the personal and the emotional. Yet Patrick Bizzaro (1993: xv), in *Responding to Student Poems: Applications of Critical Theory*, says that poet-teachers rely instead on their own experience as writers and as students, much of it gained in classrooms where teachers did not talk about their practices. Consequently, their teaching is likely to include 'a wide range of activities, some beneficial to students, others not, but almost all of them unexamined as tools of instruction'. And why have these tools not been examined? He writes:

> Generally we have left determination of how to safely enter, return from, and lead others back into the realm of poetry in the hands of a very few. Such territory has long been seen as sacred, and therefore beyond the scrutiny of any except the acknowledged experts. There are, for certain, no mapmakers among us to ease our anxiety over this journey.

Well, we do have a few mapmakers. Bizzaro is one, and he draws upon William Stafford. Victor Hugo and Donald Murray also described their practice and their theory. More recently, and at greater depth, Wendy Bishop and Katharine Haake have done the same. Scholars in composition such as Peter Elbow, Lad Tobin and Robert Brooke have also charted regions our field shares with theirs. Others in both creative writing and composition are cited in the following pages.

It was Bishop (1997) who did the most to 'ease our anxiety over this journey'. She also issued the particular challenge to which this book responds:

> In my years as a student and teacher of writing, I've often wished that I had been given more encouragement for investigating the personal, therapeutic, and affective aspects of our field. Daily, I find I need to know more about the least talked about and least researched areas of writing – how writing includes and celebrates the personal and how authoring, writing instruction, and program administration are thoroughly connected to our personalities

We in creative writing have resisted investigating the personal, Bishop supposes, because we don't know enough about therapeutic processes or remain unsure how they might be applied to our teaching. She goes so far as to propose 'a course of study that includes introductions to personality theory, gender studies, psychoanalytic concepts, and basic counseling, even if such study mainly confirms that there are large differences between a teacher/administrator's and therapist's roles' (p. 143).

This book applies several areas of Bishop's 'course of study' to choices we make and problems we encounter while helping persons become writers in the artistic genres. I pass along practices and perspectives of thoughtful teachers in our field, offer some of my own practices and thinking and bring in the most reliable ways of finding our way that I can locate in creative writing pedagogy, composition theory, psychology and cultural theory.

A particularly intractable problem

Most of us can identify with the response of Srikanth Reddy (2004) to my asking why pedagogy had had little influence on his teaching:

> I guess I just haven't had any exposure to composition theory and creative writing pedagogy so far. I've pretty much been dropped into the classroom and allowed to sink or swim on my own. But I've had many wonderful teachers when in college and graduate school, and I try to model my teaching on their techniques and strengths. In the end, I don't feel like I missed out terribly by not being exposed to composition theory and creative writing pedagogy because my own classes seem to work pretty well without such a background. I feel like a good teacher will figure these things out pretty well on their own by being attentive, thoughtful, and creative – and by consulting their fellow teachers for advice and counsel. But if I ever did feel like I encountered a particularly intractable problem in the classroom, I certainly wouldn't hesitate to check out some books on comp theory or creative writing pedagogy; in the end, whatever helps seems worthwhile to explore.

Figuring things out on my own is usually my preference too. Yet pedagogy attracts me because it offers the fascinations, perspectives and insights of fellow teachers who have observed and thought both carefully and provocatively about learners and scenes of learning (revealing, for one thing, that we are never 'on our own' in figuring out our teaching but are ourselves a text written upon and revised by long experience as students and as writers). Inspired by their wondering and guided by their perspectives, I have spent long hours pondering what was happening in my classes. I even wrote a dissertation that was a study of my teaching of first-year writing.

One result is that I *assumed* that I had my classroom persona and approach pretty well thought out. Nevertheless, I encountered what Reddy mentions as a 'particularly intractable problem' – a poetry class that I expected to go well because I knew and admired many of the students who had signed up for it, including several who were my advisees. I wanted to teach that class better than I had taught the course before. But I did not stop to consider that these students also respected me, wanted to write well for me, and doubted they could meet the expectations they imagined I must have for them. Nor did I consider the confusion they would feel when their adviser and advocate also became their evaluator. Once the course began, they also found themselves surrounded by others whose writing seemed more eloquent than their own. So they tried harder and I tried harder until eventually all of us were trying so hard that our words failed us, lurching into circularity, lumbering along or lapsing into silence.

Complicating matters, each side, certain that they *meant* well, blamed the other, and once the blaming started, I and a few students nearly turned into our evil twin.

That was the motivating incident for this book. The class wasn't a disaster, but we suffered enough for me to promise the students who were most affected that I would re-visit what had happened to us, analyze it and try to tell a true story about it.

As I carried out this promise, I encountered potentially destructive dynamics that must operate to varying degrees in any academic course in creative writing – double binds, transference, mimetic rivalry and mimetic contagion (all explored in Chapter 7). I also became aware of a powerful paradox: choices I had consciously made to respond to writers more personally, to offer them more support – in sum, to try to establish what O'Reilley (1993) calls 'the peaceable classroom' – had actually *added* to the hazards for some students by raising the stakes (see Vandermeulen, 2005).

Consulting fellow teachers for advice and counsel

My experience naturally led me to wonder whether other teachers of creative writing had encountered similar problems. To identify good subjects to interview about personal aspects of our teaching, I constructed a survey to which 150 creative writing teachers responded. Fascinated with their responses, I emailed follow-up questions, and many teachers sent thoughtful and generous replies. Some attached syllabi, assignments and handouts; 35 agreed to personal interviews and nine of those invited me to sit in on a class session. As a result, this book offers the good company of these teachers' voices, saying in different ways what Randy VanderMey (2004) put succinctly as: 'Forging relationships with some of the college's most difficult personalities but brilliant minds is one of the greatest pleasures I know in teaching, the hope for and dedication to which causes me to return year after year.'

I also found a benefit I had not anticipated: with a complete survey (and sometimes syllabi) I could get a read on a teacher's teaching. I noticed that some teachers' practice had been carefully composed and revised, in light of powerful ways of thinking about the range of experiences that enable a group of students to become writers; however, the text of others' teaching reads like a rough draft, sometimes including practices that appeared to contradict each other or the teacher's stated goals. I often asked follow-up questions to probe those gaps. I hope that one result is that readers of this book will develop a greater fascination with reading the text of their teaching and revising it toward greater depth and coherence.

Teachers and prospective teachers who care about those 'difficult personalities' who have the desire and energy to do strong artistic work are also the ones I imagine as my readers, especially teachers still finding their own way, or those who continue to revise their approach just as they ask students to revise work they care about.

The scope of the survey

Because I originally constructed the survey to identify subjects for interviews, and because time and money for travel are always limited, most invitations went to teachers in Midwest states – from the Dakotas and Nebraska, east to Ohio and Michigan. I used email addresses of faculty that college and university websites identified as teachers of creative writing. The survey included a space to list email addresses of other teachers whom the respondent thought might respond, and that gave me several more names. When I saw how valuable the survey responses themselves were for my study, I broadened geographical representation by searching for creative writing syllabi on the internet and sending an invitation to the teacher.

Thus the survey does not draw upon a random sampling of the US and Canada, let alone of other parts of the world where creative writing is commonly taught such as the UK, Australia and South Africa. On the other hand, I doubt that a more careful sampling of a wider population would get strikingly different results. Institutions and students likely vary from place to place, but creative writing *teachers* in the Midwest are probably not that much different from teachers in other parts of the world, although teachers in the UK and Australia appear less inclined to claim that creative writing cannot be taught, so they appear to share a greater interest in thinking and talking about ways to teach it.

Because the survey asked for thinking about teaching practices, it stands to reason that it would be ignored by most of those who view teaching only as something they do but not as something they think about. Thus, when I use the survey to generalize about our profession, it is more accurate to say that I am generalizing about mostly Midwestern teachers of creative writing who view teaching and learning as worthy of examination. Several teachers even added to their survey response a comment indicating their pleasure in having the opportunity to think about practices that they had taken for granted. Patrick Hicks (2004a) wrote, 'Getting me to think about these things is self-servingly beneficial.' Mary Biddinger (2004b) concluded a detailed reply with, 'Sorry to ramble, but this is such an interesting subject'. This book everywhere illustrates the benefits and pleasures of talking with colleagues, visiting their classes and seeking out their counsel.

Overview of the Book

This exploration of the personal in our teaching begins, in Chapter 1, with who we are as writer-teachers, including the influences that have formed us, the stated and tacit goals that shape our teaching and the 'artistic personality'.

The next four chapters seek ways of responding that are likely to be transformative for beginning writers. Chapter 2 questions three practices widely accepted in our teaching: the full-class workshop, early emphasis on critique over other kinds of response and the tradition of the silent writer. I prefer an active writer, questioning her writing in order to set some of the agenda for response. Writers best learn to question by writing reflections about their writing that are addressed to their peer responders and teacher. This will be covered in Chapter 3, which also discusses how reflection makes creative writing *teachable* – by making writers more open to response, by getting them response they can use and by giving teachers a window into their thinking and feeling about their writing.

Introduction: Negotiating the Personal and Interpersonal

When writers learn to set an agenda for response, small writers' groups are more productive for beginners than the workshop. This will be seen in Chapter 4, which also illustrates ways of setting up groups and training them in reader-response so that their members are more able to support each other as persons and writers, especially early in the composing process. Chapter 5 proposes that teachers should also primarily respond as readers and in other ways *accompany* writers, not just critique their finished writing. The chapter also explores how teacher response can interact with response in writers' groups and how one-to-one conferences contribute to the process of becoming a writer.

Chapter 6 discusses the various kinds of authority we need to negotiate within mentoring and master-apprentice relationships. Chapter 7 explores the sometimes paradoxical interpersonal dynamics that can develop within such relationships. And Chapter 8 looks at a particular problem associated with the location of creative writing within academia – the expectation that teachers come up with a legitimate and meaningful grade.

Chapter 9 presents ways teachers help students form the identity of writer – keeping a journal, learning to observe and remember, and telling the story of the journey of becoming that the course enabled them to construct for themselves.

The book leaves out one aspect of the personal – what to do with the highly personal and 'risky' writing our students sometimes produce and how to respond to the unusual number of troubled and depressed students who pursue study in the arts (see Anderson & MacCurdy, 1999; Lindner, 2004; Payne, 2000; Perry, 2007; Webb, 2003). I could not deal adequately with those aspects of the personal without greatly expanding the book and losing focus on its central concerns.

In these pages I not only present the thoughts and practices of many other teachers but also describe in considerable detail practices of my own that illustrate an alternative to the dominant workshop approach. In the past two decades there have been countless critiques of the workshop but only a few detailed accounts of what teachers might try instead. Tom C. Hunley's (2007) is one, Michelene Wandor's (2008) is another, though she invests more in critique of the workshop than in describing her alternative. The need for alternatives is evident not only from the various critiques of the workshop but also from good indications that the workshop approach simply doesn't work in some of the contexts where creative writing is taught. For example, David Starkey (2010: 152), a veteran workshop teacher in four-year colleges, reached this conclusion after experience teaching in a two-year college: 'For *most* community college creative writing instructors *most* of the time, extensive or sole reliance on the writing workshop is a mistake.' He adds, 'More effective methods of instruction for my students include individual conferences, small peer groups, in-class invention exercises, and, above all, in-depth discussion and analysis of professional writing with an emphasis on the vocabulary writers use to talk about their own work.' This summarizes much of the approach I describe in this book, although it leaves out my emphasis on reflection and dialogue.

Chapter 1
Considering Where We're Coming From

> *Learning to teach better is tough, exhilarating, and possible.*
> Wendy Bishop (1994a: 291)

> *One thing, for example, I have come to understand is that when I write, language accumulates along a metonymic register and gathers a particular force or momentum that almost always culminates in something that feels, stunningly, true. I pause for an instant, savoring the moment, then, driven by a kind of perpetual curiosity about whatever in the world might be coming next, breathe deep and begin again, knowing that what seemed in the instant before both fixed and inevitable is left over now, more or less, as a remainder, as delicate as a whisper or wish. This is something I know about writing and I also know that, for me, the same is true of teaching.*
> Katherine Haake (2000: 143)

We come into teaching *from somewhere*, with our own becoming as writers perhaps only partly examined, employing teaching practices picked up from models whose influence we only dimly grasp, going on shared assumptions that are mostly tacit. To become *authentic* as teachers, we need to do what writers do: name and know our sources, consider how they have shaped us, and integrate their influence, our own experience and our best thinking into a coherent text we can claim as our own.

Influences on Our Teaching

A section of my survey asked teachers to estimate the influence of each of eight factors on the way they teach creative writing: their experience as a student, their experience as a writer and reader, conversations with colleagues, observations of colleagues' classes, composition theory, creative writing pedagogy, informal analysis of student response and teacher research. Their responses show how much more we rely on *experience* (as students, as writers and as observers of our own classrooms) than on the means of seeing, questioning and reflecting upon experience that are summed up in the word *pedagogy*.

Indicate the degree of influence of each of the following on the way you teach creative writing (much influence = 5; some influence = 3; no influence = 1):	5	4	3	2	1
Your experience as a student in creative writing courses	60, 38%	39, 25%	29, 18%	10, 6%	19, 12%
Your experience as a writer and reader	117, 74%	32, 20%	7, 4%	0, 0%	1, 1%
Conversations with other creative writing teachers about your courses and how you teach them	20, 13%	43, 27%	60, 38%	27, 17%	7, 4%
Observations of others' classes	3, 2%	17, 11%	39, 25%	57, 36%	40, 25%
Books, articles, conference sessions, workshops or courses in composition theory and practice	7, 4%	16, 10%	39, 25%	52, 33%	43, 27%
Books, articles, conference sessions, workshops or courses in creative writing pedagogy	14, 9%	34, 21%	44, 28%	38, 24%	27, 17%
Informal analysis of student work and response during the course and of student self-evaluations or evaluations of the course	55, 35%	64, 40%	30, 19%	5, 3%	3, 2%
Teacher research (a more formal and multi-faceted study of a class or classes you've taught)	8, 5%	17, 11%	33, 21%	29, 18%	69, 43%

Learning to teach from experience as writers and readers

Creative writing teachers say that their teaching is most heavily influenced by their experience as writers and readers. Of those responding to my survey, 73% rated 'My experience as a writer and reader' as having 'much influence' on their teaching, and most of the rest gave it the next highest rating. This is consistent with the belief that a teacher of creative writing should first of all be a writer (some even assume that's the only requirement) and that our teaching is viewed in large part as an apprenticeship.

Hugh Cook (2004) sent me a list of ways his experience as a writer supports his teaching. Some have to do with being a model: 'experiencing how competitive getting something published is'; gaining 'respect in students' eyes simply for having published three books. They know I've "been there"'. Other items from his list relate to an insider's grasp of process: 'understanding how difficult it is to write well'; 'understanding the process of writing'; 'understanding that what works for one writer may not work for another'; and 'encouraging student writers not to be satisfied with a first draft'. Jim Heynen (2004) told me that he even bases writing exercises 'on problems I have just run into in my own work. It's one of the strongest arguments, if my experience is representative, for the writing teacher to be a writer'.

Convinced that it takes a writer to teach writers, we may fail to consider limitations of basing our teaching upon that experience. One is that writing may always have been easier for us than for most of our students – or if we had difficulties learning to write, we may have forgotten them. Stephen Brookfield (1995: 50) cautions, 'One of the hardest things for teachers to do is to imagine the fear that students feel as they try to learn what we teach. If we have been teaching in a particular discipline, content, or skill area for a long period of time, we have most likely forgotten what it feels like to come to this learning as an uncertain novice.'

Another limitation is that what works for the teacher may not work for the student. Thus, W. T. Pfefferle (2004) said he's willing to 'talk about my own processes as examples' but focuses on helping writers 'discover their own idiosyncrasies', and then he attempts 'to get inside what these writers already do, and try to maximize those things'.

An implication is that we are unlikely to teach effectively 'from experience' without informed reflection upon that experience. Patrick Bizzaro (1993: 27) observes that even expert writers can have plenty of difficulty with knowing where to begin 'in helping students read and evaluate poetry' until their own ways of reading are *visible* to them. He concludes that teachers need 'a systematic analysis that will enable them to recognize their own reading habits' as well as 'determine when such habits can be useful pedagogical tools'. In this way they empower themselves 'to let such readings go (and to perhaps offer more appropriate readings) when the readings threaten to be ill-advised or ineffective'. When he did such a systematic analysis of his own revision process, Bizzaro concluded that he needs a prewriting stage, and that it begins long before what beginning writers might see as 'the actual writing'. Some time later, reading a poem may trigger a memory, and it is this new event that occasions the poem that begins to take shape on the page. At that point, his poems talk to him, and their further shaping emerges from a dialogue between the writer and the work. A particular kind of form that often emerges consists of two strong sections connected by language bridges. Thus, what originally triggered the poem often falls away as the activity of writing generates the real discovery.

One application Bizarro made from this reflection was that the usual notion of prewriting and revising is too static in that it lacks the recursiveness as well as the distinct stages that he finds in his own process. Another outcome of his reflection was the ability to articulate why a particular way of teaching works or fails to work. He doesn't use photos in his teaching, for example, because 'writing should not be a response to a prewriting activity. Rather, the activity should help students see their own experiences as subject matter suited to writing, poetic or otherwise' (p. 25).

Learning to teach from our experience as students

In any practice we tend to follow our models, raising our children as we were raised and adopting a persona and a practice of teaching from our most influential teachers – unless we deliberately question their example or its aptness for us, and then construct our own alternative. As Andrew Scott (2004) observed, especially when starting out, our mentors' decisions 'can deeply influence' us and 'in ways perhaps unexamined by all parties'. Among respondents to my survey, 37% said that the example of their teachers had much influence, and 25% indicated a level between much and some influence. Only a total of 18% indicated little or no influence, and half of those hold a degree in another area so they may have had few or no courses in creative writing.

Often it is our mentors' attitudes and values that influence us most deeply, or at least most consciously. Jim Heynen (2004) told me his strongest influences were teachers of literature 'who relished the material'. Andrew Scott (2004) said his 'first principles' as a teacher of creative writing 'stem from those held by my teachers'. These include: 'Everyone has something to say, and something of value', 'The only way to become a better writer is to become a better reader' and 'When workshopping student stories, and when reading published fiction, class members should attempt to meet a story on its own terms'. Hugh Cook (2004) wrote that he learned from his mentors' 'sensitivity to the writing of others; the need to affirm good writing – or even to find something *to* affirm in bad writing' and 'making sure the very first response does not begin with negative critiques'.

Our mentors subtly and powerfully influence even our conception of who we should be as teachers. Audrey Petty (2005: 79) tells a fascinating story of returning to her undergraduate college and discovering that she could not be the creative writing teacher that her mentor had been for her. Her conclusion:

> As that first term progressed, I began to accept that that way of teaching wasn't me, all the while appreciating that my mentor/colleague's authority was, in part, rooted in a powerful intimacy forged between himself and his students. I began grasping the fact that my mentor/colleague's experience as well as his race and gender were crucial to his approach and to the reception he received.

Once she made herself aware of how her mentor's practice expressed who he was as a person and of how she differed from him, she could construct for herself a teaching persona that fit.

When Lad Tobin (2004: 132) surveyed a group of graduate students preparing to be teachers of writing, he discovered that although the *group* of them described 'a wide range of methods', *individually* they 'revealed a lack of recognition of alternatives'; instead, each instructor 'seemed to be proceeding the ways she had always proceeded (and presumably the way she had been taught) with very little recognition of the assumptions and implications of (or alternatives to) a particular technique or method'. For those of us who have taken creative writing courses, it is likely that our mentors there shared three assumptions – that the full-class workshop is the best arrangement for responding to writing, that critique-and-advice is the best kind of response, and, as Cook mentioned, that authors should 'remain largely silent while their piece is being discussed'. If so, those practices probably seem 'obvious' to us. I will question them all in the next three chapters.

Learning to teach from our colleagues

Only 20% of respondents reported little or no influence from 'conversations with other creative writing teachers about your courses and how you teach them'. Several fondly recalled grad school conversations about teaching, some of these later moving to phone calls and emails. But we seldom take the next step of visiting each other's classes. Frase and McAsey (1998), in urging this practice, observe that 'there are colleagues we have known for years but whose classroom persona we don't know at all'. This observation may appear to be confirmed by the fact that 60% of creative writing teachers responding to my survey reported little or no influence from visiting colleagues' classes. Yet 40% reported at least some influence, suggesting that collegiality among creative writing teachers may be relatively high, perhaps because we're used to inviting writers to our classes. Heynen (2004) mentioned, as a benefit of being a visiting writer, 'I love to sit in on other people's teaching'.

If the ability to write is caught as much as taught, we ought to watch how students catch it from other teachers. Tom Kealey (2004), who reported that visits to classes strongly influenced his teaching, commented, 'I don't necessarily pick up writing assignments or exercises from these classes. Instead, I watch how teachers interact with their students'. He noticed that one teacher took several minutes at the start of class for casual conversation about news or about their weekends. 'They warmed to this greatly, and it seemed to me that the discussions about fiction were made easier by this initial interaction.' He observed another teacher who often asked a question and waited only a few seconds before answering it himself. 'It seemed to me that students came to expect him to answer the question. I learned to be comfortable with the silence instead.' From another he picked up the practice of taking roll at the start of class. 'It helps me learn their names, and more importantly it shows that I know who is there and who is not there and who is late.' Specifically about the workshop, he noticed that one teacher often began by asking, 'What do we have here? What's this story about?' He liked this approach. 'Students began by defining what they had in front of them. I think this was helpful for the writer to hear, especially when the opinions were different.'

We can hear in Kealey's comments that he's also learning a habit of questioning that will continue in his own classroom and move back into conversations with colleagues. This may be why Frase and McAsey suggest reciprocal visits, followed soon after by conversation over lunch (which the campus center for teaching might fund) to discuss such questions as whether and how students were engaged and what thinking lay behind particular strategies and approaches the teacher used.

Because we teach kinds of writing that are difficult to teach, to students who may be too desperate to write well, and through relationships fraught with contradiction, things sometimes go wrong. At such times, conversations with colleagues can help us know how to respond. Without such help, we're likely to blame either ourselves or our students, and blaming soon becomes poisonous. But most of us do appear to have such help. To my survey statement, 'If something goes awry in my teaching, I have people I talk to who help me sort it out', nearly three-quarters either agreed strongly or agreed, and only 10% said they seldom or never have such help.

Learning to teach from our students

Asked about the influence on their teaching of 'Informal analysis of student work and response during the course and of student self-evaluations or evaluations of the course', 75% of respondents indicated either 'much influence' or the level between that and 'some influence'.

However, not many creative writing teachers have taken the next step of doing teacher-*research* – a careful study of one's teaching of a particular course, examining, in addition to student evaluations, student work, a survey of students, journaling or reflection by the teacher, and in some cases participant-observer reports and interviews with selected students carried out by a co-researcher. Patrick Bizzaro's (1993) *Responding to Student Poems: Applications of Critical Theory* and Katharine Haake's (2000) *What Our Speech Disrupts: Feminism and Creative Writing Studies* rely partly upon teacher research, as does this book. Teacher research is also included in essays in Anna Leahy's (2005) collection, *Power and Identity in the Creative Writing Classroom: The Authority Project*. However, Leahy also observes, 'With few exceptions, creative writers have not studied, documented, and analyzed their teaching' (p. xii).

Stephen Brookfield (1995: 50) suggests an in-between step, a continual seeking-out of our students' experience of our classrooms. He asserts, 'Of all the methods available for changing how we teach, putting ourselves regularly in the role of learner has the greatest long-term effects.' The means he suggests is to distribute periodically at the end of class what he calls a 'Critical Incident Questionnaire'. It asks students to report, anonymously, particular moments of their recent experience, including when the student felt most engaged in and distanced from what was happening in class, what action anyone took that seemed most affirming and helpful, what action seemed puzzling or confusing, and what about the class was most surprising. He says the intent 'is not to determine what students liked or didn't like about the class' but to get them to 'focus on specific, concrete happenings that were significant to them' (p. 114). He later summarizes back to the class what he learned and what he plans to change.

Learning from Pedagogy

We might expect that teachers faced with the complex challenge of helping students become writers in the artistic genres would seek provocative ways to view their practice and examine its underlying assumptions – in a word, pedagogy. Yet only a minority of creative writing teachers have learned to value pedagogy. Patrick Bizzaro (2001: 241) writes that he came into creative writing presuming that study of teaching was 'as much of an ongoing effort as is investigation into how to teach composition' and that 'reflection by creative writing teachers on how they teach students to write and how they respond to student writing was a natural and widely-accepted practice'. This is what he found instead: 'It might be an understatement to say that most teachers of creative writing are not particularly enthusiastic about inquiries into their classroom practices' (2004: 295).

Although many of us have been exposed to composition theory, nearly 60% of teachers responding to my survey indicated either little or no influence upon their teaching of creative writing from 'books, articles, conference sessions, workshops or courses in composition theory and practice'. We do claim to have paid more attention to creative writing pedagogy. The number who reported that 'books, articles, conference sessions or courses in creative writing pedagogy' had either little or no influence on their teaching of creative writing was about 40%. This more favorable response may be due to books about writing and teaching by the likes of Victor Hugo and William Stafford, who at least placed in our minds an image of teachers who enjoy writing about their teaching. Consider, for example, John Wylam's (2004) acknowledgement of his debt to Stafford: 'It's the way he brings what he believes to bear on the classroom and the texts at hand that moves me. Generous without becoming lax, careful without appearing merciless. Those are traits I admire.'

One reason *courses* in pedagogy have had limited influence among us is that few MFA programs have required them, and when they have, they usually sent students over to rhet-comp rather than offering their own course in creative writing pedagogy. This *should* change now that, as Kelly Ritter (2001) observes, the PhD in creative writing appears likely 'to match or even eclipse the long-standing terminal degree in writing, the M.F.A'. Because the PhD 'stands as an intellectual, scholarly terminal degree in the English studies community', it is clearly a degree for would-be *teachers* (p. 209) – confirmed by her finding that current openings for teachers of creative writing stated 'a preference for the PhD' (p. 206). Yet her survey of PhD programs in creative writing turned up little preparation for *teaching*. She infers, 'Even though nearly all new PhDs in creative writing have taught in their field, they more than likely have *never* been guided through that teaching; more than likely they have stumbled along, without formal, professional training or guidance' (p. 210). She pulls no punches: '... most U.S. universities have no specific training in place that would prepare candidates to enter the creative writing classroom even remotely as well prepared as their rhetoric and composition PhD counterparts' (p. 213).

Why so little attention to understanding what we do day after day in the classroom? Hans Ostrom (1994: xv) says our resistance to pedagogy is part of an ideology that goes back to Romanticism:

> The author, as defined in Romantic terms, has no particular use for teachers or workshops; 'he' was born with author-ity, with authorizing talent, with genius, with a potency, with a 'repetition in the finite mind' (as Coleridge would have it) 'of the Infinite I Am.' He is godlike – Dionysian, Promethean, mercurial. He is gifted and blessed; he's got what it takes.

If writers are born, not made, all they need from a creative writing course is the pleasant company of other geniuses reading good books and each other's writing and talking about what works, what doesn't and why. The writer-teacher would anchor the conversations and offer a Promethean blessing to those few who display genius. Such a teacher would appear to have little need or desire to engage in informed reflection about the actual process by which students with lesser talents might nevertheless become persons who can write.

My position is that trying to teach without pedagogy is like trying to live without literature. James Seitz (1999: 26) admires in literature what he calls a dialogic metaphor because it requires 'that *readers also be made spectators of their own forms of participation*'. Pedagogy helps teachers to become spectators of their forms of participation in their students' learning. Pedagogy provides *terms* for naming what we do and *perspectives* for seeing ourselves and our teaching. Said another way, it helps us to view our teaching as a *text*. Lad Tobin (2004: 130) urges new teachers to learn to *read the classroom*, that is, 'learn to read the complex of interpersonal relationships – teacher-student, student-student, teacher-teacher – that shapes all academic work'. As grad students they observed these relationships 'as consumers rather than producers of pedagogical theory and practice', and 'since very few teachers attempt to demystify the process of teaching, few graduate students have read the world of the classroom in a systematic way'. Take just one teaching practice, response to student writing, and consider the questions that Louise Weatherbee Phelps (1989: 47) asks as part of *reading* that practice:

> What am I doing when I read a student paper? Why am I doing it – what are my goals? What is the nature of the text I am reading? How do I read? How is my reading related to other actions? For whom do I

read? How is my reading (and related actions) interconnected with the student's actions as a writer? What, after all, is writing? How do students learn to write, and what does my reading of student texts have to do with it?

If we are not asking such questions, can we really claim to be teachers of writing? And can we be sure that our practices of teaching do more good than harm?

Composition pedagogy and creative writing

Ritter (2001: 220) found that when PhD programs in creative writing included a single course in pedagogy, it was usually composition theory. This is a start, partly because those hired to teach creative writing may also teach first-year writing (nearly 60% of creative writing teachers responding to my survey did). Thus a background in composition theory should help candidates to get a job and to teach courses in composition. It should also, as Ritter observes, give them some help teaching creative writing:

> Generally, the teaching of a composition training course focuses on important practical issues such as constructing a syllabus and articulating policies and procedures, facilitating and moderating a classroom discussion, grading student papers, managing student-teacher conferences, maximizing learning for special needs students, such as second-language students, and building a course plan rooted in writing fundamentals but taught through a variety of learning activities, including group work, peer workshops, close reading, and drafting and revising.

This is a significant list, although its emphasis on 'practical issues' might underwrite the notion that if 'things seem to be working' a teacher has little need for pedagogy. A good course in pedagogy should also offer provocative ideas and principles. Consider, for comparison, the ideas that Jim Heynen (2004) drew from composition pedagogy – in his case, primarily from six years with the Oregon Writing Project. One is that 'to be a teacher is to be a participant, so there are particular things you do such as writing with students'. Another idea was 'taking away the element of judgment coming too early'. Related to that was the ideal 'of helping students become their own doctor', which means that the teacher must *disseminate* his authority and later 'get it back to empower the student to be his own best critic'. As Heynen illustrates, composition theory has great potential for helping creative writing teachers rethink who they are and what they can do to enable a journey of becoming for writers.

But a problem with only requiring a composition theory course is that creative writing teachers may assume that its ideas and practices are suited only to composition, not to creative writing. I discovered from interviews that some teachers used 'composition' practices in their first-year writing course that they had never tried in creative writing; for instance, having students write 'writers' memos' (or 'author letters') to accompany drafts submitted for response. One said, 'I do that all the time in freshman comp, I don't know why I haven't thought about trying it in creative writing.' Others were similarly puzzled about why they used continuing *small* groups for response in composition but only the full-class workshop in creative writing. Thus, merely requiring MFA and PhD students in creative writing to take a course in 'composition' pedagogy may have little impact on their creative writing teaching.

Wendy Bishop (1994b: 287) helps explain this lack of transfer by observing that within the culture of English a 'line' has been drawn between composition and creative writing that has been difficult to cross. Nevertheless, she crossed it, reasoning that if writing in any genre is a process and if holding conferences with composition students to discuss essay drafts helped them to learn that process, then 'I would need to have poetry students in my office doing the same'. Consequently, she 'asked creative writing students to read a draft aloud and talk about it', and when that worked, she 'asked for portfolios that showed the process of writing poems and stories'. By these means drawn from composition she 'tried to learn where (creative) writers' ideas came from, what they didn't understand, what they did'.

The need for pedagogy specific to creative writing

Bishop's teaching was changed by this cross-fertilization, and yet she found that something was still missing: '... because the culture I inhabited – English studies – didn't support such commonalities in instruction, I hadn't examined very well my growing beliefs that it was more productive to cross the line than to create a separate teaching persona on either side' (p. 183). That's the other danger of offering prospective creative writing teachers only courses in composition theory: they may import its practices and assumptions into creative writing without considering how they work *differently* there.

Identifying differences between composition and creative writing would be a good place to start a course in creative writing pedagogy. The obvious difference is genre. Donald Murray (1989: 102), who also taught and wrote about first-year writing, says that students coming into fiction must first *unlearn* what they have been taught in composition. The problem 'is that the students have learned to write. They bring with them knowledge which may be true for some of the writing they have done but which makes the writing of fiction difficult'. As a result 'the better educated the student, the harder it is to return to the natural, magical art of narrative'. Before that can happen a 'process of unlearning has to take place', one that is 'painful and frightening for students'. A similarly baffling unlearning must, for some students, precede their learning to write poetry. Students good at saying directly what they mean now have to set aside abstractions and generalizations and instead create patterns of words and images that engage a reader's imagination. In teaching the artistic genres, then, we need to remind ourselves to worry about some students who in a composition or journalism course would be among the *good* writers.

A quite different and more significant difference from composition is that creative writing students may be much more highly motivated – and thus have more at stake. While many in first-year writing see the course as required, as something to 'get out of the way', most creative writing students have *chosen* the course. They may even think of themselves as *writers*, and now they are in a course that places their self-identity at risk, especially if they have little experience in the genre. Self-doubt may magnify their fears. Jane Piirto (2002: 64) observes, 'Writers need ambition, as do other creative producers, but that ambition often produces horrible feelings of inadequacy and anxiety.' Those feelings may be amplified when they find themselves among students who they perceive as having a more legitimate claim to the title of 'writer'. Thus, we need to take seriously Wendy Bishop's (1994b: 182) observation that 'students who enroll in creative writing classes for the first time may have to overcome an overwhelming sense of unworthiness'. Some or many students are likely to feel (and try to conceal) deep anxiety – a condition that may spread to and be amplified by others in the class. One likely consequence is self-doubt and anxiety that burdens or blocks their writing, further confirming a fear that they cannot write. Murray (1989: 104) observes that students in a fiction class must 'learn to seek, respect, and make use of doubt, questions, wonder, surprise, failure, accident, and discovery to explore the uncomfortable, exciting territory of the fiction writer'. Yes, but how do we help anxious and self-doubting students to relax enough to do that?

The highly motivated writers in creative writing are also much more likely to care that their teacher is a writer, and they are more likely to want to be *like* their teacher – which further raises the stakes for them. An added consequence is that they are more likely to form real or imagined hierarchies among themselves, defined partly by degrees of 'in' with the hero-teacher, and the teacher may enjoy that status too much to see its risks. Further, writers who find themselves blocked in their writing may blame a hero-teacher, who *should* be able to rescue them from such a predicament.

In short, this is not freshman composition.

So neither is it adequate for graduate programs in creative writing to send prospective teachers downstairs for a course or two in composition theory. That's a start, but it needs to be followed up with one or more courses that address challenges specific to creative writing.

The good news from my survey is that a total of 30% of creative writing teachers reported either 'much influence' or a level between 'much' and 'some' influence on their teaching from the developing field of creative writing pedagogy. Creative writing teachers who have been influenced only a little by pedagogy were likely to mention composition theory, while those who have invested more and gained more from pedagogy were more likely to credit creative writing pedagogy. This suggests to me that those who think in an informed way about teaching creative writing appear to realize that they need a pedagogy attuned to its differences.

A personal motive for writing this book was to think through my own adaptation to my creative writing courses of such composition practices as the use of writers' groups rather than the workshop, doing reader-response while delaying 'critique', and rejecting the 'silent writer' tradition in favor of having students actively reflect on their writing and question responders about it. I learned that these practices make creative writing more teachable, but they also make it even more personal, underlining the need for teachers to *negotiate* the personal.

What We Say We're After in Introductory Courses

Another source of our teaching is our stated and unstated sense of what our courses should do for our students. My survey inquires about the goals of helping students become published, become better readers, become better writers in non-literary genres, become more self-aware and thoughtful persons, enjoy the satisfactions of performing within a community, and learn to use writing as a means of personal transformation or healing:

We imagine students being better off in certain ways after they finish such an introductory creative writing course. Indicate the importance for you of each of the following goals. (Highly important=5; somewhat important=3; not important=1):	5	4	3	2	1
Students should want to publish and master the craft of the genre well enough to become more likely to be published	11, 7%	19, 12%	49, 31%	37, 24%	39, 25%
Through the process of writing literary genres, students should become more engaged and perceptive readers of literature	102, 64%	29, 18%	18, 11%	4, 3%	2, 1%
Students should become better writers in non-literary genres	33, 21%	38, 24%	43, 27%	22, 14%	19, 12%
Students should claim the genre as a valuable mode of thinking, feeling and knowing, contributing to their becoming more self-aware, sensitive, thoughtful, imaginative	93, 59%	35, 22%	17, 11%	4, 3%	4, 3%
Students should gain the satisfaction of discovering and performing their gifts as valued members of a writing community	64, 40%	46, 29%	37, 23%	6, 4%	2, 1%
Students should learn to use writing as a way to gain courage or to bring about personal transformation or healing	16, 10%	23, 15%	48, 30%	32, 20%	36, 23%

I realize that the value of this section of the survey is limited by ambiguity. Some respondents interpreted 'goals' as intentions made explicit in the syllabus. Although that describes most of these statements, the third, 'Students should become better writers in non-literary genres', probably would not be listed, although I think we would agree that it is a desirable outcome. The same goes for the last, 'Students should learn to use writing as a way to gain courage or to bring about personal transformation or healing'. Although two-thirds of respondents gave it little or no importance as a *goal*, many would welcome it as an outcome. To me, what we announce as goals matters less than what in practice we encourage – or discourage.

Personal transformation as a goal

Because my focus is on the personal side of our teaching, I was interested in how teachers would respond to goals related to personal transformation or healing. Many were clearly opposed to either stating or implying that the course might be a place for students to pursue such goals. Michael Jarrett (2004) articulated 'a fundamental distrust in the redemptive powers of writing and literature', adding, 'I do not doubt that writing can bring about transformation and healing and self-knowledge, only that this direction is assured, even inevitable and, therefore, ought to be a classroom goal. (I have a hard time setting a goal that is ultimately metaphysical, that I have no way of assessing.)'

Also accounting for resistance to goals related to healing is our assumption that within the academy, we deal with *minds*. 'Healing' is associated with bodies and emotions. Yet art operates through the senses, not only through the mind, so becoming an artist includes coming to one's senses: learning to be fully present, noticing, feeling, remembering, caring. For some students, developing those capabilities requires not just learning but healing.

It can also be seen that more teachers checked 'not important' than the category between 'not important' and 'somewhat important', indicating that many actively reject the idea that creative writing teachers should make room for personal transformation and healing.

Publication as a goal for the introductory course

I was surprised at how little we support the goal of publication in the introductory course. Only a fifth of those responding marked either of the two ratings at the 'important' end of the scale for the statement, 'Students should want to publish and master the craft of the genre well enough to become more likely to be published'. Half chose either of the two ratings at the 'not important' end of the scale. Granted, 'master' is a strong word for an introductory course, but the phrase that follows is 'more likely to be published', not 'likely'. I expected greater identification with this goal, partly because of our emphasis upon hiring successful writers as teachers and partly because books and articles about teaching creative writing have pointed to publication as a value we share. Katharine Haake

(1994: 80), for example, writes that we 'regard publishing in more elevated terms than other forms of writing achievement' and we assume that workshops will be composed of 'talented students with strong vocational commitments to writing'.

When I asked respondents to my survey why they downplay publication in introductory courses, most replied that at that level, good process matters more. Simone Muench (2004) wrote that although she stresses publishing in advanced classes, she wants introductory classes to 'recognize that the ability to communicate via writing is important in almost any field and it can be invaluable for many reasons including catharsis and healing, though certainly not limited to self-therapy'. She added, 'I find it fruitless to stress publishing at a beginning level. Most students aren't ready at that level to send work out. They end up getting rejection letters and find themselves discouraged from continuing to write'. So instead she gives 'high priority to helping students write the kind of poetry that could get published, but low priority to encouraging publishing'. Mary Grimm (2004) offered a similar explanation: 'A lot of my students tend to think of publishing as something they could do anytime, with a little effort and a few tips – they're wondering if they could become writers and support themselves by selling their novels to the movies, after they've been on the best seller lists.' Her concern 'is to get them thinking about the writing itself, not what will happen (maybe, if they're lucky and work hard) afterward'. Phil Hey (2004) said he makes the point up front. An 'attitude list' he hands out includes the statement, '*We're not here to make literature.* We're here to make writers. If you want to be a star, do it on your own time'.

Todd Davis (2005) does what I also do: suggest that students first write for people they know. He's likely to tell students about a poem he's writing to his mother or father or sister or wife, explaining, 'Those poems will have meaning whether I get them published or not'. Before they care about impressing a wider audience, he wants students to value the writing for more immediate reasons. It's a question of helping writers find their best motivation. He tells them that biographies of writers teach this lesson: 'If your goal is only to be published, most of you will stop writing very quickly'; however, if a writer 'is more concerned about the writing than the need to be validated by an outside source, usually the publishing takes care of itself'.

This lack of emphasis on publication within introductory courses prompts a question: Then why do so many of its teachers use the full-class workshop, an approach better suited for touching up near-finished products than for developing a good writing process? That will be covered in the next chapter.

Other goals for introductory creative writing

Most teachers agree that learning to write is a great way to become a better reader. In my survey, the goal of becoming 'more engaged and perceptive readers of literature' was rated by two-thirds of respondents either 'highly important' or at the level just below. Jim Heynen (2004) said that when he considers what educational purposes an introductory class is serving, 'I realize that maybe two in a class of 18 have the talent and commitment to be writers'. So how do we justify the course for the rest? His answer is that it makes them better readers. 'Going through the process and studying intimidatingly good models – there's no better way to study literature.' This is also why some teachers of literature ask students to try writing the genres they study. Laura Apol (2004) said she asks students of children's literature to write poetry in order to 'help them think about how authors work through words and how words work on readers'.

Almost as highly supported was the goal, 'Students should gain the satisfaction of discovering and performing their gifts as valued members of a writing community'. Yet this is also a *personal* goal: 'satisfaction' is personal, 'performing their gifts' involves celebrating their own and others' uniqueness. And doing so 'as valued members of a writing community' emphasizes mutual identification and empathy. I would add that where this goal matters, students will come to know and trust others enough that some are more likely to disclose highly personal, even shameful, experience even if that is not the teacher's intention.

In the introduction to their essay collection, *Can It Really Be Taught: Resisting Lore in Creative Writing Pedagogy,* Kelly Ritter and Stephanie Vanderslice (2006: xiv–xv) worry about the 'annexation' of creative writing by professional writers who are more concerned about writing than teaching and who perpetuate the view that the creative writing classroom should be 'a space that privileges artistic production over intellectual development'. Perhaps few such 'professional writers' bothered to respond to my survey. The teachers who did respond deemphasized publication, at least in introductory courses. And the survey statement, 'Students should claim the genre as a valuable mode of thinking, feeling, and knowing, contributing to their becoming more self-aware, sensitive, thoughtful, imaginative', was rated 'highly important' or 'important' by a total of 80% of respondents, suggesting that many or most of us do honor the broader intellectual goals of our departments and institutions.

Who We Are By Degrees

Since creative writing is an academic field, its teachers need to present credentials. Considered from that perspective, we're a motley group – some having taken no courses in creative writing, others holding an advanced degree with multiple courses. Judging by my survey, just over half of us have a PhD or MFA in creative writing. Most of the rest have a PhD in literature or theory (34%) or rhetoric/composition (only 3%). Another 15% have a postgraduate degree in some other area – most in theatre or playwriting, a few in education, the rest in other fields. Of course, many of us have more than one graduate degree. See below:

72, 46%	MA English
30, 19%	MFA Poetry
38, 24%	MFA Fiction
53, 34%	PhD Literature/theory
5, 3%	PhD Rhetoric/Composition
18, 11%	PhD Creative Writing
25, 15%	Other

The degrees we hold influence our choice of colleagues to converse with and align with. In *(Re)writing Craft: Composition, Creative Writing, and the Future of English Studies,* Tim Mayers (2005: xv) argues that we in creative writing have most to gain from alliances with rhetoric/composition because that field also focuses on written production. In addition, he favors elevating production over interpretation – writing over literature – making literary study 'at best a peripheral part of the discipline, important only insofar as it helps students and teachers understand more about writing'. However, such an inversion of English department priorities is unlikely to gain much support within creative writing as long as the PhDs in literature among us outnumber by as much as ten to one the PhDs in composition/rhetoric. Such a ratio favors identification with literature. Peter Vandenberg (2004: 12) confirms that where composition programs have attempted to join with creative writing to create a writing major, the merger was fraught with difficulty because creative writing faculty associated their subject with the liberal arts and literature and felt that composition 'smacked of vocational training and the social sciences'.

Given the diversity in our educational backgrounds, it's odd that our way of teaching creative writing is so similar. This fact gives credence to the observation of Ritter and Vanderslice that our teaching is dominated by lore, a pattern of practice that is handed down, undergoing little critical analysis along the way – a pattern that they find 'is systemic, pervasive, and rooted in creative writing's isolated academic status' (2006: xiii).

Who We Are As Persons

Parker Palmer (2007) says that his thesis in *The Courage to Teach* is that 'good teaching comes from the identity and integrity of the teacher'. He explains that 'in every class I teach, my ability to connect with my students, and to connect them with the subject, depends less on the methods I use than on the degree to which I know and trust my selfhood – and am willing to make it available and vulnerable in the service of learning' (p. 10). Even the value of techniques we use depend upon who we are, and 'as we learn more about who we are, we can learn techniques that reveal rather than conceal the personhood from which good teaching comes' (p. 24). Tobin (2004: 100) writes, similarly, that 'trying to embody attitudes or techniques that we believe in but have not yet integrated is ... difficult to pull off' and that consequently, 'a new teacher's attempts to act objectively, authoritatively, professionally' are 'bound to be clumsy'.

It matters even more in creative writing that our way of teaching suit our personhood because we teach what we do and teach it through the person we become doing it. Our reading life, writing process, ways our writing draws upon and transforms our experience and perhaps even our writing itself are part of what we teach. All this makes it hard for us to resist Palmer's conclusion: 'Good teaching requires self-knowledge: it is a secret hidden in plain sight' (p. 3).

The artistic personality

Jen Webb (2003) begins her article, 'Depression and creative writing students', by lamenting the 'disturbingly large number' of her first-year Australian students 'with documented depression, anxiety, obsessive-compulsive disorder, bipolar disorder' and other mental disabilities. Although she can identify external causes – rapid change in postmodern times, the 'suffering and struggle' that characterize life under capitalism, a 'pre-eminence of informational values' that crowds out our role as storytellers and keepers of social memory, and loss of community that comes with pursuing such a solitary activity – she also lends credence to evidence that artists and especially writers 'are more anxious, depressed, and manic-depressive than anyone else'. Similarly, Jane Piirto (2002: 70), in *'My Teeming Brain': Understanding Creative Writers*, says that in personality tests, writers revealed 'many of the characteristics of manic-depressives', with the exception that 'their ego strength and intelligence were higher'. In addition, she reports that creative writers 'were "markedly deviant" from the regular population, and the distinguished writers seemed to have tendencies to be schizoid, depressive, hysterical, or psychopathic ...'. Well, perhaps. To depict the human does require a sympathetic apprehension of the depths as well as the heights of the human condition.

Piirto also lists other personality traits that characterize creative writers:

> (1) independence/ nonconformity; (2) drive/ resiliency; (3) courage/ risk-taking; (4) androgyny; (5) introversion; (6) intensity or OEs; (7) naiveté or an attitude of openness; (8) preference for an intuitive and perceptive way of looking at the world; and (9) energy transmitted into productivity through self-discipline. (p. 30)

Those 'OEs' are 'overexcitabilities'. Other traits she lists are imagination, insight, 'passion for work in a domain', as well as 'perceptiveness, perfectionism, persistence, resilience, risk-taking, self-discipline, self-efficacy, tolerance for ambiguity, and volition or will' (p. 23). The resilience, risk-taking and tolerance for ambiguity resemble Keats' (1899: 277) 'negative capability' – the capability of 'being in uncertainties, mysteries, doubts, without any irritable reaching after fact and reason'.

One inference is that artists who teach may dwell uneasily within academic institutions, partly because deans, assessment coordinators and tenure review committees do a good deal of 'irritable reaching after fact and reason'.

Independent nonconformists tend to dwell on the margins of institutions and to prefer the company of others like themselves, which often includes their best students, who are likely to be drawn to each other for the same reason. Yet close relationships among passionate and 'overexcitable' students – who are also trying to impress their heroes (which may include their teachers) and to compete with each other – can be volatile. Piirto notes that while attending writer's conferences, 'I observed jealousy and anxiety among the participants, who may see each other as rivals. Perhaps it was my own jealousy and anxiety projected onto others' (2002: 64).

Further, many teachers with traits such as non-conformity, risk-taking, openness and tolerance for ambiguity concern themselves less with 'professional boundaries'. Thus their relationships with students are likely to go wonderfully well – or terribly wrong. And in the latter case, introverted, non-conformist, overexcitable teachers may sink into self-accusation or denial rather than seek out a colleague for help with working through the problem. Dynamics that threaten relationships between master artists and their apprentices are explored in Chapters 6 and 7.

If we as artists are quirky and somewhat erratic persons, teaching an art that is learned interpersonally, to students who, like us, take their work personally and often go about it passionately, and since we do all this within academic institutions that resist the emotional and the personal, then we will certainly need those strong traits Piirto lists: volition, resilience, courage and insight – especially insight.

Chapter 2
The Workshop: 'More or Less Unfortunate Misunderstandings'

> Resistance to change is a natural part of the human condition. Whenever I hear someone described as 'not taking criticism well', I want to ask, 'Who does take criticism well?'
>
> Mary Pipher (2003: 154)

> I don't believe in classes where students criticize each other's manuscripts. Such criticism is generally composed in equal parts of ignorance, flattery, and spite. It's the blind leading the blind, and it can be dangerous. A teacher who tries to impose a way of writing on you can be dangerous too.
>
> Flannery O'Connor (1969: 86)

Lincoln Konkle (2004) wrote at the end of my survey that he was curious whether others' responses confirmed his impression:

> that most of us teach creative writing in pretty much the same way. We assign students to read and discuss examples of genre, styles, etc. (some by famous writers, some by not so famous, some by students); we assign exercises as warm-ups for the workshop; finally we workshop works in progress. Then we also require a revision or portfolio to show how students have made use of the feedback they received. These classes are usually taught in a more informal, discussion-centered manner, with some mini-lectures by the instructor.

I wrote back that the survey confirmed his impression. Only 8% reported little or no use of such a workshop and just over three-quarters said they give it either 'much emphasis' or a level of emphasis between 'much' and 'some'.

Indicate the emphasis you give each of the following practices in your teaching of an introductory level creative writing course (much emphasis = 5; some emphasis = 3; not used = 1):	5	4	3	2	1
Whole-class workshopping/critique of students' drafts	93, 58%	27, 17%	21, 13%	7, 4%	6, 4%
Oral or written response to student writing in impromptu small groups	41, 26%	31, 20%	40, 25%	16, 10%	26, 16%
Oral or written response to student writing in small groups whose membership remains the same for at least half the course	38, 24%	23, 14%	18, 11%	17, 11%	58, 36%

Dianne Donnelly (2010) did a survey of a similar number of creative writing teachers for the introduction to her edited collection, *Does The Writing Workshop Still Work?* She found that 'only 10% define their model to be markedly different than the traditional workshop' (p. 3). Thus, both our surveys confirm this assessment from Katharine Haake (1994: 80):

> Since the first classes were developed at Iowa, teaching creative writing in America has largely conformed to the model of a text-centered workshop where apprentice writers come together to craft poetry, prose, and drama and offer it for criticism to peers and the master writer. As it is now conceived in the familiar institutional context of our post-secondary academic system, creative writing has become so closely affiliated with this view of the 'workshop' as to seem very nearly indistinguishable from it.

If creative writing is 'nearly indistinguishable' from this workshop, it must embody our deepest – and perhaps least-examined – assumptions. Hans Ostrom (1994: xix–xx) is among those arguing that these assumptions and much more *should* be examined. Introducing *Colors of a Different Horse*, the essay collection about creative writing pedagogy he co-edited with Wendy Bishop, Ostrom suggests that 'all of us could probably benefit from taking a hard look at precisely how "the workshop" functions in our classrooms', asking questions like 'What are our guidelines, and what assumptions underlie them?' and 'What is our role in workshops and group work, and how productive has this role been?' Also, 'What do we know about group dynamics and what should we know? Who gets silenced in our workshops and why?' And even, 'What might be gained by dismantling the workshop model altogether and starting from scratch?'

The increasing seriousness of his questions adds urgency to his ultimate suggestion that we take the workshop apart to consider how it might be remade. That's my project in this and the following two chapters.

First, a clarification. Although the creative writing 'workshop' has been discussed in numerous articles recently, different writers mean different things by the word. Philip Gross (2010: 55) helpfully lists four workshops categorized by purpose: the 'open workshop', where participants bring works-in-progress and each 'is critiqued as if finished work'; the 'set-agenda workshop' in which writers compare their responses to a set task that confronted them with a 'technical or other challenge'; the in-class 'writing-and-sharing workshop'; and 'the ideas workshop', in which writers 'pitch a set of possibilities for future writing' and the teacher and group respond in different roles – reader, fellow writer and critic. In Donnelly's edited collection, when Gaylene Perry (2010) praises 'the workshop' for being 'robust in nature' and 'underpinned by the very notion of creativity' (p. 128), she is referring as much to a writing-and-sharing workshop as a peer-review workshop. Another source of confusion is group makeup. In composition, a 'workshop' approach typically involves *small* groups, which may be why Bizzaro (1993: 161) uses 'workshop' to mean 'the time in the course when students comment on each other's poems, either in small groups or as a class led by the instructor'. In most creative writing discourse, however, 'workshop' refers to *teacher-led full-class discussion and critique of student writing* – Gross's 'open workshop'. That's what Haake and Donnelly mean, and Ostrom likewise distinguishes 'workshops' from 'group work'. That is also what I mean by 'workshop'. The form of peer response I later offer as an alternative I'll call 'writers' groups'.

Attractions of the Workshop

When I confirmed Konkle's (2004) impression that our courses typically rely on the workshop, I added that some teachers, especially those with a background in composition, prefer writers' groups (nearly 40% say they give more than 'some emphasis' to such groups). He responded that he had 'tried that once' but was dissatisfied for two reasons: '1) I didn't think students were getting very good discussion of their manuscripts since I wasn't conducting the workshop in the groups; 2) I missed conducting those discussions, which usually are enormously enjoyable. So I returned to the practice of conducting workshop with class as a whole.'

I agree that leading a workshop discussion can be 'enormously enjoyable', especially with small classes of capable, motivated and experienced writers. For students too. Donnelly (2010: 4) reports that teachers responding to her survey said that their students 'always say on evaluations that the workshop portion of the class was the most enjoyable part' and that students are 'almost universally motivated' by the encounter, to quote two. Gayle Elliot (1994: 113) offers what may be one explanation: that the workshop's circle with everyone included changed the power dynamic between teacher and student because in such a learning community, students are given roles they seldom get to play in other courses:

> Member writers base their trust in one another on *mutuality*; each – including the professor – will alternately be in the position of writer, each of critic; roles interchange session by session. The dynamic of the workshop revolves not around any single 'knower', but around the interchange within the circle itself. And while it would be false to claim there is no competition amongst writers, competition is not the ethic or motive force of the workshop: the work creative writers do is not oppositional by nature. (p. 114)

Elliot sums up the workshop as a *gift exchange*, which implies an exchange among equals:

> ... the group readily accepts that the workshop piece, or 'gift', will circulate – passed along in manuscript and conversation from person to person around the circle till it returns, eventually, to the writer who sends it forth. Each writer/critic gains through this interchange: the writer receives critical insight into her own work; the critic formalizes a critical approach which benefits both her own – and the other students' – writing. (p. 123)

That's the ideal. But how often does the workshop live up to it, at least for beginning writers? The members of the group are rarely equals; competition may be a stronger motive than Elliot allows; only in some classes do writers manage this level of engagement; and if being in 'the position of writer' means submitting their own writing, few professors occupy that position because they know better than to ask students to critique work by the member of the circle who gives the grades.

A workshop-in-progress

Workshops certainly can be admirable in practice. Observing Gina Franco teach a fiction workshop at Knox College, which offers a major in creative writing, I could appreciate why teachers are drawn to the approach.

The class was gathered around tables pushed together to form a square, so her arrival seemed less like a professor assuming control than like a leader joining a meeting. She greeted a few of the students, remarking to one sitting in a different place, 'You switched sides. I'm disoriented when people I know move'. The comment acknowledged that the workshop is personal and interpersonal – and it might have made students new to her teaching wonder whether the familiars owned an advantage.

At home in her authority, she talked a little about her expectations for the course. To ease fears about evaluation, she emphasized that it is preceded by a long process of learning and that 'I don't grade anything until the final portfolio'. She also checked attendance to remind students that a workshop is an event created by its members.

Then she introduced the workshop session in a way that directed students' attention to the event they would enact: 'I thought we'd try to see what it's like to work together as a group.' Although this wasn't the first workshop course for many of the students, it was the first workshop session for this one, and since in earlier meetings the class had seemed hesitant, Franco focused on helping them monitor their feelings, gain confidence and learn good practice ('When you read your piece, read slowly so that people can take it in.')

Response began with reader-response, not praise or critique. She asked, 'What struck you, what stayed in your head?' When that response moved toward questions about the main character, Gina pushed them deeper: 'What do you know about her? What's her position in the world, her relationships? What do you think she wears?' These questions led to a quite different one: 'What's her *problem*?'

One student replied, 'She doesn't like to face reality?'

'What do you think about that?'

'She creates others' lives in her own mind.'

Another: 'I get the feeling that the character lacks a sense of self. She's wearing the same jeans. She keeps piling on t-shirts. She doesn't pay attention to her own appearance but notices minute details about others around her.'

Gina: 'There's more there. That's an interesting statement. Now I ask you, Who is she? Do you have trouble saying? You point out that character and identity are difficult to get to. Why? She's tuned in to how *others* live?'

Student: 'I don't think that's necessarily true. She's perceptive of how her hair is straightened and her t-shirts don't quite match. She's tuned into *everything*, the real and the unreal.'

Gina: 'There seems to be some kind of emptiness. Can you point to what it is?'

I admired her grasp of the story and ability to use follow-up questions to draw students deeper into the text. She also illustrated that although workshopping devours class time, it does provide opportunities for the alert teacher to offer powerful generalizations. Explaining the 'What's her problem' question, Gina said, 'If you're going to write good fiction, you have to have conflict. Usually it's a hang-up, something the character is afraid of. What is this character hung up on?' She offered a larger point about fiction as a lens for reading the story before them.

In workshopping another story, a student asked a question about language: 'Most Spanish words I liked, but what about *cascada* and *cerveza* when earlier it was "beer"?' Gina: 'Problems come up with the use of foreign words, particularly Spanish. The question of whether such a word is used in an appropriate, culturally evocative kind of way doesn't seem to come up with European languages. What you have to consider is, "Am I being honest with the voice of this character?"' This workshop was clearly an apprenticeship, and Gina was able to demonstrate that a perceptive and alert writer-teacher can use the workshop to help students grasp principles that have broader application.

Even when she asked students to shift from reader to critic, she continued to address them as writers – implicitly as *fellow* writers. For instance, she asked them to point to 'things you would steal if you could'. One student pointed to a particular sentence. Others talked about what its important words implied.

When another student said he had difficulty making a transition in the story, Gina pursued that turn toward critique: 'What's confusing, what doesn't work?' A student answered, 'Confusion between the person she lives with and the guy at the desk.'

Gina: 'Assuming this is not a poor transition, we have to ask about its purpose. Why *not* make the two characters distinct? What's lost, what's gained?' She asked whether the characters were merging – whether what had seemed to be two characters was actually one. To engage non-participants, she asked for a show of hands for MERGING versus NOT MERGING. A few voted each way, most didn't vote. 'Both?' she asked. To get more to respond, she said, 'Let me make sure all of you are following. What's being merged and to what purpose?' After further discussion of whether readers heard one character or two, she summed things up: 'How many *he*'s do we have? There's a distinction between who she *imagines* and who she's actually living with. When we get here, we don't know which *he* she's writing about. Fantasy and reality run together. If you make a distinction between those two characters, what's lost?'

    Student: 'The possibility that there's only one *he*.'

    Gina: 'Yes. Isn't that an interesting hang-up to have?'

    Then she again invited them to see the workshop in relation to good writing: 'When you are reading things cold, you tend to form a consensus. The consensus will tend to push toward the story's accessibility.' When this happened, she said, 'I will try to push back. Accessibility will not necessarily make a piece better. It's important to *work* at the complexity, to think about it. I'm not saying I'm not interested in clarity; I'm saying I am interested in complexity.'

    All the while, she helped them observe their workshop and their own participation in it: 'I structure things this way – what's working, what's not working – but eventually I hope I can do less leading and you can just talk.'

    Clearly, engaged and thoughtful interaction with a text and with each other can happen in a good workshop. In Franco's we can experience the value to writers of hearing the voices of peers engaged in the activity of reading and interpreting their works-in-progress as well as of learning to read in ways that they can carry back to both published work and their own works-in-progress.

    In addition, we can observe Franco's pivotal role, both in helping students attend to and interpret the story before them and in coaching them in effective group process. Her contribution underscores Konkle's concern about how writers can get *good* response without the steady presence of an insightful and authoritative writer-teacher. I'll address that in Chapter 4.

Criticisms of the Workshop

    If some graduates of creative writing programs tell glowing stories of finding self, voice and artistic direction in the presence of wise teachers and an engaged workshop community, too many others tell a different story. Barbara Bogue (2004b) told me she was among the older students in graduate school, so she came in already feeling like an outsider. And then she had to endure *several* 'bad experiences in workshops'. The worst was the first one. The teacher was a well-known writer – 'very glamorous'. He decided after some time who were the five real *writers* – and he put their names on the board. 'The rest of us were just scum, I suppose.' He would sometimes say to male students, 'You have no balls at all'. He told her she 'didn't deserve to represent herself as a graduate student'. This is hardly the kind of workshop that Elliot extols as a 'gift exchange'. Bogue said that such teachers taught her 'everything I never wanted to do'. She added, 'I do my best to treat all my students equally, as writers and as individuals'.

Granted, her story may be about bad teaching, not a flawed approach; and her response was not to reject the workshop but to do hers differently. And perhaps any approach, in creating a certain kind of space for good things to happen, also opens itself to certain problems. For instance, in giving power to participants, the workshop is vulnerable to those who misuse that power. Robert Vivian (2004) wrote that two of the three workshops he participated in as a student did not work 'largely because of some rather ungenerous and egomaniacal classmates – it really wasn't the teacher's fault'. Pat Emile (2004b) had a similar complaint: 'Always, at least one person thinks they are the greatest writer in the school,' she told me. 'They tend to go after people in order to make their own stuff stand out. They denigrate others' work and like to talk about their own work that is being published.' She added, 'Sometimes it's a person who's not a very good writer, so I suppose it's a defense mechanism.' Vicious or thoughtless comments from such participants can do a good deal of damage, especially if they start a trend. Jeff Barker (2004a) remarked that 'while the teacher attempts to mitigate both cruelty and ignorance, sometimes the floodgates get opened and it's tough to close them because of the weight which students give to one another's opinions'.

We also have to consider the possibility that the peculiar dynamics of group critique may bring out the worst in some participants. Carol Bly (2001: 16), who apparently first encountered the workshop as a teacher, describes how disquieting that experience was:

> ... first, the room was filled with the smell of fear, and second, I didn't care for the expressions on the other students' faces. They had the look of cats near a mousehole. I couldn't quite identify it at the time, but in retrospect and with much experience since, I know that at least one dynamic in that room, whether conscious or unconscious, was low-level, mild, politically sanctioned sadism.

I take that last phrase to mean that the dominant writers colluded to put down weaker ones, perhaps expecting the teacher's gratitude for helping to expose pretenders. Teachers may sanction sadism more than they admit, even to themselves. To justify an agonistic workshop, we might point to the one or two top writers whose talents appear to be confirmed by it, but if one thing those writers learn is to likewise disdain the less talented, then the ones disdained have less reason to join the audience for literary writing. A good creative writing course should augment that audience, not discourage potential readers.

Ostrom (1994: xiv) lays a quite different charge: that as a result of the common assumption among creative writing teachers that what they are paid to teach is not really teachable, they seldom bother with reflection about *how* to teach or with planning to teach well but instead 'fall back on the workshop in its simplest form: "going over" poems and stories in a big circle, holding forth from time to time, pretending to have read the material carefully, breaking up squabbles like a hall monitor, marking time'. A workshop leader who won't teach can frustrate and anger students who want to learn. For a telling story on this theme, see Wendy Bishop's (1994a) 'Afterword' to *Colors of a Different Horse*. She describes what I hope was her own worst workshop experience as a student, sitting in a circle with a 'famous white-haired poet' who just smoked, did not intervene, did not teach: 'My second year of graduate workshops consisted of hours of meeting with a group of other aspiring poets not to be taught. Our egos grew to the degree that they were not sated. Cliques, competitiveness – some of us thrived, at a cost.' They read and waited for their master to say that their work was good. 'He did not teach us, we assumed, because we were not ready, worthy, or worth it' (p. 283). Adding insult, a poem by this poet labels creative writing a 'weed' in academia, a communal pursuit that offers:

> A Built-in therapy for all and sundry,
> Taking in each other's laundry.
> No schedule, no syllabus, no curriculum
> No more reading (knowledge has gone elsewhere).

Bishop reports, 'This teacher, in the years I studied with him, returned no annotated texts, gave no tests, shared no grading standards, kept to no schedule or syllabus, designed no curriculum' (p. 284).

Two further allegations against the workshop, sameness in the writing and coteries and rivalries among students, may be interrelated. Among teachers, the conflict inherent in taking money to teach what they say is unteachable may be one cause of coteries and rivalries because our unconscious tends to displace our inner contradictions onto the social scene: the teacher's failure to teach all but the privileged few gets refigured as 'some people just aren't writers'. And when students sense that a teacher's focus is on separating who's hot from who's not, the ambitious ones either elbow their way toward the top or become angry and resentful at their failure to get there. One interviewee recalled such a workshop: 'The group who drank with the prof could do no wrong with their writing and the rest of the class could do no right.'

A class divided in this way would also produce sameness in the writing. The outsiders, too worried about judgment, would be unable to find a voice. The expressions on their faces, too, would be reduced to a timid – or angry – sameness. And no one would be surprised if those eager to be seen as the 'real writers' produced work that resembled the teacher's. Bizzaro (2004: 305) writes that influence in the workshop 'no doubt works vertically, where sameness is passed from teacher to student who, in turn, becomes a teacher who passes certain literary biases to yet another generation of students'. Elsewhere he (Bizzaro & McClanahan, 2007: 86) makes the accusation stronger, charging that the kind of master-apprentice relationship fostered by the workshop approach 'has produced a generation of clones – students who sound amazingly like their teachers'. Eve Shelnutt (1989: 11) writes that hiring star writers adds to this problem because they tend to talk about the living writers they know and compete with rather than helping their students to locate themselves within the literary tradition. Consequently, 'intellectual isolation is programmatically reinforced'.

Feminist critics have charged that the competitiveness and cliques associated with the workshop are especially alienating for women. Katharine Haake (1994: 77) writes that her own early workshops as a student were 'painful and discouraging' and that even later ones were 'vaguely disappointing – apexes for the most gifted writers, nadirs for everyone else'. In *What Our Speech Disrupts: Feminism and Creative Writing Studies* (2000: 143), she writes that using the workshop as a teacher forced her to confront 'the inequities of a system that worked, paradoxically, for those who did not need it, those who already knew, as if by some genetic memory or code, how to write. What I began to see was that what worked in teaching "the best" writers was of little value to the rest'. In seeking to explain the failure of the workshop, Haake (1994: 80) initially looked to 'the dissonance that exists between the traditional male "mentor" and his often female students', but she later arrived at a more inclusive indictment: that 'the ideology embedded in the very way we conduct ourselves as a discipline is alienating and problematic for male students as well'.

Bly (2001) even wonders whether workshops make writing worse. Even though she includes 'literary fixing' as a late stage in the multi-stage writing process she proposes, she 'can't help noticing that groups aren't really much good at doing literary fixes'. Her students 'report impatience with the halting pace of group critiquing', and she observes that groups seldom suggest a change 'that hasn't been suggested a thousand times'. Further, groups 'miss, or at least give too little attention to, the subtle points of a writer's prose', and they 'balk at saying anything unusual, lest they look like fools' (p. 45). They easily fall into small talk, watering down writers' most genuine ideas instead of helping the writing to go deeper. Jim Heynen (2004) offered a similar observation: 'A wise person once said that whatever your peers find most problematic in your writing is probably your gift.'

The critique workshop's poor fit for beginning writers

When Mary Swander (2005) examined the history of the workshop and its emphasis on critique, she reached a provocative conclusion: *it was never intended for beginning writers*. She reports that the approach was designed a half-century ago at the Iowa Writers' Workshop for writers who were presumed to be accomplished but who needed toughening up for the beating they would later take from critics. But when graduates of Iowa and similar programs taught creative writing courses elsewhere, they brought the workshop format with them – using it even in beginning classes, and as a means of *teaching*, not just as a final toughening up.

Swander writes that she used the critique workshop herself – until she became a writer in the schools:

> I couldn't ask second graders to go write a finished poem and come back for a critique. So, I had to give the students building blocks in direct, understandable ways. I developed exercises and series of hands-on demonstrations of ideas and concepts. We wrote together collaboratively as a class, and I had students write in pairs to develop confidence and generate rough-draft material. (pp. 168–9)

Next she 'carried this building-block approach back to the university setting' and found it worked better there too (p. 169). Jill Baumgaertner (2004), a creative writing teacher who is now an academic dean, told me that she 'was highly suspicious of courses that use nothing but workshop' because 'undergrads need more direction' as well as 'more hands-on'. Don Bogen (1981: 13), who calls for an emphasis not on products but on process – much of it involving imitation of published writers' ways of finding ideas, getting started actually writing and doing revision –

charges that the workshop at its best 'produces superficially proficient but empty work, and at its worst it gives young writers a narrow and distorted idea of what writing actually *is*'. Paul Brooke (2004) describes a similar process-emphasis approach in 'Travelling Theory: Exploring the Deep Rainforest of the Creative Writing Classroom'.

Swander came to think of the critique workshop as a 'shame-and-blame method', one that 'merely covers up the instructor's inability to guide the student from point A to point B' (2005: 173).

One place we can hear that shame-and-blame tone is where Louis Catron (1984), in *Writing, Producing, and Selling Your Play*, satirizes 10 types of writers who resist criticism, including 'the negatively deaf', who *act* appreciative but secretly feel abused; 'the wall' type that 'used to be human' but now has become a shield that 'hides the tender self from comments'; and 'the porcupine' – a 'surly brute' who 'responds by tossing barbs for every barb received'. Female students would feel especially targeted by two other types: *'Who, Li'lOl' Me?* Break out the Kleenex because this one will become a rain cloud at the faintest hint of a discouraging word'; and '(Wide-eyed and with an oh-so-meek tone) *But Mother Liked My Play. And My Friends. Just Everyone.* You feel like a cad to disagree with mother' (pp. 231–32).

What kind of guilt or frustration in a teacher precipitates such sarcasm?

Part of the 'ideology embedded in the very way we conduct ourselves as a discipline' that Haake (1994) questions is the seldom-examined assumption that advice and critique are *good* for writers. In reading roughly a hundred syllabi for introductory creative writing courses, most available on the web, I found a litany: criticism is helpful, you need to learn to take it, some day you'll be glad you went through it ... Nobody wrote 'no pain, no gain', but that's what I began hearing. I thought, 'If this many teachers devote this much rhetoric to *defending* critique, shouldn't they also inquire whether there are problems with it that cannot be attributed to an excess of tenderness in those who have to endure it?'

At the least we should ask *when* critique is valuable. Bizzaro (2004: 296) observes that our foundational idea is that master teachers 'teach what they do when they write'; however, given our emphasis on critique it is more accurate to say that they teach what they do as they prepare manuscripts for publication. What they do when they *write* starts much earlier, and in early stages writers benefit less from critique than from response that offers *accompaniment* – as I'll explain in Chapters 4 and 5. And yet my survey suggests that roughly three-quarters of creative writing teachers rely heavily on the critique workshop, even for introductory courses. If Haake is right, that such a workshop works only for the best writers, then the question is, how many others, given less critique and more accompaniment early on, could *become* good? I notice that more teachers who use the workshop and think carefully about it are asking that question. For instance, Anna Leahy (2010) calls the workshop 'our profession's signature pedagogy' (p. 65), but she adds that in an introductory course, 'I delay the sharing of student work until students have begun to learn together to read as writers and to use common vocabulary to talk about writing concepts' (p. 72).

Fine-tuning the Practice of Critique

Since most agree that critique does have a place late in an introductory course and in advanced courses, I'll review ways teachers try to make it succeed. Robert Vivian (2004) wrote that 'what's at stake is so important and valuable, especially at the beginning, that a teacher is a caretaker as well as a catalyst'. He explained, 'Workshops are excellent for creating space, time and (hopefully) mutual support between and among a host of different writers. More and more I see my role as one who is duty-bound to create this important and supportive space ... [T]here's a delicate balance to be achieved and honored in a workshop.' Good workshop leaders are acutely aware of that 'delicate balance'. Some guide not just practice but also attitude. I admire the 'guidelines for workshop etiquette' sent to me by Paul Hedeen (2002):

- **Respect the space and the sounds**: actually, it is both a privilege and a necessity 'to hear' creative writing. Be a respectful audience: considerate, affirming, constructive. Be a practiced reader: rehearse your work.
- **Doing unto others**: every writer wants his/her work to be dealt with decisively (to the point) but with tact and sensitivity. Often, the workshop criticizes or praises immoderately, especially the former. Temper criticism with praise. Choose language that is accurate but sensitive. Believe as well as doubt. Be precise: point to places in the language that are successful or that are weak. Offer the kinds of commentary that you find most useful to receive. Even though we would rather be ruined by praise than saved by criticism (to paraphrase Lincoln), our job in this class is 'to grow'.
- **Amazing grace**: accept criticism graciously. It is offered with love of our common and complex endeavor, trying to perform a difficult task well. Shun defensiveness – even though it sometimes feels sooo good.

- **Be extravagant**: spend your language 'like there is no tomorrow' or like you wish you could spend money. Every writer must risk failure and then having failed, or only narrowly having succeeded, be willing to revise (to re/see) his or her work.

Hedeen acknowledges that critique and learning from critique are always threatened by the emotions it arouses. Nicole Mazzarella (2004) involves students in designing ground rules. Her classes 'spend a day talking about how we're going to workshop'. She describes her own workshop experiences and asks students what kind they want. For example, 'I let them express their concern that others will be too nice to them' as a way of encouraging everyone to be specific and helpful.

Most teachers try to make response and critique less personal, especially by urging students to distinguish the work from the writer. Laura Apol (2004) stressed that 'it's off-limits to ask about the experience itself'. If a respondent does need to refer to the writer, she suggests that they do so 'in the third person as "the author" or "the writer" rather than addressing them directly as "you"'. Another way to make response less personal is with I-oriented rather than you-oriented statements, as Andrew Sofer's (2002) 'Intro to Creative Writing' syllabus illustrates:

> Use the language of response rather than the language of judgment ('The rawness of the language distracted me from the content' beats 'This piece is really offensive'; 'I had problems investing in the characters – what's at stake for them?' beats 'Your characters suck!'). Be precise: 'I felt the imagery lose steam in the third stanza' beats 'The language is kind of vague.'

Such I-oriented language comes across as one reader's experience of the piece rather than as the judgment of an authority. The language of response is discussed further in Chapters 4 and 5.

Teachers disagree whether indications of problems in a piece of writing should be accompanied by proposed solutions. Jim Heynen (2005) wrote in the survey that one of his guidelines says, 'Critical responses should state or imply alternatives. "I don't like this" is not a useful response.' However, because a critique *with* a solution threatens to appropriate the text, Barbara Bogue wrote in the survey that one of her guidelines warns, 'No "re-writing" another's story – stick to the story on the page.' One way out of this dilemma is the rather demanding guideline that Elizabeth Slattery (2004) noted in her survey: for any piece of criticism her students offer, 'at least two solutions must be suggested'. One respondent wrote that she asks for 'a discussion of the most compelling ideas/ feelings/conflicts the piece is struggling with and *possible* ways of exploring them'.

Response roles and written response

Rather than simply inviting discussion, some teachers assign one or more students to take particular *roles* in responding, especially in initiating response. Some teachers make this respondent a partner with the author. Donald Platt (2004) noted in a survey comment, 'Workshop discussion is always initiated and directed by a student who has been paired with the author as his or her partner.' Platt allows these partners to rotate during the course of the semester. In email, he elaborated: 'Guidelines for the partner/introducer are simply to read the poem closely with the class, explain the poem's formal and psychological dynamics as completely as possible, offer an interpretation of the poem, identify the poem's strengths, and then offer a few suggestions for revision.' The advantage, he finds, 'is to engage the students more closely with each other's work and, incidentally, to eliminate any awkward moment when we're all wondering who is going to be the first to lead off the discussion'. Another advantage I see is that at least one student will feel called upon to respond in some depth; in addition, the teacher's comments are less likely to dominate.

Some teachers have several or even all students *write* a critique, usually in preparation for the workshop session, and if these critiques go to the writer, the teacher usually asks that they be signed. An advantage of pre-workshop writing is that students are better prepared. A risk is that they may come *too* prepared – too committed to their initial way of reading. Assuming that the teacher also reads these critiques, a related risk is that the student may respond to impress the teacher, which may or may not assist the writer.

Moving written response onto a listserv allows writers to address the whole class. Posts prior to a workshop might do some of the preliminary work of the workshop. However, Natasha Sajé (2005) wrote that she asks students to post their comments *after* the workshop discussion. Her 'Introduction to Creative Writing' syllabus calls for weekly posts 'giving feedback to one of your classmate's one-pagers, or addressing an issue we did not get to in class'.

An advantage of a listserv over workshop response is that introverts, who like to think things through before speaking and who, consequently, are likely to offer responses worth hearing, have more opportunity to contribute. When they find their contributions valued, most contribute more to whole-class discussions.

Listserv discussion also poses risks: in a workshop, because visible reactions usually signal when a comment is unclear or even hurtful, it can be immediately clarified or modified. However, an injudicious post is out there in everybody's inbox, and responses from others may pile up more damage, perhaps dividing the class between sympathizers and those who think that *some* people are just being too sensitive. Teachers who use listservs learn that they need to monitor them.

Departures from the Standard Workshop

Earlier I cited Ostrom's (1994) question, 'What might be gained by dismantling the workshop model altogether and starting from scratch?' Michelene Wandor (2008) would dismantle it. Her mantra in the later chapters of *The Author is Not Dead, Merely Somewhere Else* is 'The workshop must go' (p. 219). She would replace it with in-class writing, followed by students' listening to each other's pieces as they develop, and she would replace critique with informed *noticing*: 'All the pieces are heard again, and I draw attention to relevant stylistic/linguistic features to draw out the aesthetic and convention-distinctive implications of the appropriate genre, and to generate observation of these aspects of the language' (p. 213).

Rather than starting from scratch, I'll describe, in Chapter 4, one alternative structure for response – writers' groups. Here I'll consider two modifications that suit either the full-class open workshop or writers' groups: emphasizing kinds of response other than critique; and teaching writers to solicit the response they think they most need.

Response other than critique

A good way to reduce the damage critique can do – as well as prepare students to do critique better – is to emphasize other kinds of response, especially in introductory courses.

Clearly teachers do other things *besides* critique in the workshop. Some begin with a close reading of the work-in-progress, as Gina Franco did in the account presented earlier. One wrote in a survey comment, 'I also ask students to think about the piece intellectually – what argument is it making? What values or beliefs does it advocate or challenge?' Tom Kealey (2004) said he begins by having respondents say what they think the story is *about* – a question that may reveal as much about the reader as about the piece being discussed. And a significant number of teachers say they emphasize reader-response. Of those completing my survey,

38% checked, 'Except with near-final drafts, responders should describe their response as readers instead of offering criticism or advice for revision.' The way Joey Horstman (2005) does this is illustrated by his questions: What is the most interesting thing you find? A good word or sentence? What's working? Tell the writer how you were interpreting the character. What's the tone of the piece? The pacing? Where did you lose interest?

Some teachers use reader-response to lead up to critique, but Juliana Spahr (2004) stays with reader-response. Normally, if a teacher asks, 'How does the piece work?' students hear '*How well?*' Spahr's approach keeps responders in the *how*. Before workshopping, she asks students to post listserv responses of at least 500 words, explaining that 'responses can be detailed discussions of how a poem or the poems are made'. She also lists 'some possible questions to answer', and these integrate aspects of Elbow and Belanoff's (2000) 'descriptive responding':

- What do you notice about this poem?
- Say back to the author what the poem is saying.
- What is almost said in this poem?
- What is lurking underneath the poem? What is unsaid in the poem?
- What is the center of gravity in the poem?
- What moves the poem along?
- What line can the poem not live without and why?
- What line would you remove if you had to remove one line?
- What word is central to the poem?
- What word would you remove if you could?
- What is missing?

Only a few of the later questions call for anything like critique or advice. Primarily, the question of whether and how the piece should be revised is left to the writer.

Notice in addition that a particular *kind* of reader is assumed for this reader-response, one who is also a writer examining how poems work. In fact, Spahr also draws upon Charles Bernstein's (2006) 'Experiments' for what might be called *writer*-response, including 'creative rewrites of a poem or poems':

- Reverse the poem. Change a phrase like 'turn of day' to 'straight of night'.
- Take the poem and put blanks in place of three or four words in each line, noting the part of speech under each blank. Then have someone else replace the blanks with random words.

- Write an entirely new poem by imitating the poem.
- Change all statements to questions. Or vice versa.
- Change the location of the poem.
- Change the tense of the poem.
- Eliminate parts of the poem.

She tells students that the idea is 'to get you examining how a poem is made in close detail'. Such experiments should also expand their repertoire of re-making moves. Perhaps an inventive responder might do something so interesting that the writer feels pushed aside, but a spirit of playfulness should limit that risk.

Asking the writer to set the agenda

When the addressee in *Letters to a Young Poet* asks for critique, Rilke (2000) responds, 'There is nothing that manages to influence a work of art less than critical words. They always result in more or less unfortunate misunderstandings' (p. 9). That he later offers criticism doesn't mean that he contradicts himself. I think it means that he believed that before giving over work to another for judgment, writers should first consider how the writing matters to them and what they are trying to do in it or through it. Rilke urges the young poet, 'Go within. Search for the cause, find the impetus that bids you write' (p. 11). This search within reminds writers to listen to criticism in relation to the impetus for the piece so that they avoid letting response appropriate their work.

As important, when readers know something of the writer's impetus, they can relate their response to the writer's sense of where the piece is coming from and what it needs to become. One result is that 'unfortunate misunderstandings' are avoided on both sides.

Nevertheless, most teachers follow the practice Nancy Kuhl (2005: 5) describes: '... participants share work with the group, then listen silently as group members discuss the merits and weaknesses of the piece.' Of those responding to my survey, 68% agreed that the writer should be silent, although some invite the writer to respond at the end of the session – if time allows.

A few let the writer say a little more. Adam Brooke Davis (2004) wrote that he allows the author to 'respond to critiques in class with questions, not defenses or explanations'. Ann Frank Wake (2004) goes a little farther: 'The poet has the opportunity to "explain" anything he/she deems relevant after listening to initial responses.'

By contrast, only a small minority, 13%, said they at least some of the time give the guideline, 'The writer should lead the workshop session and actively seek specific response'. Thom Tammaro (2004) said that in his classes 'writers are encouraged to indicate "problem" areas they are having in their work that's submitted for critique'. Why don't more teachers give the writer a voice in the workshop session?

One reason is that writers facing critique can behave in irksome ways. Thus Paul Willis (2004) admonishes, 'The writer should not apologize for the draft before presenting it to the group', and Jessica Farquhar, in a survey comment, said she warns, 'No elaborate defenses from the writer'. Defensive writers may not *listen* very well either.

A more principled reason for the silent writer tradition is that workshopping is considered a time for *readers* to have their say. Dawson (2005: 77) argues that although early creative writing teachers doubted that writing in the artistic genres could be directly taught, they did believe that writers benefited from learning to read like a writer, and they saw the workshop as opportunity to learn this kind of reading. He cites Tate, who said his aim was 'to prepare students to teach themselves to write by a particular practice of reading'. I do not believe that this worthy aim is sacrificed when the writer sets an agenda for response, though the range of response is likely to be reduced – resulting in fewer 'fortunate misunderstandings', but also fewer irrelevant ones.

We might ask ourselves whether another reason we resist letting the *writer* set some of the agenda for response is that the teacher may have less opportunity to direct the discussion and offer impressive insights.

The most substantial reason to silence the writer is an understandable ambivalence toward a writer's intention. Richard Robbins (2004) indicated in my survey that in responding to student drafts he would be unlikely either to 'Speculate on what the writer seems to want to do in the piece but hasn't yet done' or to 'Respond to the writer's comments, concerns, or questions about the piece'. His reason is that he wants to focus on how the *work* can be construed, not on what the writer intended:

> I like to think of the poem as a private utterance trying to become something that will have a public life beyond the writer. So I don't care what the writer intends so much as what the poem's language is telling me it is trying to be. I would be very careful about interpreting the meaning of an unfinished poem, because there actually may be no real meaning until several stages of revision have been completed. Questions from the writer are useful sometimes, but only at the end of discussion, after the uncued readings and misreadings of peers have let the writer know how the poem, *on its own*, is telling readers. Ultimately, there will not be writers around telling readers how

to read their poems. The writer's job is to create compelling, telling language and then let the poem go.

I agree that an artistic piece needs 'to become something that will have a public life beyond the writer' and that writers need readers' help in listening to what a work is becoming. If, as has often been said, we write in order to discover what we have to say, then the process of composing in language must be richly generative, outrunning – and thus revising – our intentions. But here we encounter a paradox: the work must speak for itself, yes; but it must also speak for the person who revises it and signs it. Thus Catherine Wiley (2005) asks, 'Why should the writer stay quiet when others are discussing her/his work? It is going to be her/his job to revise, after all.' Juliana Spahr (2004) took a similar position, adding that writers are best able to *hear* response when they ask for it:

> They come to the workshop and get the information they need. It does not matter if we think their work sucks or is perfect. This judgment is not our job; the general and larger culture publication machine will sort that out for us. Our job is to tell them how their piece works; how we read it; how we misread it. This is best done when they are saying, Here is what I wanted to do, is it happening?

Worth adding is Steve Westbrook's (2004: 3) observation that in spite of typical textbook exercises that 'present students with the illusion of purposeless writing', we would be hard pressed to find published writers who are not trying to make something happen through their writing.

An approach that foregrounds the artist's intention

Observing Carolyn Holbrook's creative writing workshop, I noticed that writers presenting work for response first talked about what they were trying to do and then indicated what kind of response they thought would be helpful. Then they listened, without defending their writing, and sometimes asked follow-up questions. Said another way, readers and the writer engaged in *dialogue*.

Their practice illustrated what Holbrook had written on her survey: 'For a long time, I used the model which demands that students remain silent. I now find the model that allows the student to be in control of the critique of their work far more productive and empowering.' She later emailed that she had 'seen students crumble under the "take your medicine" model' (2004a). She had used it for a time, but it 'never hit the right spot with me and I kept looking for a better way'. She found that better way in choreographer Liz Lerman's rethinking of assumptions about how performers and fellow artists can best support an artist's desire to advance a work-in-progress and at the same time to grow as an artist. Her rethinking challenges the assumptions of critique workshop.

Lerman (2003) writes that after several years as an artist, 'I finally acknowledged to myself how uncomfortable I was around most aspects of criticism'. She had been creating art, performing art and teaching the making of art but remained troubled by 'the array of feelings brought up by both giving and receiving criticism'. Critique sessions were 'often brutal and frequently not very helpful'. In the role of critic, although she 'had plenty to say', she 'kept wondering why' she was saying the particular things she said. In the role of artist, the longer she worked as a choreographer the fewer people she trusted to tell her about her work 'since much of what I received in the form of criticism from others seemed to tell me more about their biases and expectations than about the particular dance of mine being discussed. It didn't seem to me to really be about helping me to make the best dance I could from my *own* imagination'.

So Lerman evolved an alternative grounded in the artist's questioning. 'I discovered that the more I made public my own questions about the work, my work, the more eager I was to engage in a dialog about how to "fix" the problem.' She had learned from conversations with friends and with other choreographers that 'often, just talking about the messes that are an inevitable part of creating new work, talking about it out loud from my perspective, pointed a way out of the dilemma'. As a result, she 'began to wonder what would happen if critical sessions were indeed in the control of the artist'. She experimented with response in the form of questions rather than advice and found that this got the group deeper into the work because its 'motivation and meaning to the creator became the basis on which feedback was given'. She found that with her students' work, not only could she raise all of her concerns through questions, but that also, to her amazement, there was no resistance: they engaged with the questions rather than defending their work.

Whether a response session was productive, Lerman decided, depended upon two 'preconditions': the first is that artists seeking response need to *publicly* question their work as part of inviting response; the other is that the responders must 'want this artist to make excellent work'. (She observes that sometimes 'people looking at work don't want the artist to succeed, especially on his or her own terms'. This may be especially true when artists are students, competing for grades or attention.)

Her response session itself has four stages. The first is 'Affirmation', by which she means that responders should mention aspects of the work that gave them satisfaction. She explains that artists 'want to hear that what they have just completed has meaning to another human being', a desire she describes as 'so intense at times as to appear desperate'. Because affirmation easily becomes trite, she offers the model, '[W]hen you did such-and-such it was surprising, challenging, evocative, compelling, delightful, unique, touching, poignant, different for you,' and so on.

Stage two she calls 'Artist As Questioner.' Her observation is that '[t]he more artists clarify what they are working on and where their own questions are, the more intense and deep the dialog becomes'. Like the affirmation, the questions must be *specific*:

> It doesn't work to say 'tell me what you think' since in my experience people don't really mean that, and if we do tell them what we think, they get defensive. But if a person says, 'Do you think my arm should be this way or this way?' or 'I'm working right now on the way I express a strong feeling, what did you think of this section?' the respondents are given the opportunity to say exactly what they think in a way the creator is prepared to hear.

Lerman finds that 'usually the artist has the same questions that those watching do', but when the *artist* asks first, 'the opportunity for honesty increases'.

At this stage she defines an additional role, *facilitator*, because she discovered that while some artists are fully able to analyze their work and move from their dissatisfactions into specific questions, for others 'it is a new experience'. So working from a general question from the artist, the facilitator 'can help make it specific and find the real heart of the matter'. But the facilitator 'needs to probe with more questions, not with answers'. In a writing workshop, this facilitator role might be played by the instructor or by a student paired with the writer.

Stage three is 'Responders ask the Questions'. Rather than offering criticism or advice,

> ... responders form their opinions into a neutral question. So instead of saying, 'It's too long', a person might ask, 'What were you trying to accomplish in the circle section?' or 'Tell me what's the most important idea you want us to get and where is that happening in this piece?'.

The facilitator may also need to help responders with question-forming because for many, 'forming a neutral question is not only difficult, but a seemingly ridiculous task if criticism is the point'. Lerman notes that this role can be difficult for participants 'who are used to giving feedback from a position of authority: teachers, directors, folks called in to "fix" a piece', perhaps because they feel that they are 'giving up the right to tell the truth very directly'. Lerman counters, first, that she can say 'whatever is important' through questions – that what she can't say 'probably couldn't be heard, or isn't relevant'; second, 'the actual process of trying to form opinions into neutral questions is precisely the process necessary to get to the questions that matter for the artist'. Hearing compelling questions, the artist becomes 'more open to the possibility of hearing what others are saying, and actually learning from it'.

Stage four Lerman calls 'Opinion Time'. If a responder 'really has an opinion that can't be stated as a neutral question and this person feels that the artist really needs to hear it', then he or she *asks permission* to offer it. Lerman believes that there are 'times when artists can use these opinions to help place the work in a larger context' or 'to weave his or her own solution'. In Lerman's experience, artists are always willing to hear from everyone offering an opinion. She adds, 'It is curious to note that often during this opinion time, people choose to do more affirmation.'

Lerman holds off discussion of subject matter or content until after stage four, finding that it can break the momentum of response if it comes earlier.

Implications of Lerman's practice for creative writing

Lerman's beginning with affirmation of aspects of the work does more than gratify the artist and confirm that responders want the artist to do good work. It also brings them alongside, experiencing the work as readers or fellow writers rather than as critics. I think that this is also why, for responders, 'the actual process of trying to form opinions into neutral questions is precisely the process necessary to get to questions that matter for the artist'. Questioning helps them think *with* the artist and imagine what the artist is trying to do.

I also find provocative Lerman's discovery that some artists seem unable to question their own work. How can they revise if they don't know how to question/examine the work in some other light than the glow of inspiration? If an agenda-setting role for the artist is crucial for getting response that the artist can work with, and if that agenda-setting role depends upon the artist's capability to publicly question the work, then an introductory course in artistic writing ought to teach questioning and reflection. That is the focus of the following chapter.

If writers can learn to ask questions that get genuinely helpful responses from fellow writers, then response can take place not in the teacher-led critique workshop but in more supportive writers' groups. That's Chapter 4.

And writers asking good questions can reposition instructors from the role of expert reader, offering free-wheeling critique and advice, toward the role of experienced writer, responding in ways that *accompany* the writer. That's Chapter 5.

Chapter 3
Reflection and the Dialogic Self

> *Speaking as a woman, what I would say is that it is never enough to know what we know; we also need always to know how we know it, and, most especially, to know what we don't know. To know the knowing as well as the not.*
>
> Katherine Haake (2000: 11)

Here's the story about how I came to ask the kind of questions Lerman asks, especially this one: What if the *artist's* questions about and vision for a work-in-progress were to guide most response to it?

I was teaching a news writing class. Early assignments provided a reporter's notes on an event from which students were to construct a news story, with the most 'newsworthy' information in the lead. Sometimes intelligent students made judgments that puzzled me, and since there were only five students, I began asking them to explain their thinking. One assignment was to write a story about a commencement at which there had been a protest against the speaker. Our textbook's advice to highlight the atypical within a routine story should have cued students to lead with the protest; however, one good student left it out entirely. When I asked why, she said, 'Well, I just thought, if that were *my* commencement, my grandmother would cut out the story for her scrapbook, and she wouldn't want that protest stuff in there!' Here was sound thinking about why a significant group of readers would prefer the routine story. We decided that a reporter might suggest running two stories, the routine one in its usual location and a story about the protest on page one.

I learned from such exchanges that I could not teach writing without access to the writer's *thinking* about the writing. I later encountered the discovery in the words of Jeffrey Sommers (1989: 175): '... the best way to get students to provide answers we would like about how they compose is to ask them direct questions'. Thus I began asking students to attach a note to the story, the kind they might give to an editor to explain certain choices they made when writing it. These notes soon showed me that much of the time I had spent pointing out problems in their stories had been wasted: the writers often recognized the problem; what they needed was help working through it. The notes let me get right to the point of giving them that help.

I began to rename what I was doing: 'teaching news writing' gave way to 'teaching *persons* how to think and act in the *roles* of reporter and writer'. In those roles, they needed to consider, for each story, the probable judgments of editors as well as what readers already knew and would want to know. To get a handle on the problems they encountered in thinking about these things, I next asked writers to include a question in the note to me. Like Lerman, I discovered that some writers had a hard time asking good questions – typically the weaker writers. The happy surprise was that as they learned to ask better questions they became better able to think in the role of news writer and thus wrote better stories.

Next I learned to read the note first and to let its perceptions and questions shape my response. I noticed that students became more eager to read my comments – and they *learned* from them. When the notes revealed difficulties shared among several of the students, I devoted class time to working through them, making that time more productive too.

But strange things were happening to my authority. *Students* were setting much of the agenda, both for my response and for my in-class teaching. They became less concerned with pleasing me but more focused on learning, on becoming writers instead of just completing assignments. I became less of an authority over them but more of an authority beside them – a resource, translator, typical reader, writing coach.

Of course this shift in authority complicated grading. Students accustomed to hiding problems in order to 'make a good impression' were being asked to *acknowledge* problems and uncertainties. They must have wondered whether they should do that or if it would be smarter to fake understanding in hopes of making a better impression. And for my part, should I give a lower grade where problems were acknowledged – or a higher one, since a problem acknowledged is closer to being solved? I'll consider such dilemmas in Chapter 8, on grading.

A 'Fruitful and Trustworthy Source of Learning' and a 'Different Way of Teaching'

I soon learned of other teachers who had made similar discoveries about the benefits of written reflection, not just to responders but also to the writer. Peter Elbow (1986: 38) described how, during a serious bout of writer's block, he found that turning aside and *writing about being unable to write* somehow brought him around to writing again. His aim in such reflecting was 'to write as honestly and accurately as I could about *what's going on* in my mind and feelings as I write – particularly at moments of frustration'. He came to call this reflection 'the most fruitful and trustworthy source of learning for me – in the personal realm or in matters of learning and teaching' (pp. 38–9).

The study of reflection that holds most promise for teachers of creative writing is Kathleen Yancey's (1998) *Reflection in the Writing Classroom*. Yancey gives equal emphasis to benefits of reflection for the writer and for readers who respond to and evaluate writers. In her case, it was work with assessment (which in the US refers to institutional evaluation of programs rather than teacher evaluation of individual students) that taught her that any attempt to assess a text is 'perilously incomplete' without the writer's 'accounts of what went into the making of that text'. But later she realized that these accounts by writers offered teachers something larger and more powerful, a *story* about students' learning, 'a story about how they learned and what they learned, about how that both dovetailed with what I'd planned, and departed from that agenda'. From reading these texts, she began to understand 'what was obvious: there was a lot more and other going on in my classes than I'd understood previously. So I began to ask about that – what's going on here? – sometimes abruptly, without warning, without really knowing what I was asking, much less what I expected to learn'. As she learned to ask more carefully, she 'became better able to read student cues as signals teaching me what was important, what needed to be asked. In time, which questions to ask of students, how to ask them, when to ask them became not a way of research apart from the classroom, but a means of learning for students and teacher *in* the classroom, and a different way of teaching for me' (p. 17).

Yancey's story about the pleasure of wondering about and reflecting upon what was happening within and among her students, leading to 'a different way of teaching', parallels my own story. One result is this book, which I hope will both provoke and inform readers' own reflections about the persons who enter their classrooms seeking to become writers.

Getting Students to Write Good Reflections

Students who are merely *assigned* to write a reflection about their writing seldom do it very well. First, they need guidance in learning what reflection is, why it is worth doing and how to go about it. Second, since they assume new authority in doing this writing, they need to feel *authorized*. Third, most of them, much of the time, need peers and teachers to *respond* so that reflection leads to dialogue, which becomes internalized as a pattern of thought that informs and deepens subsequent reflection, eliciting even better response, bolstering writers authority over their own writing ... and so on.

Explaining reflection to students

Yancey's useful definition of reflection emphasizes *time* – looking backward and looking forward:

> In method, reflection is dialectical, putting multiple perspectives into play with each other in order to produce insight. Procedurally, reflection entails a *looking forward* to goals we might attain, as well as a *casting backwards* to see where we have been. When we reflect, we thus *project* and *review*, often putting the projections and the reviews in *dialogue* with each other, working dialectically as we seek to *discover* what we know, what we have learned, and what we might understand. (p. 6)

Thus, a written reflection about a piece of writing starts with two questions: where did this writing *come from* and where is it *going* (where do I want it to go or where does it seem to want to go)?

Reflection in creative writing is likely to differ from reflection in a course in a more transactional genre such as news writing. Transactional writing comes mostly from outside the person – from a problem to be solved, a scene or event to be described or a purpose to be accomplished with a given audience. Thus in a reflection about such writing, asking where it comes from brings the writer's attention back to the problem or occasion or purpose, and asking where it is going directs attention to ways the writing still needs to change in order to accomplish its purpose with its audience. Transactional writing also happens mostly on the outside of language: it is acting by means of language more than a way of knowing through language.

Artistic writing happens more on the *inside*, emerging from the writer's own experience, motives and emotions, shaped and colored by imagination. Artistic writing also happens inside language: because the artistic genres encourage playful engagement with the materiality of language, these genres are peculiarly suited to *discovery*. The writer is more likely to be engaged with an artistic problem – say, working out the form of a villanelle or the plot of a piece of sudden fiction – than with having a particular effect upon an audience. Thus, 'Where did this writing come from?' is likely to find its answer in an experience of the artist, an impulse, an idea or an artistic challenge; and 'Where is it going?' might translate into 'What might happen next?' or 'What needs to be added or taken away for this *form* to be complete?' These questions are deliberately ambiguous about agency: the writer is responsible for revision; yet because language and the artistic process are co-writers, responders must also listen to where words or language patterns or the incipient form of the piece seem to *want* to go.

And because reflection articulates desire, including aesthetic desire, a third reflective question, 'What do I *like* about this writing?', assumes added significance with the artistic genres, where liking drives discovery and guides revision. The writer's answer to this question also matters to responders because it helps them view the work from the writer's perspective and know how it matters to him or her, which makes them less likely to appropriate the writing or to make a comment that is unhelpful or even painful to the writer, and more likely to think with the writer about what comes next.

What results is an easily remembered formula for a writer's memo that works with any genre of artistic writing at any stage in its revision:

- **'Where did this writing come from?'** invites the writer to recall how a prompt, a personal experience, an idea, an activity such as reading, an artistic challenge and so on helped get the writing started. This is a compelling question for beginning writers, who need to become aware of the sources for their best ideas and who need to learn how to move from there toward a piece of writing that is whole and complete. Richard Hugo's (1979) *The Triggering Town* gets its title from the kind of experience – in his case a kind of place – that typically triggered his writing. For writing that has gone astray, sometimes just remembering where it came from can get the writer back on track.

- **'Where is it going?'** asks what the piece seems to be *becoming*. What parts belong or are most alive? What parts seem to drift off-track? What connections and relationships hold promise? What partial patterns beg for continuation or completion? As the course proceeds, and as writers gain a better sense of genre, this question about where a work is going can be asked more in terms of criteria that define success in the genre.

- **'What do I like?'** invites articulation of *pleasures:* Were there enjoyable discoveries? What about the piece as it appears now (a character, situation, idea, image, action, aspect of form) interests the writer enough to motivate further work on it? Writers who are good critics and who too easily see what's wrong with a draft are usually better

able to revise when they identify what's strong or alive in it. Writers learn that they need to care about a piece in order to keep working on it. When a writer cannot find much to like about a draft and readers can't either, the writer can more readily let it go and move on.
- Finally, writers ask themselves, **'What kind of response will help me revise the piece toward what it needs to become?'** As I will explain further in subsequent chapters, as writers learn the discourse of the course and engage in dialogue about works-in-progress, they gain power to use reflection to generate better questions that empower both peer readers and teachers to respond in ways that are both more helpful and less intrusive.

Permitting students to speak freely

We tend to think of reflection as private – talking to oneself. That's Elbow's emphasis, so his textbooks asked students to write what he called a 'process note'. Yancey (1998) also emphasizes the benefits to the writer of stepping outside the text to write about where it came from, what is happening in it, how it is working and where it seems to be going:

> [S]tudents frequently remember ways in which they generated material that they'd been unaware of. Consequently, in the process of recording the process, students learn: about the myriad of methods they use to recall, remember, re-create. And they have a *record* to which they can return. Second, describing processes can be generative: students often create scenes or themes or insights that they can use in a later draft. And third, in such describing, students continue to develop an authority, an *expertise*, about their own writing, about how it works when it works, as well as about how it doesn't. (pp. 28–9)

I agree that reflection can help the writer in all these ways, but I think that few students would realize this potential if they wrote reflections only for themselves. What first motivates students to write good reflections is the opportunity to explain their work and their thinking to a teacher in order to get response that is relevant and helpful. Consider this little testimonial for writers' memos from my student Eileen's mid-semester constructive reflection: 'Often, I sense something missing or something not functioning well in a story. In such instances, writing the memo helps me to articulate what the problem is ... and if I am not sure how to correct the recognized problems, it serves as a way of letting you know that I am aware of it.' She is recognizing that articulating a problem may itself generate a solution, but she also likes being able to articulate her problem *to* someone, mostly, I think, because she believes the response will aid her learning, but also because in explaining herself to someone whose understanding she trusts, and, naturally, *imagining* response, she may become more able to articulate the problem for herself, and from there she may be able to find her own answer.

Because I came to emphasize the *addressed* quality of these reflections and to value the genuine dialogue that results, I decided against calling them 'process notes' or 'learning letters' and settled instead upon Jeffrey Sommers' term, 'writer's memo'. Sommers (1989: 175) also emphasizes dialogue over self-address: what the writer's memo does is put teachers in touch with 'students' other selves', the selves they keep hidden when they worry about grades. Students' impulse to hide part of themselves explains why reflections that are merely *assigned* contain little substance and have minimal value. The voice writers need for productive reflection can be addressed to a teacher *accompanying* them, but not to one who cannot suspend authority *over* them. Recall those scenes in military movies where, in the face of crisis, the junior officer approaches the commander, salutes, and asks, 'Permission to speak freely, Sir?' The permission is granted and the speech tells the commander what he needs to know to take corrective action. Teachers also need to let students know that they have permission to speak freely. One way I do this is to issue invitations that describe the benefits of writers' memos. Here's one:

> Those of you who haven't had a course with me before may think it odd that I ask for a writer's memo with nearly all assigned writing. I do this out of my sense of what a *course* can contribute to your work as a writer: it can help you analyze your own processes as well as develop perspectives from which to view your writing at its various stages – and invite others to helpfully participate in your thinking and revision.
>
> Writers' memos show whether you're asking good questions and they tell me how I can help. One thing I've learned from them is that many of the problems I used to point out were already evident to the writer. When I can find out what you already know, I'm better able to discern what you're not quite seeing, and help you solve problems you are seeing.

Giving permission to speak freely also means accepting the occasional apology. A student may write, 'I had three papers due this week, so I worked only an hour on this draft – I'll do more later.' The writer feels better for being able to explain marginal performance, and I'm rescued from trying to decide how to respond to a piece that doesn't merit response. I've found that students usually keep such promises, probably because they like being treated as responsible adults.

Dialogue becomes internalized and self-sustaining

When we face tough challenges, we naturally call to mind the words that parents, teachers or friends have spoken to us in comparable situations, using their words to 'talk ourselves through' the problem. When students write provocative writers' memos that enable teachers and others to offer response that is genuinely helpful, students *listen* to it. Then gradually they internalize the main themes they hear, and in this way the dialogue becomes a practice of thought that can be elicited by subsequent reflections. I notice that my own students learn to anticipate my response and use it to go ahead and revise further on their own. For example, one student's memo mentioned an image and observed that it needed more detail (something I had observed about her previous poems). She noted, 'Funny how I realize things while typing this.'

Students who 'realize things' while writing reflections then become more motivated to write reflections for themselves. Occasionally I encourage a class to try this in order to call up and think with those inner voices that the dialogue of the course helps to form. Here's an example:

> If you're stuck, try starting, 'I want to write a poem about ____ (or that ____) but what I seem to be up against is ____.' It's odd, but sometimes writing about your stuckness gets you unstuck, and writing about what you want a poem to do helps you figure out how to make that happen – or discover something else you want to do instead.

Students who 'realize things' while reflecting are also more likely to draw upon other resources of the course. Yancey (1998: 6) reminds us that good reflection employs different *ways* of seeing, calling upon 'the cognitive, the affective, the intuitive, putting these into play with each other: to help us understand how something completed looks later, how it compares with what has come before, how it meets stated or implicit criteria, our own, those of others'. Much of 'the cognitive' and especially those 'stated or implicit criteria' are supplied by a text or readings. A practice of reflection encourages students to draw upon such perspectives in order 'to theorize from and about [their] own practices'.

In sum, students doing reflection move from passively complying with our expectations and judgments to thoughtfully soliciting our perspectives.

They also become more attentive readers, better able to learn from theory and from the example of published writers. In this way they become more responsible. Said another way, they act less like students and more like writers.

Reflection in an authentic voice is generative

A freely spoken memo not only tells a teacher more but also has greater generative power for the writer. Peter Elbow (1991: 150), commenting on a study in which students spoke about their composing process, remarked that 'the students probably wouldn't think so clearly and frankly about their own thinking and discourse if they weren't using ordinary language. The vernacular helps them talk turkey'. Jeffrey Sommers (1989: 184) says good reflection speaks in an 'authentic voice' – which can put writers in touch with generative inner voices.

One occasional happy result is a writer's memo with literary potential – sometimes greater potential than the piece it accompanies. Students often conclude from prior experience in English classes that good poems defy understanding, so when they are first asked to write a poem, they may concoct an unreadable jumble of images presented in unpunctuated sentence fragments. Something closer to a readable poem may occur in their writer's memo. After writing haiku in a country cemetery, a student wrote these words in her writer's memo:

> It was getting dark
> while I was watching,
> and the headstones
> were falling in
> with the shadows
> and the cold ground
> that held them.

I broke the writer's paragraph into these lines to illustrate that she had another poem. The rhythm is simple and effective, and the final 'held them' is nicely ambiguous: held the headstones? held the shadows? held the bodies buried beneath those stones and shadows? 'Falling in' fits this pattern too. Andy Mozina (2004) told me about similar experience. He assigned students writing a poem to present their subject first in prose. When one writer 'described what was *there*, just presented it in simple detail' in the prose account, 'the result was beautiful'; however, the poem, Mozina said, was too cryptic – 'she mucked it up'. Similarly, what my student, Jon, submitted as a poem for his first assignment, labeled

'Kitchen Poem', begins with a list of striking images but so random that it mostly defies readers' efforts to identify the speaker and the 'she' who is described, let alone grasp their relationship and find meaning:

> Chipped chairs empty round
> Dinner Table
> Scraps of a meal wait
> To be rescued
> Brittle crumbs and favorite
> Casserole dish
> Still warm still full of
> Greens and carrots
>
> Stumbles and sighs she
> Rubs her tired eyes
> Inspects an index
> Finger and hums
> A Russian sailors'
> Dance dull finger
> Traces circles
> On a calloused palm

His writer's memo begins, 'I brought this poem with me from my youth'. The memo continues in a voice whose rhythms and images reveal the emotions stirred by this writing, but now the situation is readable. Again I have only broken this part of his memo into lines:

> I remember well the table waiting to be cleared
> late in the evening, long past the dinner hour.
> The woman in the scene is a woman who helped shape me.
> Despite fatigue, she always made certain the tasks were completed
> before the end of her day.
> She could have used some help,
> deserved a hand with all the work.
> But she did this work alone, and she hummed.
> Often she hummed the tunes
> she had heard me practicing
> on the piano earlier in the day.
> I learned a Russian sailors' dance
> when I was 12. It sounded foreign to me,
> but I liked it. The melody was contagious.

Here we can identify the speaker and the speaker's relationship to the person the poem describes. We also encounter in 'contagious' the speaker's sense of what mother and son *caught* from each other. In what Jon turned in as a poem, the second stanza has music and promising images but no hint that the Russian Sailor's Dance has anything to do with the speaker – or even who the speaker is or what moved him to utterance.

When I can point to something in a writer's memo and say to a beginning writer, 'Look, you're writing *poetry* here', then the writer can quit trying to be mysterious and simply write under the spell of the emotion, allow himself to be carried along by language. William Stafford (1986: 97) calls poetry 'language with a little luck in it'. A writer's memo is a good space for getting lucky, but writers may at first need help to notice what luck has brought them.

A Way of Thinking About How Creative Writing Can Be Taught

The kind of reflection I have been discussing is *reflection-in-action*. It focuses on a single composing event as it moves forward. Yancey (1998: 14) describes two other kinds: *Reflection-in-presentation* accompanies finished work (often a portfolio) presented to an audience, perhaps an audience not known to the writer, which will evaluate the writer or perhaps assess the course or program. I'll say a little more about it in Chapter 8, on grading. The third kind, *constructive reflection*, will conclude the book. A constructive reflection tells the story of 'the process of developing a cumulative, multi-selved, multi-voiced identity, which takes place between and among composing events, and the associated texts'. When students write a story of their becoming in the course, they gain insight into their own development as writers but also help the instructor construct his or her own story about how the course works – or fails to work – with different writers.

Said another way, these stories help me to theorize about how creative writing can be *taught*.

As Ritter and Vanderslice (2006) show, part of our *lore* – the set of stories we repeat to each other – is that creative writing can't be taught. The dominant assumption is that a group of would-be writers can enjoy camaraderie and productive interaction, pick up aspects of the craft of writing, be inspired by the presence and example of a teacher who is a successful writer, and – largely by critiquing works-in-progress – learn how to *read* the way writers read. This accounts for the workshop – which, when done well, does appear to help some of the best writers to continue to teach themselves through reading and writing. But what about the rest?

The story told by my students' reflections leads me to a quite different conclusion about how a course can help *most* students, not only to produce better writing but also to develop the identity of writer: by writing, reflecting on their writing, bringing those reflections and questions to readers, getting response that becomes better informed and more precise as the course proceeds, and gradually internalizing this response until it becomes an interior dialogue that guides them as they write and revise. The internalized dialogues are the 'voiced' part of what Yancey refers to as the 'multi-selved, multi-voiced identity' of the writer. Now, with help from the ideas of Mikhail Bakhtin, I'd like to theorize about the multiple selves of the developing writer.

A 'multi-selved, multi-voiced identity'

Patrick Bizzaro (1993: 26) decided that he wrote with two selves: the self actually *doing* the writing (an inner self speaking freely in a certain voice); and what he calls a 'guide' self, coming alongside that writing self to bring in different perspectives, or standing over it to direct revision. Bizzaro's provocative conclusion is that his role as a teacher is to serve as students' guide self 'until they are ready to perform in that role by themselves'. Earlier I described how my students' reflections likewise led me to shift from critiquing writing to coaching writers in their thinking and decision-making, so I agree that temporarily serving as students' guide self is perhaps the most significant contribution we as teachers can make to their becoming as writers.

But I believe that the teacher of creative writing, as well as a writer's peers, must also accompany, encourage and draw out that 'writing' self Bizarro mentions, especially in an introductory course.

In addition I would personify what Yancey calls 'goals we might attain' as yet another *self* – namely, the writer we hope to become who has completed some wonderful writing and knows what's good about it. Let's call this the ideal self.

This notion that composing writing and composing the identity of writer both depend upon an inner dialogue among these three interdependent selves I draw from Bakhtin's 'novelistic' theory of human becoming. As explained by Michael Holquist (1991: 38) in *Dialogism: Bakhtin and His World*, Bakhtin views self-change as depending upon an ongoing dialogue among, essentially, three selves: the self I am aware of being at any given moment – the self drawn by fascination and desire, the self audible when my most authentic voices speak; an *ideal* self or hero self, partly projected from the self I have been and now am; and a *guide* self that actively negotiates progress toward that hero self, the self that does the looking when I say, 'I took a good look at myself', the self that observes, reflects, questions, solicits response and directs revision.

A good course addresses the tripartite self of the writer

If writing itself as well as growing and changing as a writer depend upon an open and lively dialogue within a tripartite self, then one way this model helps us to actively *teach* creative writing is by suggesting that a good course will give each self its due:

The inner *writing* self: We can help students develop good habits of attention and perception and provide warm-up exercises and building-block experiences (as Swander suggests). We can provide good working conditions, including encouragement, provocative assignments, inviting models, a milieu in which writing matters. We can encourage solitude and the habit of regular writing as well as help students find *pleasure* in the process (Chapter 9). We can allow writers considerable freedom to explore the subjects they need to take up, perhaps even subjects we or their peers find threatening. To give this self space and time to develop, we can delay not only critique but also grading (Chapter 8). (See Perry, 2010, for in-class writing and interactions to provoke and nurture the writing self.)

The ideal self: While the writing self is drawn by desire and the pleasure of discovery, it is the ideal self and its quest for perfection that drives revision. Thus, part of the business of any creative writing course is to help students, especially through close reading of good models, to develop their aesthetic sense. Further, a good course articulates – and helps students identify with and learn to think with – the criteria that those who love literature use to define excellence. Many or even most students enter our courses with the hope of producing writing that they and others will recognize as *good* – as well as with the hope of becoming someone they and others will see as a *writer*. They are more likely to become that hero-self if they articulate their desires and goals early in the course, and they will be better able to grasp what they have accomplished if at the end they tell the story of their achievement and their becoming in a *constructive reflection* (Chapter 9).

The guide self is the self that negotiates between the writing self and the ideal self – the self that actively questions and reflects, seeks response and then uses response to re-vision the work-in-progress. Clearly, this is the most teachable self and part of what a course can teach it is a more precise and powerful language for reflecting about and questioning works-in-progress. In a course students learn a *discourse* – a shared language for talking about the subject or activity – and although students should write reflections that speak freely they should also learn to speak powerfully, insightfully. Here is a reminder I've given to let students in on my thinking about how the course works:

> Carefully follow guidelines for writers' memos. I often specify them in ways that get you to integrate ideas from the text with your thinking about your stories. For instance, this time I asked you to describe your story in terms of conflict/crisis/resolution or connection/disconnection so that you learn to think in those terms and so that I can hear your thinking (like a track coach watching you in practice, seeing how you stretch and set and move, and listening to you talk about what's happening). I think that most of our learning occurs in such thinking-space, connected to but a little removed from the object or action we're thinking about, dwelling upon, mulling over.
>
> You will also find that when you briefly represent your story for a reader, you can sometimes name what's central to it and from that naming get a fresh start.

The next two chapters view peer response and then teacher response primarily as means to help students to develop the kind of reflective guide self that will help them revise within the course and continue to teach themselves and grow as writers beyond the course.

A way of thinking about *time* in a good course

Another way the three-self dialogical model helps make creative writing teachable is by suggesting how a course should *move* from start to finish.

Too often teachers feel compelled to stake out a fixed position between those who call for a 'nurturing' approach and those who advocate 'discipline'. The discipline side accuses the nurturers of being soft-headed, overly concerned with self-esteem and tolerant of sub-par work. The nurturers respond by wondering how insensitive teachers can ever hope to develop students' confidence to the point where they can *write*. Elliot (1994: 119) is among those who ask why we can't have it both ways:

> Must we agree so readily with a dominant critical view that disparages 'nurturance' (of talent, of ability) out of hand, immediately

consigning this aspect of our labor to a lower, 'feminine' realm? ... Why not consider the ways in which the instilling of discipline and the nurturance of talent *complement* one another, admitting that as instructors we provide not only structure and rigorous critique, but also a context and climate within which a natural gift – and a community of writers – can flourish?

The three-self model suggests how we can 'have it both ways': early in the course, especially an introductory course, teachers should create space to nurture and encourage the writing self; later they should shift emphasis toward criteria that define the excellence sought by the ideal self. As Jerome Bruner (1993: 54) observes, the selves we imagine we might become 'tempt us to action occasionally, and more often they challenge the mundane acts of the Now self'.

One problem with the dominant workshop approach is that it too early and too exclusively addresses the *ideal* self: it tries to tell students whether their writing has arrived and where it falls short before they are ready to see that for themselves. At the same time, it slights the *writing* self that needs safety, opportunity, help to find subject, voice and angle of vision. A third problem is that a workshop course – unless the teacher does conferences and encourages writers to set an agenda – does too little to develop the *guide* self. Yet that is one place where teachers *can* emphasize discipline early on. The guide self might also be called the 'disciplin*ing*' self because it oversees revision. At the start of the course, teachers can insist that students give careful attention to questioning and reflection and to inviting responders, including teachers, to question their drafts with them. If writers do this, by the end of the course most should have at least a few pieces of writing that stand up to scrutiny.

Balancing Individual Writers' Inner Dialogue

A further benefit of the three-self model is that it helps teachers understand and assist different students as they deal with their own peculiar issues.

It's important to notice that the three selves need an equilibrium. The guide self's executive role is crucial for questioning the work-in-progress and soliciting response but a too active guide self can hamper the writing self, resulting in language with little real discovery and in contrived plots. At the same time, a free-rein writing self may utter little more than dazzling nonsense; it needs the guide self to shape the writing for readers. And what about that ideal self, intent on a great finished product?

Kenneth Burke's (1966: 18) famous observation that humans are 'rotten with perfection' suggests that although we need aspirations, they can become obsessive. Aspirations that are too high or too imposing can block the writing self.

Each writer needs just enough tension among the three selves to keep the inner dialogue going and to keep the writer moving ahead with writing and revising. Yet, at the start of the course or in response to components of the course, some are likely to have an inner dialogue that is dominated by one of the three selves.

Avid readers in a creative writing course often have a too-dominant ideal self, a condition that can be exacerbated by a course whose readings are so virtuosic that would-be writers can only admire, not hope to imitate them. One of my students, Ryan, found that with another teacher's workshop approach, little class time was left for finding good models and learning how to read them. Consequently, many students did not learn to read well and as a result were not very authoritative in responding to each other's writing. By contrast, my course allowed more class time to discuss strong models, so his perception was that my students learned earlier to talk about how the writing of their group members worked. The disadvantage for some was that they saw too clearly how far short of the models their own stories fell. As Ryan put it, they had to 'get out from under' the achievement of published writing in order to move ahead with writing of their own.

But an additional benefit of freely spoken writers' memos is that they give me a window on each student's struggle, generally enabling me to respond in ways that help them get their three selves back in balance. Early in the course I might remind writers who are oppressed by great writing that its authors probably also started with what Anne Lamont calls 'shitty first drafts' (quoted in Burroway, 2003: 18). And later on, I may need to tell them, 'Don't worry so much about *constructing* a good plot – just put your characters in a tight spot and see what happens'. Or in poetry class, 'Just start with an image or phrase or line you like and ask it what kind of company it wants'.

Because I emphasize faithfulness and persistence, I also have to be alert for students who already rely on those virtues. Jeannine came into the course with a highly-disciplined guide self as well as with the high expectations for performance that I have associated with the ideal self. She was the kind of student who reads the text, follows directions, asks good questions. Hardest for her to learn, then, was that artistic ways of making often have as much to do with letting go. Both her poem, written in imitation of and homage to Billy Collins, and the memo that follows it are about learning to be drawn by pleasure, not driven by discipline:

All I Ever Needed to Know, I Learned from Billy Collins

Billy Collins came over for dinner last Friday night.
Sure, some girls had dates, but I had the Poet Laureate –
what's better than that?

And after dinner there was dancing, as there usually is.
And good ol' Bill showed me the steps
of all the dances from the old days:

the jitterbug, the fox trot, and the elephant sway,
(that one I think he made up just to see
if I would do it, and I did.)

He in a tuxedo and I in a gown, we twirled around the ballroom
that had become a page – and our shoes
with ink pads fastened to them.

'No worries,' he said,
and we kept on dancing – he showing me
where to pause, where to stop, and where to push on through.

And when to call our dance something else,
like a leather-bound book, a soaring balloon,
or a juicy watermelon (be careful not to trip on the seeds).

We whisked, we turned, pivoted and stopped,
cheeks pink from exertion and breath running
away from us.

'Well,' I panted, 'that sure was educational.'
But William, sweet William, bowed, took my hand,
and kissed it, saying, 'But my dear, the point is to have *fun*.'

Jeannine's writer's memo also emphasizes letting go:

> This poem was written as an imitation of Billy Collins. It was fun because, through Billy Collins, I was given permission to cut loose and write candidly without worrying about sounding 'like a poet'.
> My response group helped me to refine the metaphors in the poem, which was the most challenging part.
> I like this poem because I believe it was my 'breaking through' point to writing my own kind of poetry. I believe that I found my own

voice when it comes to writing poetry; before I'd been trying so hard to present deep thoughts in a deep way, in a voice that really wasn't my own.

Notice how helpful it is for Jeannine to have this space both to acknowledge what her problem had been and to say why she believes she has put it behind her (see in the last chapter her constructive reflection about the course, which also views this poem as a breakthrough).

As her account illustrates, our *writing* self runs largely on pleasure and tends to go silent without it. Yet, in academia we easily forget – even in the arts – how much pleasure matters. We know it is vital to reception – just listen to people talk about their favorite movies or the books or music they keep close by. But we also know as writers the ecstasy of receiving, seemingly as gifts, the apt word, a fresh and evocative image, an astonishing idea. As long as words come and the work moves, we can write without rest or repast. Yet apart from a writer's memo or a conference, what invitation do students in academia receive to express the *pleasure* they have found in doing things with words?

Amanda was the opposite kind of writer, the kind whose inner writing self was capable of carrying her away, so she was also good at writing memos that are freely spoken. Notice how, in the memo following her poem, her associative mind goes sailing on language:

Writing on the Wall

Carlin once got a spanking
when he took a crayon
to the wallpaper in the corner
he had been sent to sit in.

Did he, as he viewed
those bold purple marks
of his own hand, foresee
a bending over your knee?

I wonder this now as we
sit opposite each other,
your stubborn deafness
like a wall. I press my words

against it – they are almost
visible in the air between us.
Whose unpleasant fate are they
spelling? Mine? Or yours?

Okay, so one afternoon I'm sitting in front of my computer, studiously deconstructing *O Pioneers*, and somehow all of a sudden I'm revising 'Flutterings', a poem which has absolutely nothing to do with Willa Cather, and, next thing I know, the good ol' American Heritage dictionary is open in front of me, and I get distracted in the 'w' section as I am trying to decide whether or not 'wonder' is the right word, when suddenly my eyes fall upon the phrase 'writing on the wall'. Now this is a saying I have heard many times, but for some reason I never thought about its meaning. So naturally I follow the directional cross-reference to 'handwriting on the wall', and after observing that words prefixed with 'hemo' are usually the sort that make you wrinkle your nose and say 'yech', attempting to master the pronunciation of 'haute ecole', and appreciating the sounds of 'harliquinade' and 'happenstance', I learn that 'handwriting on the wall' is 'an omen of one's unpleasant fate'. Curiosity sated, I put my deconstruction hat back on. Six or forty minutes later, *O Pioneers* still has a center; however, this poem is on my screen.

I guess the poet is the speaker, and I guess this is partly based on fairly recent memories of talking to my parents, particularly to my mom about post-surgery caretaker options. I don't remember any of us kids scribbling on the wall, but I'm sure that every family must have a wall scribbler, and in my family it would have been Carlin because I was perfect and Andy wasn't as naughty as Carlin was. Fictitious or not, the first two stanzas set up the last two well, don't they? The connection between 'bold purple marks of his own hand' and spanking imagery was accidental, or at least subconscious. I like the play with the literal and figurative writings and walls. I do not like the phrase 'unpleasant fate' – it is straight from the dictionary and too heavy, but the best I can think of. My group members were confused about who the speaker was speaking to in the second stanza. I was intending it to be the speaker's parent, but they thought it was still Carlin. What do you think: do I need to make this clearer?

This isn't a perfect poem, but is much improved from the horrible word poem I wrote during the semester's infancy.

Amanda's writing self wanders happily. To write, she needs a sense of freedom – and she also tends to resist revision. But at this point, late in the course, the desire of her ideal self to write *well* helps to motivate her guide self to reflect and question. Her memo also illustrates the power writers gain as their guide self learns to use the discourse of the course.

The Status of Reflection in Creative Writing

It is difficult to overestimate the value to an artist of a richly informed habit and practice of reflection – and equally difficult for me to imagine helping students become writers without having them do writers' memos. Stafford (1986: 73) writes, 'I'm interested in the psyche that hasn't done something and then does something. What does it do in between? So I always try to get the people to relax enough to pay attention to the things that actually occur to them during the process of writing.' I know of no better way to help students pay attention to this 'in between' than teaching them to write reflections that can also serve to guide response from sympathetic readers. In fact if I had to sum up in a single sentence what a good writing course is, I'd say this: *It's a community in which provocative perspectives and dialogues about writing become internalized, developing in students a reflective capability that equips them to sustain a writing life.*

Yet the literature of creative writing pedagogy, at least until recently, has included few references to written reflection – except in the writings of those who are also steeped in composition theory. Donald Murray (1989: 108–9) writes that he and his students 'share our drafts and our *written* commentaries about how we have written that day or that week, how we have felt, failed, attempted; what problems we have defined and solved or failed to solve, what questions we have answered – or not answered'. Wendy Bishop (1990: 163) mentions a 'writing process cover sheet', which she describes as 'a written narrative that traces the generation, revision, and development of that piece of writing over the time period when it is composed'. And Bizzaro (1993: 73–4) refers to an 'interactive journal': 'Once an exchange took place between us, though, often through an interactive journal ... I could better "see" what they intended. Then I could continue our dialogue in a way that enabled me to participate with them in the meaning-making process'. Paul Brooke (2004: 19) also describes having students use their journals to address him, 'asking me questions about particular stories or poems that they are working on'. These examples of reflection-in-action correspond to what I call a writer's memo.

The idea that students benefit from writing about their writing and their learning shouldn't come as a surprise to creative writing teachers. Aren't the genres of artistic writing themselves forms of reflection, images of life to hold up to life? Yet only a minority among us ask students to reflect about their writing. Because reflection goes by different names, my survey describes five kinds of 'supplementary writing' that teachers might ask writers to submit with works-in-progress:

When students submit drafts or revisions for your written response, how much of the time do you ask them to submit with it each of the following kinds of supplementary writing? (Always = 5; sometimes = 3; never = 1):	5	4	3	2	1
An account of where the piece came from, where they think it's going, anything else they want to explain	9, 6%	16, 10%	33, 21%	22, 14%	73, 46%
A summary of how you and others have responded and of how they have used those responses in revising	4, 3%	16, 10%	27, 17%	28, 18%	79, 50%
Their informal assessment of the strengths and weaknesses of the piece	12, 8%	33, 21%	30, 19%	21, 13%	59, 37%
A critique of the piece, using criteria developed in class or drawn from a text	6, 4%	17, 11%	27, 17%	19, 12%	84, 53%
The concerns and questions they would like you to address in your response	33, 21%	35, 22%	30, 19%	15, 10%	41, 26%

Teachers who ask for more than the work-in-progress itself are most likely to ask for questions: 44% said they ask writers for 'the concerns and questions they would like you to address in your response' either always or much of the time. However, 37% of teachers seldom or never ask even for concerns or questions. Nearly three-quarters of teachers say they seldom or never ask for 'an account of where the piece came from, where they think it's going, anything else they want to explain'; only 16% say that they always or often ask for such an account.

Reasons we resist reflection

One reason we might resist the idea of asking for students' reflections is that they often make us a coach of students' writing process, something we may feel less equipped to be than a critic of their writing. A related reason that I have discussed is the preference to listen to what the text has to say, apart from the writer's intentions.

But I think that the deepest reason we resist asking for reflections is one I mentioned at the beginning of this chapter: giving writers means to understand their process, question their work and invite others, including teachers, into that process gives writers added authority, *apparently* at a cost to teacher authority. Jeffrey Sommers (1989: 184) emphasizes the freedom teachers and students gain: 'Ultimately, the writer's memos change not only the student but also the teacher, freeing both from their academic roles and encouraging both to assume the more productive roles of writer and reader'. But a quite different way of saying this is that writers' memos reduce the authoritative distance between students and teachers, making even more *personal* a course that is already highly personal in its subject matter as well as in the extent to which writers take their work personally.

I realize now that the changes in role and relationship that occurred when I began asking for writers' memos also influenced me to invite students to address me by my first name. I remember how strange it felt at first seeing *'Carl'* at the top of a writer's memo. Often it and the words following felt *voiced* – sometimes vibrant with emotion, as though the writer had charged into my office, grabbed me by the arm and said, 'Carl, look at what I've written! Tell me what you think!' Here's a recent example from Margareta:

> Now, Carl, honestly, is this a good story? Is it going somewhere? Is it stronger and more mature than just a sappy romance/redemption story? And, can you explain to me how this happened? How a story just poured out of me without prior thought or preparation? I think I like it. How can I keep exercising that skill and train it to be more useful to me?

Reading and responding to such insistent memos made my teaching more intensely personal. Also more meaningful, more satisfying, more productive.

Only later did I realize that it meant that I also needed to think more carefully about how to *negotiate* the personal, because what Yancey's rather intellectual account of reflection does not imply and what Sommers' optimistic account of change in teacher role does not acknowledge is that we must at times reclaim the disinterested and distant role of *Authority*, especially when we assign grades. And *shifting* distance within close relationships can cause uncertainty and then raise suspicion, leading to breakdowns, sometimes plunging an interdependent class into confusion, even resistance. I'll consider these risks in Chapter 7.

Chapter 4
Response in Writers' Groups

> We don't need fixing, most of us, as much as we need a warm space and a good cow. Cows cock their big brown eyes at you and twitch their ears when you talk. This is a great antidote to the critical listening that goes on in academia, where we listen for the mistake, the flaw in the argument.
>
> Mary Rose O'Reilley (1998: 29)

In creative writing, the dominant format for peer response is the full-class workshop. However some creative writing teachers prefer a practice common in composition – the continuing small group or writers' group. This chapter considers its advantages and offers ways to make it work.

Two Alternatives for Peer Response

As I reported in Chapter 2, only 8% of creative writing teachers say they give the workshop little or no emphasis. Thus, if they do use small groups, these tend to be impromptu groups focused on a specific task.

Impromptu groups work for getting heads together around a defined task or question, so they can respond to exercises and early drafts if given guidance. Another use is to prepare students to engage in the workshop. One teacher said she started the course with small groups focused on works by a limited number of writers, and then each group reported to the class what they discussed. Beginning writers could get comfortable hearing response and responders had a kind of rehearsal space where they could discover that what they offered could be understood and valued.

But the kind of small group that is my focus in this chapter is the *writers' group*. Due to limited class time, writers' groups are less likely to supplement than mostly replace the workshop.

The obvious reason to choose writers' groups is that they save time. Assuming a class of 16, a workshop course would require three or four one-hour classes to respond to a short piece from each writer, whereas four writers' groups could get through their members' works in one period, opening up class time for exercises, writing, discussion of process and discussion of published writing.

A related factor is group dynamics. A class of 12 can do a good workshop, and a class of 16 might manage. With a class of 20 or larger, Joey Horstman (2005) told me 'they don't talk and I don't know how to get them to talk'. Even if some do talk, the reticent students easily become marginalized. However, in writers' groups all members are likely to contribute.

Writers' groups work differently

Earlier I discussed Lincoln Konkle's (2004) realization during a trial run of writers' groups that he missed the pleasure of leading the workshop. I identify. I do rely primarily on writers' groups for response, but when I walk out of class early to leave time for groups I usually go to my office – and feel like I'm missing something. I sometimes announce that any group that wants another responder can ask me to join, but they generally prefer to manage on their own and I remind myself that I do want students to learn to write, as Elbow (1973) put it, without teachers.

Konkle's other concern is more fundamental: 'I didn't think students were getting very good discussion of their manuscripts since I wasn't conducting the workshop in the groups'. My colleague, playwright Jeff Barker (2004a), articulated the same concern:

> When I've taken writing courses, I've felt that my money was paid so that I could be taught by an experienced, trained teacher. Frankly, I didn't trust the other student writers, because they were possibly no better than I was. I wanted feedback from a master, so that my writing could improve appropriately. I didn't want to turn to my neighbor whose taste had been honed by multiple viewings of 'Zoolander' to hear them pronounce, 'I think that ... um ... you know, the thing you've written ... is boring'.

That's a compelling objection – how can writers take seriously the response of someone whose textual authority they distrust? Reinforcing such skepticism, as Bizzaro (1993: 42) reminds us, is the influence of New Criticism, which favors the *exemplary reader*, the one who knows the norms governing ideal texts and can use them to evaluate works-in-progress.

Nevertheless, in *What is English?* Peter Elbow (1990: 133) says that teachers (at least in composition) have 'slowly built up enough experience and wisdom (and courage) that it is now impossible for teachers to say, as only recently they used to say, "Groups can't work – it's just the blind leading the blind". There are too many teachers who are making them work'.

The thing is, writers' groups work *differently*.

If teachers imagine writers' groups as the workshop broken down, *but still doing criticism and advice*, they probably won't work, at least in introductory courses. At the start too few students know those 'norms governing ideal texts' well enough to offer good criticism and advice; so instead most will offer vague praise, along with conventional or superficial suggestions.

However, what members of writers' groups *can* do from the start is offer *good company for finding potential* in early drafts, and they can do this by offering their questions and describing their responses as *good readers who are becoming writers*. Such accompaniment depends partly upon good questions from writers, which means that writers must learn to reflect about and question their work publicly. If the questions are genuine and provocative, then most readers will be able to get beyond the superficial. Offering good company further means that the others in the group should primarily describe for the writer their experience of trying to read the text – not play critic and try to tell the writer how to fix it.

Over time, through their experience in the course, writers learn to articulate better questions about how their writing works, and the responses of their group become more informed by the norms governing ideal texts.

Writing as relationship-forming

What writing groups offer is depth of relationship, making possible real revision of writing and writers over time. Consider Elbow's (1973: 128–9) reasons in *Writing Without Teachers* why response from a writers' group can be more beneficial than response from a teacher:

> They see your writing every week. They hear you read things out loud. They hear you react to other people's writing. They can listen fully to your words – just listen and attend to their reactions – because they don't have to try to evaluate or give a grade. They get to know your language, your way of handling words, so they can hear ideas, feelings, and nuances that are only partially encoded in the words.

I would add that it's also easy for members to bring back to the group a piece they have revised to learn how the group responds to the revision.

As they come to know each other and the kind of writing each does, they can learn to hear a new piece in relation to what the writer *wants* to accomplish in it. At the same time, each writer also comes to know the ways of reading of the other group members, ways they can then internalize and bring to their reflection on their own writing. An added advantage is that promising but rough writing stays *publicly* in-process longer, with each group member contributing to the development of at least a few pieces by each of the other members. When pieces dramatically improve as a result, the group gains a sense of accomplishment along with added awareness of how others revise and of how they used reflection and response to inform their revision. It matters that each of the members have had a *role* in each writer's production. As Brooke (1991: 11) explains, 'Learning is influenced more by the roles offered in school than by any particular content or material being taught, because it is in negotiating a response to these roles that individuals work out their future stance towards knowledge, towards authority, and towards academic learning.'

Because they have time to form relationships, members of writers' groups can also encourage and support each other. Members of writers' groups typically speak of 'my group' in ways that suggest a team or club. Thus writers' groups more easily meet Lerman's precondition that responders must *want* the artist to make excellent work. A small group of compatible writers can play the roles of fellow dreamer, listener, reader, interpreter, encourager – and later on, helpful critic. Working writers know the value of such response. Jim Heynen told my students that he will join a writers' group 'when the fires aren't burning and I need support to get going'. He said he knew of a writing group that 'has nudged several novels out of each other'. He added, 'To fire each other up is at least as important as saving each other from each other's clunkers. What's important is that you realize that the greatest support is not going to come from your instructors but from each other. You are each other's best friends when it comes to sustaining the writing life.'

Close groups can even enable a different kind of thinking. Anne Ruggles Gere (1987), in *Writing Groups: History, Theory, and Implications*, reports that when individual minds 'enter into close relation with and work upon each other' there arises 'a new kind of psychic life' that is 'clearly distinguished by its peculiar intensity from that led by the solitary individual'. She believes that this 'psychic life' helps account for the creativity of some writers' groups, as well as for the sense of empowerment members report. 'Individuals feel empowered because they discover new capacities in themselves as they collaborate' (p. 64). Gere even argues that writers' groups 'contribute to our understanding of what it means to write' in that they 'highlight the social dimension of writing' (p. 3). Even finding a voice, she says (1999: 28) implies connection: 'To describe a voice as authentic is to put it in relation to other voices.' If writing is best viewed as *forming a relationship with readers*, then it makes sense to learn writing with a few others who are one's readers and fellow writers.

A small and supportive community is also a better space for students to compose the identity and practice of *writer*. Holquist (1991: 28), interpreting Bakhtin, writes, 'I see my self as I conceive others might see it. In order to forge a self, I must do so from *outside*. In other words, *I author myself*.' A good writers' group offers productive space for self-authoring because it allows each writer to *become known* by a few other writers. Like a good teacher, a good group listens; then, too, feeds back what they're hearing, including their sense of who the writer is and might become.

A good group can even help members to push back against the influence of the teacher, a theme I'll take up in Chapters 5 and 6.

Making Writers' Groups Work

For writing groups to work, they need members who are compatible but who also complement each other; they need to learn to respond in ways other than critique-and-advice; and, as I've said, they need an active questioning and agenda-setting role from writers.

Forming the groups

I've never asked students to form their own writers' groups. They would be too likely to choose people they already know or to form a group too homogeneous to offer each other new perspectives. I also worry that those who fall outside the dominant group or its social networks might be excluded. Such students can feel painfully isolated when a class is told to 'partner up' and nobody invites them. In addition, if the best writers form a group, they may compete with each other more than collaborate, and then the other groups will lack their gifts.

Yet I always give students a say in the matter. They write about subjects close to them, in a genre that may be unfamiliar, so they have reason to want readers who they believe will be receptive, helpful and trustworthy. But before they can decide who they would like to work with, they need to know each other, so, for the first two weeks, I begin most classes with a small-group activity, rotating membership so that each student gets a chance to work with most others. Then I hand out a sheet with everyone's full name and an invitation to mark two or three they would like to work with and one or two they would prefer not to have in their group. I suggest, for instance, that they might want to avoid being in a group with a close friend, since they can already easily get response from each other if they want to.

I also tell them they may choose to leave the grouping to me, and I describe how I go about it: 'mix sexes where possible; try for differences of style and personality great enough so that members can offer each other new perspectives but not so great that clashes or failures to communicate are likely to occur; try to include in each group people who have had training or experience in responding'.

I prefer groups of four. A group of five takes too long to get through everyone's writing, and a group of three may offer too few perspectives.

To form the groups, I first make sure no one is grouped with a person they vetoed. Next I add to each tentative group persons who requested or were requested by someone already placed. Finally I fill in gaps with those who expressed no preference, still with an eye to both diversity and compatibility.

The only difficulty I recall was placing a student who acknowledged he had problems socially and who was vetoed by most of the class. I negotiated to allow two strong female members to work together if they would also work with him.

Although some groups work better than others, I've never had to shuffle group makeup part-way through a course.

Once groups are formed, I do attendance by asking students to check for missing group members. It reminds students that they have a place and role in the class.

Teaching reader-response

Most students assume that responding to writing means praise, criticism and advice, so that's what they will offer unless given an alternative with reasons to prefer it.

The best alternative I've found is reader-response. Steve Coyne (2002/2008) said he explains such response this way: 'Put a window in your brain so the writer can see what his or her work did to you while you were reading, I tell them. Where did you laugh? Where did you feel suspense? Where did you find the visual impact of the piece intense?' In his experience, such responses are 'much more useful than pronouncements about the success of the piece'. Of course, since not all such responses are valuable, he also tells students that 'the price of doing business as a student in a creative writing class is patiently enduring comments from people whose perceptions are not astute or not useful to the writer'.

Another way to teach reader-response is with a set of strategies that Elbow and Belanoff (2000: 521–9) call 'descriptive responding'. This summary for my students is adapted for my poetry class from their composition text, *A Community of Writers*:

- Pointing: simply list words or phrases as well as images or details that caught your attention. Sometimes say why.
- Center of Gravity: what *single* detail, image or physical quality or impression seems to you to be the generative center or source of energy?
- Summary: what do you hear the piece *saying* (message, attitude or both)? If the *speaker* is saying something different from what the *poet* is saying, summarize both. (Notice that center of gravity is concrete; summary is abstract.)
- What's *Almost* Said or Implied: what do you think the writer might *want* to get at but doesn't quite? The other side of the question is, Where do you as *reader* need more information before you can make sense of something in the poem?

These are distinct ways of responding that also complement each other. Readers can learn them and writers can learn to ask readers to do one or more of them. They are ways of noticing how writing engages readers.

I also remind students for the first several weeks to *avoid praise and criticism* of the piece as a whole. As Catherine Wiley (2005) said, 'I think evaluative language (which is usually positive) is useless for getting students to revise. Students have a tendency to over praise each other's work in a bland way that does not help the writer "re-see" the piece.' Readers offering descriptive response do praise or question *particulars*: some pointing will be to words, phrases, details that appeal to – or puzzle – the reader. In addition some 'almost said' questions are *implied* criticism. As Wiley observed, often writers

> think they are saying one thing, but their readers are getting a different message, which is why descriptive language helps. If three peers say, 'I think this poem is about the pain of leaving childhood and looking toward growing up', and the writer has tried to write a poem about first love, or puppy love, clearly the poem is not working.

The writer gets valuable feedback, and from a kind of response that keeps everyone *in the writing*.

The occasional student who is a good enough critic to be able to tell someone how to fix their writing – and who assumes that this would be a favor to them – is an odd kind of problem. I meet with such students to persuade them that they can offer more by asking good questions and, in particular, by helping others in their group to find their questions.

Since students tend to mimic a teacher's ways of addressing writing, my written comments on drafts are mostly reader-response as well. However, my position as teacher and evaluator sometimes compels me to do more. For instance, if a writer prefers a kind of writing (much fantasy fiction, sentimental poetry) that fails to meet criteria for literary writing, I need to tell them so. I also do more analysis of underlying problems and offer more advice than I expect peers to offer.

Practicing reader-response

My classes begin practicing the modes of descriptive response on a piece of my own journaling. I would not ask a class to *critique* my writing, but my aim is to demonstrate that reader-response helps writers know how a piece of writing engages readers. I assign each mode to a segment of the class, then I read and ask members of each group to respond. As we work through the modes, I explain differences among them. They confuse summary and center of gravity at first, so I show how summary presents an overall sense of aboutness and is thus an abstraction *from* particulars, while the center of gravity is concrete, sensual, so it may be the most resonant detail or a pattern of details. A good center of gravity response helps writers know how the concrete experience offered by the work is noticed and interpreted by readers. A fringe benefit is better thinking about titles. Beginning writers too often write summary titles; better titles name or relate to the center of gravity. A writer who 'can't think of a good title' may find that the problem is that the piece lacks a center of gravity.

We often observe that descriptive responding generates a large quantity of response – especially with an early, wandering draft – so the writer needs to select what fits with his or her own developing intention for the piece.

Students next practice descriptive responding on each other's writing in impromptu groups.

From receiving descriptive response, describing their own response to others' writing, and learning to read published writing the way writers read, students learn to reflect upon and question their own writing, which gets them better responses, leading to better revisions.

An agenda-setting role for writers

When students are ready to respond in their new writers' groups, I hand out a set of guidelines to help writers set an agenda for their group's response. These are from my introductory poetry course:

- Select poems or journal entries moving toward poems for which you genuinely *want* response (if the writing is too close to you, you may tell your readers you just want them to listen without responding).
- Get response early, before you're so committed to the current version that you're unwilling to revise.
- Provide readers with a copy unless you just want them to listen.
- Before reading, tell your group where the piece came from, what changes have occurred so far, where you think it may be going, maybe something that keeps you interested in it; and something that concerns you to which you'd like response.
- Read the piece *twice*, once to let it be experienced, once more to let readers see each part in relation to their sense of the whole. Pause after the first reading to give readers time to think and collect their thoughts.
- Lead the group when your work is discussed. Ask a few follow-up questions. Be prepared with *specific* questions so they can answer helpfully. Either ask readers to use particular modes of response such as pointing, center of gravity or summary, or give them specific questions or both. Do *not* say, 'Tell me if you think it's any good'. They will just tell you that it is, and you won't know if they're telling the truth or being nice.
- Resist defending or even explaining. Mostly, *listen* and ask questions. Your goal is a performance on the page that needs no explanation.
- Keep track of time: divide time remaining by the number in the group (or first decide who needs how much time).

Notice how the practice of reflection is central to setting an agenda for response. My remaining guidelines address responders:

- Stay within the agenda set by the writer. Remember that the piece belongs to the writer; don't charge in and try to fix things according to your own vision. As you get to know each other, you will get better at knowing when to go a *little* beyond what the writer asks for, but do it by *asking questions*, almost never by giving advice.

- Listen carefully, attentively, actively. Take a few notes or make a few marks as you're listening.
- Try for detailed and sustained response so that the writer gets a clear picture of how a reader works at experiencing and interpreting those words on the page.
- Start with (and keep starting with) descriptive response: describe your own activity as a reader, using I-language, not You-language (for instance, instead of saying, 'You're not clear here', say, 'I get confused here', and then tell how your thoughts run so that the writer understands where and why you get stuck).
- Remember that the 'I' of the poem is not the writer and that what that persona does is not necessarily what the writer did.

Such guidelines seem to be enough to get groups started. As they get to know each other, writers discover what kinds of response each of the others does best. Responders also learn how to complement other responders in the group.

I believe – and Lerman confirms – that part of the empowerment writers' groups offer derives from each writer's sense that he or she stays in charge of the work and its revision. When writers articulate their real questions they usually also listen to the response, especially from fellow writers they trust. And response is richer and more helpful. Karen Spear (1998: 61), a compositionist, writes that because group members want to avoid embarrassing each other, they 'need permission from writers to review their work'. Writers give that permission by saying where the piece came from, where they think it is going, how it matters to them and what questions they have about it. Then peer responders know what the writer is ready to hear and can also better sense what the writer needs to know. 'By learning to accept this role rather than evasively opting to play student', Spear argues, 'writers can begin to move their groups toward mature collaboration'.

Genre differences?

Does response in writers' groups work differently from genre to genre? I don't change my basic approach when shifting from a class in poetry to fiction or non-fiction except by sometimes adding guidelines for the writer's memo or for response that are specific to the genre. But my colleague Jeff Barker mentioned that because plays are meant to be performed responding to them requires a theatrical imagination, which students in a beginning playwriting class probably do not have.

It seems to me that if readers need a theatrical imagination in order to adequately respond to a draft of a script, then writers of scripts also need to develop such an imagination and responding to others' drafts should help them do that. And the teacher might select for full-class workshopping those texts that most require a theatrical imagination.

A writers' group might even do a reading performance of a script as a form of response.

Monitoring and Coaching Writers' Groups

Teachers do need to monitor writers' groups, not only to discover and address problems but also to help students pay attention to group process.

Some teachers assign a reporter to summarize each group session: who read what, the central question the writer or others raised and so on. This lets the teacher know whether all writers had pieces ready for response, whether the group finished them and whether they encountered any problems. Assigning such a role also helps groups monitor their own process.

I monitor groups primarily through writers' memos. I ask writers to summarize their group's response in the memo in which they invite my response. If what group members offered seems relevant and helpful, I assume the group is working.

In addition, early in the course I ask students to mention in their writers' memos any difficulties they are having with responding as well as any concerns they have about the response they are receiving. Then we talk about the concerns in class. A fairly common complaint is 'My group isn't helping me'. When we talk about what that means, it's usually that the group isn't telling the writer what to do to fix the writing. So we talk about whether that's what they really want. Students readily understand that if they go to another person with a problem in their life, they seldom want that person to simply tell them what to do. They want to be listened to and they value ways of thinking about the problem, but they also want room to decide for themselves. They can see why they would want the same for their writing. Sometimes I remind them that we are becoming writers, not just fixing one piece of writing.

One means to investigate further how writers' groups are working is a short survey. I designed this one partly to remind writers of their responsibilities and partly to help them notice benefits they might easily miss:

Response in Writers' Groups 79

Quick survey on writers' groups

1. If you agree, write A; if you disagree, write D; if neutral, write N:
   ___ I've had writing ready to present when groups were scheduled.
   ___ I become more aware of my writing just from reading it to others, even apart from any response.
   ___ I get ideas for my own writing from other writers in my group or from their writing.
   ___ Group members help me re-see my writing, discovering in it what I hadn't known was there.
   ___ They help me see where my writing has gaps or leaves questions.
   ___ From hearing how others reflect on and think about their writing, I get better at reflecting on and thinking about my own writing.
   ___ I need more help knowing how to respond to others' writing.
   ___ We should spend more time in writers' groups.
   ___ I feel that other members of my group write better than I do.
   ___ I usually make clear what kind of response I want from group members.

2. Check how well you think your small group is working:__very well, __well, __okay, __not well. Comment or explain:

3. How might I help?

Summarizing their responses back to them usually makes for a productive class discussion. If particular groups seem not to be working, I may meet with them to work through the problems, though I've rarely found this necessary.

How teacher response can engage group response

In the workshop, the teacher's responses to each writer help to teach the whole class ways of reading works-in-progress. One apparent sacrifice of going to writers' groups is that each student normally has direct access only to the teacher's responses to his or her own writing. A way to partly overcome this limitation is to ask each writer to summarize for their group those parts of the teacher's response that group members may find interesting or useful.

One benefit is to the writer, who has to think through carefully what the teacher has said in order to relate it to what the group said when they responded to the piece. In advocating this practice, Spear (1988: 145) suggests to teachers, 'Let them read your comments and explain to each other what the comments mean. They are giving feedback on feedback this way, and they are getting inside *your* frame of reference to understand better the values and expectations you hold for their writing.' Once the group has heard the summary of the teacher's comments, all the members should have a better grasp of the teacher's values and expectations.

A second benefit is the feedback that Spear mentions. Since writers' memos include a summary of the group's response, my own response often picks up on that conversation, taking issue with parts of it, more often agreeing and building upon it. From this feedback, group members form an impression of how their response contributed and of how their group process is working and might improve.

A third benefit is that my response enters and extends the group's dialogue. My response may give a writer courage to resist any limiting or misleading response from the group. On the other hand, if both the writer and the group disagree with my response, then the writer gains support from the group for resisting my reading. In either case, writer and group think about *reasons* for deciding one way or the other, which in turn helps them to think about what makes writing good.

It has been charged that peer response is merely 'the blind leading the blind'. Early in the course, it can seem that way, to the writers' group members too. But as they learn to read better in the genre, become better writers, talk about how they read each others' developing drafts and share what they have learned from instructor response, response becomes 'the dimly seeing helping each other to see more clearly'.

Making Room for Critique and Advice

About halfway into an introductory course, groups can bring critique and advice into their repertoire of response. By then they understand criteria for good writing in the genre well enough to begin to explain their judgments. As important, writers have learned how to ask better questions – and gained enough confidence to resist bad advice. Group members have had time to develop a depth of relationship that enables them to be honest and helpful. And writers have become more invested in their best pieces and want to bring them to completion.

I don't believe that groups should 'switch over' from reader-response to critique, but simply provide it when writers ask for it – and as portfolio time approaches, they do ask for it. I offer as a model Lerman's approach: responders pointing to particulars they liked or saying how the piece mattered to them, the writer asking questions, the responders asking questions and responders offering advice if the writer assents.

A good way to help students state and defend their judgment is through comparison of poems that deal with the same subject but at a different level of artistry. This practice is most valuable with poetry mainly because students learning to write poems are less confident in their ability to recognize what's good than are writers in other genres.

Beginning students tend to associate judgment with individual taste. They observe that 'different people have different opinions' but fail to examine the assumptions behind such differences. Robert Scholes (1985: 24) shows in *Textual Power* that the values that support criticism can be best understood by tracing them to the *group* that upholds them: 'My point here is that criticism is always made on behalf of a group. Even "taste" is never a truly personal thing but a carefully inculcated norm, usually established by a powerful social class.'

Different groups have different values. I've made this point by having students rate a set of photographs. Included are 'Kodak moments', 'calendar photos', photojournalism or illustration images, perhaps a family photo of little interest except to the relatives of those pictured, and two or three images with greater artistic interest. First I have students rate these on a scale of 1 to 3, just going by what they like. I record the scoring, casually asking one or two who rate a piece high or low to say why.

Then we rate the photos again, but this time I position them as members of a review committee choosing images for a show in the campus art gallery. This role significantly changes some of their ratings, and by talking about why, we identify the reading practices and values of those who frequent art galleries: photos of merely personal value to the photographer get lower ratings because gallery display implies that the image can be read by and have meaning for multiple viewers. Also losing value are photos whose appeal depends upon sentimentality, as well as the 'calendar photos' that appeal to what we already like instead of enabling us to view the familiar in a new way. Craft counts too: photos that demonstrate awareness of timing, lighting and composition gain in value.

About making judgments about poetry, Juliana Spahr (2004) observed:

> My job as a teacher of creative writing is to let students know they've got a whole lot of options for writing out there and to talk about what ones do what (what sorts of writing have what sort of politics; what sorts of writing tend to be used for critique; what ones to seduce beloveds, etc.). I often talk in creative writing classrooms about what institutions support what sorts of poetries.

I agree – and yet I say to students that our location within an English department restricts what we can call good (and underlies criteria I will later use to evaluate their work). Cathy Day's (2005) syllabus makes a similar point through comparison: 'If you signed up for ballet class, you'd never expect that you'd be given permission (not to mention a grade) to simply "do your own thing". The same goes for a class in art, in acting, etc.'

An added benefit of tracing criteria to the shared values of a community of readers is that students are less likely to assume that a teacher's judgments reflect merely personal tastes.

Concluding with workshop

Another way to make room for critique is to conclude an introductory course with a round of full-class workshop. I tried this with a poetry class as I was finishing this book, devoting the second-to-last week to workshopping one poem by each of the 13 members.

Our workshop did not *emphasize* critique and advice. Primarily we followed Lerman's structure: the writer said a little about where the piece came from and then read it; responders said what they noticed on first reading; a volunteer read it again, and responders talked more fully about what the piece enabled them to experience – what pleasure it gave them, what connections it enabled them to make and so on. This was typically the longest stage. Next the writer asked questions, often indicating at the start that many had already been answered. Then responders stated their suggestions and concerns in the form of questions. Finally, there was opportunity for any further criticism or advice that readers thought the writer would appreciate. This stage was brief, usually bringing up observations about word choices, questionable lines, apparent inconsistencies.

Afterwards 11 students responded to an anonymous survey. One question asked how the course should work in the future – all writers' group, all workshop, or writers' group with an episode of workshop at the end. All favored the third choice, even though only a slim majority had voted ahead of time to give up some writers' group time for workshop.

Their responses to questions about writers' group versus workshop emphasized ways each structure complements the other. They were adamant that a workshop would have been a bad experience early in the course: their writing was not ready for that much exposure to readers they didn't yet know and trust, nor did they know then how to talk about someone else's writing. They also valued getting response while their writing was still rough or incomplete, as well as the opportunity to develop enough trust to be able to speak frankly to each other about their writing.

As important, they confirmed that they became advocates for their group members. A question on the survey asked about the level of competitiveness in their groups and everyone marked the least competitive choice, 'I was as pleased when another member of the group came up with something really good as when I did myself'. If Lerman is right that responders must *want* the artist to do good work, then pleasure in fellow group members' success appears to be a significant advantage of writers' groups.

They also said that over time, by talking with a few others about a relatively small number of pieces, they learned how to write and revise and be understood within their group. They had learned to read poetry and to talk about others' poems in an authoritative way. This experience enabled them to do a good workshop.

But they said that toward the end of the course, they wanted to know whether their writing would also work for *other* readers, those who did not know how they wrote. Many were gratified to discover that it did work.

A related benefit of the workshop session was fresh response. One wrote, 'I heard voices I hadn't really heard much all semester.' In addition a larger group building upon each other's comments often achieved greater depth of response.

A conclusion I reached was that writers' groups help students develop a good process, but they may offer diminishing returns toward the end of the course. One student wrote that she 'felt like I could almost predict the response I'd get' from her group and that they 'seemed to spend more time talking about the concepts of the poem, its idea, what sparked it, etc. rather than on what was actually happening inside the poem'. The workshop focused on the poem.

And, yes, I did enjoy leading that workshop. The mood was constructive, even celebratory. Students found pleasure in each other's work and enjoyed trying to help the writer imagine how it might be made still better. Coming together as a class to hear a wide range of good writing was a satisfying way to wrap up the course.

I repeated the experiment at the end of a fiction class of 14, where it was somewhat less of a success because of the added class time required (nearly three weeks) to work through fiction and respond in a way that is helpful to the writer.

My experience in both courses did confirm that the workshop deals best with near-finished drafts. Pieces that were less finished raised more questions than a large group could deal with.

The Writer's Solitude and the Influence of the Group

A familiar paradox of the writing life is that we write among others and for audiences; and we write in solitude and for ourselves. How in a *course* do we affirm solitude? Earlier I mentioned that Jim Heynen said that he will join a writers' group 'when the fires aren't burning'; he added that 'when the fires *are* burning I want to be left alone'. Response is usually a good thing, but one that a writer can get too much of. We've heard of pieces that have had the life workshopped out of them.

Carol Bly (2001) is one teacher who insists that 'a writer must write *alone*, not in a group' (p. 14); and that 'writers need to learn how to protect their own inspirations' (p. 43), at least through the first two stages of writing. Stage one she calls 'first inspiration' and stage two she calls 'self-deepening'. She urges writers to declare, 'I am not going to do any public literary fixing until I know the underside of my idea. I promise myself not to be distracted by the slightest practicality if it shows its head. I certainly will keep clear of friends and loved ones' (p. 43). She also charges that 'the majority of creative writing teachers allow a student to "put up for workshopping" work that is still so close to the original inspiration that the student's mind has not yet lived it through' (p. 40).

The way of 'living it through' she proposes is a self-questioning. She says that groups usually suggest *adding* something, but that what writers need instead is to discover what is *beneath* the original idea and the emotions associated with it – to go deeper. Here's her five-step way of getting there that she calls empathic questioning:

(1) *Decide* to really *listen.*
(2) Empty yourself of your own point of view.
(3) Ask open-ended questions (*not* Socratic questioning) to collect more information about the *feeling* associated with the writing as well as the further '*meaning attached to the reported feelings*'.
(4) Paraphrase what was learned as you understand it.
(5) Decide, based on that, on 'a good direction to take from here' – consider goals.

Bly explains that if writers practice such empathic questioning with themselves, they 'won't then have to keep returning to writing classes for another fix' (pp. 49–50).

I have several responses. First, her concern that critical response can threaten still-fragile writing offers an added reason to have the *writer* set an agenda for response and to caution responders about offering unsought advice.

Second, notice that Bly fails to imagine that groups might do something other than 'fix' works-in-progress. I've argued that writers' groups can and should describe their response and ask questions in order to inform the writer's own process of reflecting on how a piece works, how it needs to work differently and what might be done to bring that about. This practice approximates Bly's empathic questioning.

I would add that Bly's advice to avoid influence has most value for accomplished writers who are already located within networks of relationships with other writers and with readers and who thus are able to *imagine* in solitude the responses of good readers.

Bly does makes me think I'd like to try to offer an alternative to the typical writers' group of four members: allowing students of roughly equal ability to form response pairs, provided that both agree to expand the usual repertoire to include written response and empathic questioning of themselves and each other.

Chapter 5
Teacher Response to Student Writing

> [W]e must model for students the various selves they might become as readers and writers. Like our students, and perhaps because of them, we must negotiate identities during the writing course. From this perspective, the best teachers of writing are not necessarily the best writers or best readers, as we have long and perhaps erroneously assumed. Rather, the most successful teachers are apt to be those who are best able to adapt to texts their students write and model the various roles their readings require of them.
>
> Patrick Bizzaro (1994: 242)

I never imagined that anyone might try to teach writing without at least some of the time writing responses to students' drafts, so I was incredulous at Katharine Haake's (2000: 113) lament, in *What Our Speech Disrupts: Feminism and Creative Writing Studies*, that in all her years of creative writing classes – in BA, MA and PhD programs – she received 'only one written comment' on her fiction. She notes, 'It lies before me now, typewritten, yellowed and cherished.' Looking back, she realizes 'how much I wanted validation from my teachers, wanted to know they had labored over what I had written, wanted their attention and time, wanted to be viewed as someone worthy of it'. She was doing this looking back to examine whether she herself 'continued to write long notes' to her own students because she *still* wanted validation, but now as the 'good caring teacher'. She recalls that her graduate school adviser, Francois Camoin, said that teacher comments 'negated the whole value of the workshop' because 'what the student looks at is what the *teacher* wrote' (p. 114). But in spite of all this, Haake confesses, 'I continue to write comments to students because: (1) it is very hard to tell them that I won't (I am a coward), and (2) I forget I once knew that as a practice it is flawed' (p. 114). Despite these doubts, her book affirms written response. Most creative writing teachers do too. None of the respondents to my survey noted after questions about written response that they didn't write responses. The reason Debra Rienstra (2005) gave for offering 'fairly detailed response' was to make certain that writers 'always have at least one person doing her best to give them substantive response'.

In composition, Lad Tobin (2004: 12) – known for his emphasis upon *student* response – declares in *Reading Student Writing: Confessions, Meditations, and Rants* that 'reading and responding to student writing in process' is the thing we writing teachers do that 'counts most'. And Nancy Sommers (2006: 253), following an extensive study of writing development through four years of college, concludes that for first-year students, feedback from teachers 'is *monumental,* their most personal, most intimate and direct connection with their college writing culture'. Such feedback offers 'messages of hope and despair about who they are and who they might become as students'. Can teacher response be less important for creative writers, most of whom care much more about writing and take themselves more seriously as writers?

If reading and responding *count more than anything else we do*, then we ought to examine our response practice. Composition has a rich tradition of such study but, in creative writing, few teachers have examined how the roles they take as responders and the different kinds of response they offer help writers to revise texts and selves.

Roles Teachers Take in Responding

Our typical role in response is that of *textual expert*, saying how a text works and how it might be improved. Yet some of us, at least some of the time, add two quite different roles: we play the role of the *reader* that the text evokes, articulating for the writer the emotional response and interpretive process of that reader; and we try to be good *listeners*, perceiving what the writer wants to do while we also try to sense what the writing wants to become. The survey questions below focus on specific practices that relate to one or more of these roles. I'll discuss all of these practices in this chapter. I present them here as a group to demonstrate relative emphases within our response practice:

In your written (or recorded) response to drafts of students' writing, how likely are you to use each of the following strategies (highly likely = 5; somewhat likely = 3; not likely = 1):	5	4	3	2	1
Find a way to praise or encourage the writer	123, 77%	25, 16%	6, 4%	1, 1%	1, 1%
Point out what's working, say what isn't working, suggest some things the writer might try	132, 83%	18, 11%	3, 2%	1, 1%	1, 1%

Illustrate what you might do with parts of the writing if it were yours	28, 18%	27, 17%	32, 20%	37, 23%	32, 20%
Take the position of the intended reader and describe your response – say what it makes you feel, describe how you read and connect, raise questions that such a reader would like answered	62, 39%	50, 31%	29, 18%	6, 4%	9, 6%
Offer an interpretation of what the piece seems to be about that probably goes beyond the writer's awareness of what it's about	37, 23%	51, 32%	36, 23%	17, 11%	14, 9%
Speculate on what the writer seems to want to do in the piece but hasn't yet done	45, 28%	54, 34%	41, 26%	8, 5%	8, 5%
Respond to the writer's comments, concerns or questions about the piece	80, 50%	33, 21%	25, 16%	6, 4%	10, 6%
Mark or edit grammatical or stylistic lapses	59, 37%	31, 20%	40, 25%	19, 12%	6, 4%

Responding as critiquing and fixing the text

The assumption most evident in teachers' response practice is that we are textual experts and fixers. Of those completing my survey, 93% said they are highly or somewhat likely to 'point out what's working, say what isn't working, suggest some things the writer might try'.

Analyzing his own past practice, Bizzaro (1993: 45) found that he had been doing three kinds of written responses to poems, all aimed at fixing: intertextual comments, marginalia and summative statements. The intertextual comments generally aimed 'to condense lines, to refocus images, and to avoid redundancies'. He observed that 'many times I cross out not only to condense the language, but also to bring the intended image (that is, what seems to me as reader to be the intended image) into sharper focus'. His marginalia were explanatory, 'generally used to reinforce what I've done within the text' (p. 48). Similarly, he found that his summative statements 'begin with some form of praise and then point out two or three kinds of changes the writer should attend to when revising' (p. 49).

My survey suggests that the practice he describes is typical.

Fascinating, then, is his *motive* for analyzing his practice: it wasn't working and he wanted to understand why.

One reason he found was that some comments were interchangeable from poem to poem, giving students a teachers-always-say-that impression.

Another reason his response practice didn't work was that students could 'simply make the adjustments I urge and resubmit the poem as finished' (p. 53). Gina Franco also found that her students were 'likely to do only what the authority suggests'; so she was considering cutting off the supply of suggestions.

An added complication is that when writers follow advice they don't understand, the writing easily becomes a hodgepodge – and now they have someone else to blame.

There's a larger problem too: when students try to write the poem, story, essay or play that 'the authority' seems to want, they fail to develop their own authority as authors.

A related danger is that teachers may confuse the writer's intentions for the piece with their own and thus appropriate the writing. Pat Emile (2004a) wrote she tries 'not to do too much "directing" with students' poems' because one of her teachers 'would take my poem and "fly off with it" in directions he wanted it to go', and that 'tended to kill any enthusiasm I had for what I had thought of as *my* poem'.

Bizzaro charges that when we suggest how to 'improve' a story, poem, essay or play, we are actually telling the writer what we would do if the poem were ours. I wondered how many teachers do this deliberately, so my survey asked how likely the respondent was to 'illustrate what you might do with parts of the writing if it were yours'. Fully 20% said they are highly unlikely to take this tack; yet nearly as many – 17% – said they are highly *likely* to do so. No less an authority than Victor Hugo writes, 'If I can, I talk as if I'd written the poem myself and try to find out why and where it went wrong' (in Bizzaro, 1993: 55). Eliot Khalil Wilson (2004) told me that he deliberately takes this approach. When I interviewed him, he was planning to give his advanced class poems written by his beginning class that he called 'typical undergrad poems', 'very solipsistic', 'their journal in verse form'. He said that beginning students find such writing 'endlessly fascinating' because they don't read published poetry. He planned to show his advanced class 'how I would edit them if they were mine'. He explained, 'Of *course* I'm a narcissist. I can only treat this as if it were mine. I'll say, "I would cut the first four lines". We'll cut out words. Take out "neath" and adjectives behind the noun.' To justify this approach he referred to his textual expertise: 'I'm familiar with what a publishable poem is and I read a lot of lit mags. They hired me for that reason.' Appropriation does concern him – 'I do worry that I'm trying to generate 15 Eliot Wilsons here' – but he decided that his best recourse is to rely on students to resist. 'I came along imitating Sexton or Hugo. I started with Frost. I struggled under that anxiety of influence, and I have to hope that that happens with my students.'

In telling students how to fix writing, what I think we *try* to do is expressed by Carol Bly (2001: 137), who observes that a teacher 'is a mildly directive person, but only in the sense of intervening on behalf of a writer's *higher* instincts, helping the writer to do a check on his or her simpler, or lower, instincts'. An example she offers of a lower instinct is 'to write lyrically but not truthfully about life'. Put another way, our aim should be to help them see the piece, not as we would write it but as they might write it if they were the writer we help them to imagine being – an act of imagination that requires attention not just to the writing but also to the person of the writer.

Responding in the role of the reader

Like the workshop, the typical praise-critique-advise pattern of teacher response addresses primarily the ideal self – that writer-I-might-become who has produced excellent work. Consider Wilson's assumption that he was hired because he's 'familiar with what a publishable poem is' – and thus can show students how their texts meet or fall short of that ideal. Such response has real value at the right time. Flannery O'Connor (1969: 102), who was suspicious of teachers and workshops that aimed to 'improve' a writer's work, writes, 'The teacher can help the student by looking at his individual work and trying to help him decide if he has written a complete story, one in which the action fully illuminates the meaning'. Students' need for such response is a reason Bizzaro (1993: 60) believes that a creative writing course inevitably *includes* apprenticeship to an accomplished writer. Yet he also writes (1994: 234) that 'we should aim at something higher: we should aim at the writer's increased fluency with the elements of poetic writing'. By responding to develop fluency, we can hope to 'shorten the time span involved in a master-to-apprenticeship relationship'.

Said another way, teacher response should aim not so much to improve texts as to nurture students' *guide* self, the self through which they develop capability and authority to reflect upon and question their writing, to solicit response and to revise.

Katharine Haake (1994: 78) agrees with the goal of making writers more fluent, less dependent. She even says she has *abandoned* the idea that 'it is appropriate or useful to tell students how to "make their stories better"'. When I look at Haake's responses to students in *What Our Speech Disrupts* (2000: 120–39), I still find advice for improving stories, but much of it illustrates what the writer *might* do. Commenting on these 'response dialogues', she observes too that 'it's not really as if I don't make "suggestions" for revision or rethinking. But I almost always try to say "why", to locate my comments in a critical logic, which is maybe the best that we can do' (p. 120). Such a 'critical logic' would help writers to see for themselves how their writing is working and to imagine how it might work differently. However, because she draws her logic and its terminology from critical theory, her approach probably has most value for graduate courses. Bizarro (1994: 234) likewise believes that increasing students' fluency depends 'largely on the methodology teachers employ in reading and interpreting student texts', but his reader-response approach is more accessible for undergraduates because it relies on the familiar terms textbooks use to describe how texts engage, move and influence readers. Here's how he (1993: 67) summarizes his conclusion about what teachers should do: 'Rather than enforcing their readings of student poems as definitive, teachers must willingly submit to the text, participating in the development of the reader summoned by the text and evoked, knowingly or unknowingly, by the author.' The teacher then must 'reflect back to the author not what the poem, as a collection of literary devices, means, but how the poem's meaning is reassembled by an individual reader'.

Notice, in addition, Bizarro's (1993) reliance on the writer's evolving *intention*: 'Since the writer makes choices that dictate who the reader will be, the problem a student must solve in revision is how to make certain that the text will be read as he or she intended' (p. 67). This means, in turn, that teachers need to grant students authority: 'Rather than relinquishing control of the text to the teacher, students must work cooperatively with their teacher-readers in determining what the poem might become, a process that includes the critical consideration of who the poem addresses.' The teacher's commentary 'must thus be nonjudgmental and provide the writer with clues as to how the text might better create the envisioned audience' (p. 68). Bizarro adds, 'Questions based on how the reader has *construed the author's intent* better serve the reader employing reader-response methods than questions advising the author, albeit indirectly, on *how to manipulate the text* in revision' (p. 76).

But this shift in responding also involves negotiating the personal because the teacher is deliberately downplaying his or her authority. 'Interaction and shared authority,' Bizarro insists, 'are at the center of any method of evaluation and reading founded upon reader-response theories' (p. 69). But sharing authority can be disconcerting. When he first exercised less control over novice writers, he 'had to fight two overwhelming feelings': that he 'was not doing a good job of teaching' and that students who were accustomed to more authoritative teaching 'thought that I was not doing my job'. He had to remind himself that being less in control 'was exactly the point, that by relinquishing control I might actually be doing a better job of "teaching"' (p. 74).

One kind of evidence that he was doing a better job came from observing students later in the term. He 'was pleased to see a considerable amount of verbal exchange in their workshop discussions of each other's poems'. In addition, he was 'pleased to note an improved atmosphere for peer commentary, not only over what I had seen before in my teacher-oriented workshops ... but also over what my students report to have experienced in workshops in various other writing courses'. He attributes these developments 'to my students' ability to employ the kinds of comments I made on their poems when commenting on each other's poems' (p. 74). I earlier cited Camoin's remark that response from the teacher 'negated the whole value of the workshop', but that risk is greatest with critique, where the teacher's textual authority trumps that of the writer's peers. Non-experts are on a more equal footing when the question is how a text engages and affects readers.

Another kind of evidence Bizzarro found to favor reader-response was quality of revision. Once students realized that they needed to 'make the necessary revisions by themselves rather than rely on the teacher-reader's instructions' (p. 80), their revisions became 'far more extensive and far less predictable' than those 'made in direct response to concerns voiced by the reader-evaluator' (p. 83). Few teachers realize the extent to which writing for teachers prevents writers from even stopping to consider the more important question of how a text engages actual readers. As Joey Horstman (2005) observed, students 'seem not to realize how a reader is reading'. I think this is often because they are still too close to the experience to see what the writing fails to offer a reader, or they imagine as audience only a teacher judging whether the piece meets certain criteria, not a reader seeking meaning and pleasure.

By focusing on what a text does with its readers, reader-response even invites consideration of how a text operates ethically and morally. As Wayne Booth (1988) argues, the texts we read are a part of 'the company we keep'. A text invites us to become, for a time, a certain kind of person, so one ethical question readers face is whether to become the reader the text evokes. (Application: if we find a student text morally repugnant, a way to say so with less risk of alienating the writer is to describe what impedes our becoming its reader).

Worth adding is that a shared focus on how texts work with readers could draw us closer to colleagues who teach composition or literature. Terry Eagleton, in *Literary Theory: An Introduction* (1983: 205), argues for transforming literature by setting it within the wider context of rhetoric, 'the received form of critical analysis' that examines 'the way discourses are constructed in order to achieve certain effects'. That's something members of English departments care about.

My survey asked respondents how likely they were to 'take the position of the intended reader and describe your response – say what it makes you feel, *describe* how you read and connect, raise questions that such a reader would like answered'. Of those responding, 70% said they were either highly likely or likely to do so, and a total of only 10% selected either 'unlikely' response. However, I doubt that this many have adopted a reader-response *approach*; some probably do reader-response primarily to introduce criticism and advice.

On the other hand, I doubt that any of us avoid *all* criticism and advice. I like Bizarro's (1994: 243) conclusion that teacher commentary should 'cover a range of distances, from the long-range perspective of teacher-authority in text-based commentary to the up-close-and-personal perspective of shared authority in reader-response methods'.

Response that nurtures the writing self

If critique addresses the ideal self with its eye on an excellent finished text, and reader-response helps the guide self find perspectives for questioning and re-visioning the writing as a means of engaging readers, what about the *writing* self that pours forth words? Might our spoken or written response also nurture and encourage this self?

The teacher doing reader-response at least *respects* the writing self by resisting appropriation of students' texts.

But we can do more. Bizzaro (1994: 234) cites Stafford's claim that a good teacher is one who offers good *company*, which Bizzaro rephrases as 'introducing students to the many selves writers might become'. Bizzaro's emphasis is upon readers invoked by the writing, but when Stafford (1986: 17) speaks of offering 'good company', his concern is more with what I have called the writing self engaging with emotion and language than with a guide self shaping the text for the reader. In fact, Stafford delays consideration of readers: 'Each piece comes to me as a crystallization of its own, and preferably without my thinking of its effect on others.' And when Stafford describes his classroom response practice, what is striking is his emphasis on the 'impulse' that generates the writing:

> My classes became more like ballet than like workshops. What did a piece of writing mean? – not what did it say, but what did it portend, or hint, or reveal, about that surely valid human impulse that brought

it about? My job was not to correct but to understand and participate. A student's paper was a test for me and I began not to put any evaluation remarks at all on a paper. My remarks were meant to show my accompaniment, sometimes my readiness to learn more. (p. 18)

This 'accompaniment' is that of fellow artist, listener and nurturer, not that of critic or advice-giver. Starting with his principle that 'an artist is someone who lets the material talk back', Stafford recognizes that, as teacher, his students are his material, so he needs to get them to talk back so that they can learn how to listen to their writing as it talks back to them:

> I began to treat each encounter with a student as an occasion for learning as well as possible where the student was, how the material of the course was striking an individual. If I could find the periphery of a student's relation to a story, or how a phrase of my own had the impulse to join another phrase, I was ready for next steps. But this procedure required my listening in class or in conference, and my readiness to adjust my next move as a result of what I found out.

Stafford's aim is to help beginning artists perceive, trust and act upon their own impulses. As they learn to do that, he withdraws: 'Writing was in its language aspect a series of moves like dancing. Imposing my will on language – or on a student ... – was not my style. I wanted to disappear as teacher, as writer ...' (p. 21).

Responding inside-out or outside-in

As a way to learn from each other's practice, my colleague Amy McCann (2004/2005) and I each wrote separate responses to a set of poems from her class. When we later compared our responses, we noticed an interesting difference: her comments focused more on details – diction, rhythmic qualities, conciseness, specificity, concreteness. She had invited but not required writers to imitate one of four poems, and she deliberately chose difficult poems in hopes that writers would try on the language of poetry but not write a too-similar *poem*. Her working assumption was that poetry is mostly learned inside-out: that through developing a feel for language, imagery, lineation and so on, students 'catch' poetry and then gradually learn to write poems that are more unified and whole. Thus, her responses emphasized Stafford's kind of noticing-accompaniment.

My comments revealed that my working assumption is that poetry is learned more outside-in: I assume that beginning poets have wrong and vague hypotheses about poetry because they don't know how good readers read it – for instance, they fail to realize that a poem usually has a speaker whose situation provides a kind of 'ground' for whatever else the poem offers. More of my comments described my difficulty in identifying a consistent speaker and situation or in following the progress of the experience, thought or emotion of the speaker. McCann had not asked students for writers' memos and I missed them because when I could not find a whole *poem*, I wanted to know what the writer was *trying* to do so that I could help them think.

Said another way, McCann's responses mostly accompanied a writing self that needs to develop a feel for poetic language, while my comments more often addressed a guide self learning to think about expectations and practices of readers. Probably some students learn better from one approach, others from the other, and some pieces need one kind of response more than the other.

Overcoming Resistance to Revision

My survey confirmed that teachers have a difficult time getting students to do real revision. 'Students who resisted revision, apparently feeling that their original inspiration was what mattered' was frequently a problem for 19%, quite frequently for 24%, occasionally for 31%, seldom for 17% and never a problem for only 7%.

A common way to deal with such resistance is to require students to submit a certain number of drafts. The problem is that this approach doesn't fit some writers. Although most do work through several drafts, a few compose sentence by perfect sentence, the way a crystal grows. Others do their 'cooking' internally and then write rapidly, sometimes needing little revision. A former student, Jessica Laaveg (2004/2005), told me about her best piece for two different courses. One was an essay dashed off 'between lunch and band practice'. She recalled 'liking the first draft and reading it to my roommate'. Later, neither her teacher nor her other readers encouraged revision. The other, a story, came as quickly. 'I had been stood up for a tutoring appointment and had time to write.' She said that the first draft took about 45 minutes and only minor revision followed. The pieces took first prizes in successive years in the college literary competition. If she had been required to submit drafts, she would have had to manufacture 'rough' versions of her first draft.

I've begun to describe a better way to get writers to do serious revision: teach them to first question their work in writers' memos that invite response, thus improving both the quality of the response and the writer's interest in it. When Rachel questioned her title, I felt invited to suggest in my response ways she might find a better one:

> The reader can discover more if you provide a more concrete and grounded title. It will probably have something to do with light/blonde/golden/sheaves/harvest; or with hands (some of the most powerful imagery in the story has to do with her empty hands and her sense of uselessness. And her redemption comes through finding things to do with her hands. (His hands would be rough, calloused; she'd notice that, and he might too.)

Because I'm responding to her question, I'm confident she will think through what I say, and I try to give her enough options so that I avoid suggesting a particular title. The memo helps enable the 'interaction and shared authority' Bizzaro (1993: 71) seeks. You might say that it allows written response to gain some of the dialogic quality of a good conference. Next notice how much of my response to Erica's story draft is in dialogue with her memo about it:

> Erica,
>
> I so like your thinking in the presence of this story that I feel like just tiptoeing back out of the room and leaving you to sort things out in your own way. Or maybe I'll just whisper a few thoughts before I leave.
>
> I'm charmed by the boy's love of shaping things from mud and of naming his creatures according to their nature.
>
> As he builds the town and more and more details come in, I wonder, as you do, Where's this going? I also sensed the possibility of destruction when he starts hanging on to his creation, though that could take many forms, including rain and the other creatures who live along creeks and also shape or track the banks.
>
> I like that the story is moving toward something female. All this touching and shaping and making out of responsive material hints at an Adam who is waiting for the creature who is bone of his bone, flesh of his flesh.
>
> But you also have the start of something – maybe something much longer – with whatever is happening in church as he ponders good and evil (which he ponders further as he shapes his characters and imagines their lives).

My response to her begins by telling her what is also my point here: that when students become good at reflecting upon their own writing, they become capable of raising relevant questions and using others' responses as means of finding their own answers.

Turning revision into a story

In the previous chapter I suggested that members of writers' groups should bring a summary of teacher response back to their group. Now I'll add that writers, when submitting a portfolio for evaluation, should also summarize how peer and teacher response influenced revision for each piece of finished writing.

Not many of us follow this practice, perhaps because most of us rely on the workshop, whose interaction the teacher would partly recall. Half the respondents to the survey said they never asked students to summarize prior response and only 12% said they usually or always did so. A teacher who relies on the workshop as well as on conferences, Adam Davis (2004), explained that writing such summaries helped students to take revision more seriously, and the practice helped him combat overemphasis on self-expression. He said that many students:

> approach the first course in creative writing with a highly mythologized idea that the purpose is self-expression, and that self-awareness at the level of technique, the exercise of control, compromises that inspiration (and I actually believe that's often true at the discovery-draft stage). But of course if the art is merely about spilling whatever's within and pleasing oneself, there's really no role for the writing class or the peer group.

Having students write about where a piece came from and how response influenced its development helps affirm that revision of works-in-progress toward their potential is largely what a course is about.

The summary doesn't need to be lengthy. Notice how Melissa's writer's memo, following her haiku, quotes from an earlier memo and also charts how responders have contributed to her process:

Loitering

Darkness is extinguished
in the lot, when streetlight flickers,
catches, and they're caught.

Writer's Memo

The following appeared in my first writer's memo and explains where this poem came from: 'I saw a streetlight flicker on. All of a sudden, a circle of light covered a portion of the pavement, and

I thought about how surprising that would be to someone who was there doing something he/she shouldn't. Smoking ... picking tulips ... loitering ... I finally settled on loitering because it was so familiar to me – being from a small town where the cool thing was to drive down main street, pick a corner and loiter!'

You liked this haiku when I first turned it in, and suggested adding a couple words: 'is' in the first line and 'when' in the second. And I like the haiku a lot with those changes. I'm glad that I can be free to make a few changes to the 5-7-5 haiku rule!

What I like about this poem is the moment – while catching is happening in the poem, the poem also catches the moment. I also like the rhyming that happens in 'lot' and 'caught'.

Tracing the development of their work in this way, students come to understand the resources they draw upon and they gain authority for evaluating the result.

Negotiating Our Multiple Identities As Responders

I agree with Bizzaro (1994: 242) that 'the best teachers of writing are those who can play various roles in the classroom, who are capable of adopting numerous personas, and who are willing to experiment with authority both in student texts and in classroom interaction'. But he stops short of acknowledging that when our personas are numerous and various, students may find us confusing or even contradictory. Students naturally try to 'figure out' teachers, but what do they make of a teacher who *accompanies* them as fellow writer, reader and listener/counselor when they are used to having teachers tell them whether a piece is working, how to fix it and how good it is?

Explaining why we respond as we do

One thing I concluded early on in this study is that when we respond in ways that students do not expect, we ought to explain what we are doing and why. Thus, I recently wrote to a class:

> You may notice that I seldom tell you directly what to do with a poem. Instead, I raise questions, suggest possibilities, tell you what part of the poem leads me to expect, whether the rest of the poem meets that expectation, and so on. If your focus is on 'fixing' the poem, such response probably frustrates you. On the other hand, if I do tell you how to fix a poem, the danger is that it comes to feel no

longer like *your* poem. So I try to give you different perspectives and leave you room to decide.

Besides, as you must have heard by now, my focus during the course is on helping you become the sort of person who has learned what Flannery O'Connor calls 'the habit of art' – which includes habits of attention and perception, along with ways of saying and forming that will enable you to continue to write strong poems.

I also acknowledged that this kind of response seldom includes much direct praise, and that this might frustrate them:

If you've *invested* in a poem and you've written about something that matters to you and you're excited about what you've written, it must hurt if I seem less than excited – and give you a list of questions and reactions instead. But with another part of yourself, you can also understand: you don't want to quit working on a promising poem until it has really *arrived*, with the words and the form as true as you can make them.

This practice is part of being intentional about inviting students to examine classroom practices, with the larger goals of focusing attention on conditions that best serve their learning and writing and of inviting them to share responsibility for establishing those conditions.

Sayback of teacher response

Yancey (1998: 37) writes that results of studies of how students 'unpack' teacher response 'disappoint and, from a teacher's perspective, dishearten':

Put simply, whatever it is that students *unpack* in our responses, it certainly doesn't seem to be what it was we thought we had *packed*. In place of what we understood as specific responses and recommendations, students find uncertain readings, confusing advice, and another text altogether.

As remedy, Yancey suggests that we tell students, 'Talk back to me. Tell me what you think I'm saying, tell me how you are reacting to what you think I'm saying, tell me where I'm clear, where you disagree, what you want me to know.' She calls this 'sayback'.

Perhaps its main benefit comes when students go back and read teacher comments more carefully. That gets them beyond most misreadings. Any that remain we can correct before they take hold and threaten relationships. Since misreading is most common as well as most damaging early in the course, sayback should also come early. One or two episodes is usually enough.

Accompanying Writers Through Conferencing

Critics who allege that teachers are drawn to the workshop because it requires little preparation would be surprised at the commitment among us to conferencing, which demands considerable time and attention. Fully 45% of teachers responding to my survey said they give much emphasis to individual conferences and another 30% selected the next level, between 'some' and 'much' emphasis. At the other end of the scale, only a total of 7% indicated either little or no emphasis.

Some teachers said that the conference is where they do their best teaching. One wrote in her survey that in a class that fulfills a general studies requirement, her students ranged 'from individuals who consider creative writing the lesser of several evils to accomplished writers who are genuinely interested in developing their gift'. Her solution was 'teaching the entire course tutorially, privately, in my office', a decision she called 'worth the expenditure' of time and effort.

An alternative to the one-to-one conference is meeting with students in groups of three to five, functioning as a small workshop.

With the one-to-one conference, the obvious advantage is dialogue. We can ask questions, uncover assumptions, sometimes help the writer rethink them, and together come up with directions to take in revising. Liza Ann Acosta (2005) stressed that especially when classes are large, conferences 'allow for personalized attention. Troubleshooting is much better ... each student is so different in the kind of questions and blocks that they encounter that a conference allows me to tackle those questions specifically'.

Conferences also prevent misunderstandings. Anna Leahy (2004) told me that they 'have made me much more aware of how much students misunderstand when they are reading or what they have trouble interpreting from class discussions'.

A conference can also help a writer accept that revision can be an arduous process, as Joey Horstman (2005) illustrated:

> Both my experience as a writer and as a teacher say that the first edit always makes the piece worse. You're tearing it apart now. I warn them that the poem will get worse before it gets better. You have to go through that. The first thing you try isn't going to solve everything. It's hit and miss. I can't tell you what will fix this or I would fix it. I

can tell you certain things as an editor. I may be able to tell you why it slows down here. But I can't tell you what to fix it with. I can give a couple of suggestions. Maybe a metaphor here would round out the voice, but that's a guess.

He said that the question is this: 'What really is at the heart of what's weak about this piece? All of language is related so it's not just one thing, but what is the one thing they can work on that will help the piece?'

Personal and interpersonal dynamics

The most obvious way teachers *accompany* writers is in conferences. We can hear accompaniment in Bronwyn Williams' (2004) conferencing guidelines, from his syllabus for 'Creative Nonfiction':

> At conferences we will discuss reading or writing assignments for the course (or movies, baseball, or whatever else comes to mind). We will work together on paper topics, to let me know where you are having trouble, and to try to figure out the best way to improve your papers. Conference time is your time to get individual attention and advice about the distinctive strengths and weaknesses of your work.

Clearly, conferences are also where our teaching is most personal. Laurel Johnson Black, in *Between Talk and Teaching: Reconsidering the Writing Conference* (1998: 14), observes, 'In conferences, students can express both academic and personal concerns, can tell us the stories of their lives as they discuss what prompted and informed their writing. As teachers, we can respond to those personal elements confidentially and with feeling that we may not care (or dare) to show in the classroom.'

Yet Black also acknowledges that the easy camaraderie imaged in this description is deceptive. In fact, she discovered that students, when asked to write about a bad experience in school, often wrote about their worst conference. She admits that she initially chose conferencing as a research study for a course she was taking 'because I was smug in my belief that any examination would show the professor and my classmates how fair, honest, critical, thoughtful, reflective, and even nurturing I was. It would show that I could connect with each student individually and personally'. Yet when she recorded her conferences she discovered that they sounded different than they had seemed at the time – less effective, less sensitive, less egalitarian. In fact, she was struck by:

> how great a distance lay between my image and my words, my goals and my practice. Despite any perceptions I may have had about the

'personal' nature of student-teacher conferences, the academic patterning of the classroom and the cultural patterning which the classroom reinscribes carried over to my conferences and undermined my efforts at equalizing power and engaging in real conversation and cooperative learning. (p. 11)

The success of the conference will also depend on just on how well teacher and writer understand each other, which depends in turn on the emotions evoked in their relationship and by the work before them. Black writes, 'We come into conferences feeling something about this student, something about the texts at hand, just as our students come into conferences full of feelings.' She adds that when we ignore or suppress such feelings, 'we miss what prompted our students to write or what kept them from writing what they wanted; we miss developing the trust that comes from sharing feelings as well as facts and writing strategies; and we are frustrated by what has remained unsaid, unexplored, or unresolved' (p. 121).

Especially in an introductory course, one challenge is the student who, as Horstman put it, 'thinks their work is fantastic and there's no way you'll tell them differently'. He sees this as a problem of trust. 'The students have to trust that I can comment on it intelligently.' Black says that conferences 'help demystify the process of evaluation for students as the teacher reads through and responds in a variety of ways to the draft while the student listens and watches' (p. 14). A writer who thinks his work is terrific has to reconsider when a good reader cannot read it as he intended it to be read.

More common among students is lack of confidence, which tends to be self-fulfilling: writers too careful to do every little thing right avoid the risks that lead to the kind of powerful writing that would move readers and boost the writer's confidence. Then our challenge in the conference, as Horstman said, is 'not only diagnosing what's wrong but finding what I can say that will make them better rather than crush them'. He added, 'I grew up playing sports, so I think of it in terms of coaching. You approach one person differently than another to get them to improve. With some, I can say, "This is crap", but another student would be crushed by such bluntness.'

In some ways, conferencing resembles counseling – both are interpersonal processes with the goal of helping the client to make changes in thought; feeling and behavior. Both require time and trust. Mary Rose O'Reilley (1998: 32) observes, 'Our most productive comments can do no more than hold open a space into which the student may in time grow.'

One thing teachers who do conferences can learn from counselors is the value of empathy. Rollo May (1939: 97) insists that counselors *'must learn to empathize'*. He explains that this involves 'learning to relax, mentally and spiritually as well as physically, learning to let one's self go into the other person with a willingness to be changed in the process. It is a dying to one's self in order to live with others'. This capability is seldom recognized as a significant part of college teaching – course evaluations always ask whether the teacher is a good talker, but seldom ask whether he or she is an active and empathetic listener.

Strategies counselors employ may also apply to our conferences. For instance, occasionally a student seems to be in a rut, persisting in a direction that seems to offer little promise. Tobin's (2004: 54) experience in therapy taught him 'that strategically timed interruptions can be very useful. Therapists interrupt patients when they fall into repetition that allows them to avoid getting to central issues'.

Teachers might also learn strategies for persuasion from counselors. One, Mary Pipher (2003: 106), finds that using words like 'experiment', 'temporary', and 'pretend' lower the apparent risk of change. Thus, writers who cannot bear to part with sections that they worked hard to write but that turn out not to contribute might be more willing to move them to a 'temporary' file than to delete them entirely.

As with responding in writing, we may also need to remind ourselves to avoid offering more than the writer can comprehend and use. For most students, finding one or two directions for revision is usually enough. But as Horstman (2005) said, 'Some students I can give a lot of suggestions, some a few.'

Who takes the lead and how?

Most conferences follow an agenda set by the teacher, and they focus on developing the writing. For example, one respondent described a flow of interactions in his courses that usually goes like this:

(1) Discussion of a model or creative exercise.
(2) Creation of a draft by the student.
(3) Reaction in annotated form from me.
(4) Interaction based on annotations between student and instructor.
(5) Ongoing revision until near the end of the term.

The conference, coming at stage four, clearly follows up from teacher response, so much of its agenda is set by that response.

Many teachers do expect student initiative in preparing for the conference. Bronwyn Williams' (2004) syllabus tells students to 'think about how your work is going, what is working, where you are having trouble, what questions you have for me. Then show up on time, ask questions of me, and take notes about what we discuss (it is very easy to forget the details of a conference we had in January if you decide to re-write a paper in April)'.

Other teachers use conferences less to fix writing than to coach thinking; in the terms I have used, they focus on the writer's guide self. Donald Murray's (1985: 139) conferences, by his account in *A Writer Teaches Writing*, bring to the fore the student's thinking, planning and decision-making. Instead of reading the student's paper and saying what he thinks, Murray asks the student what she thinks of it and what she plans to do in revising, and then he responds to her response. Liza Ann Acosta's (2005) description of her conferences suggests that she also relies heavily on the student's agenda: before the conference the student gives her a draft along with a writer's memo that summarizes and responds to feedback from the writers' group. Then during the conference, 'I read the draft and the memo and spend the time addressing the questions raised in the memo (usually they know instinctively what is amiss in the paper).' She then uses the conference to help them think through what they will do next in revising.

Having students set an agenda helps them move from a student role to a writer role.

Whether and when to schedule

On a survey item that asked whether they *scheduled* conferences, only one teacher checked 'I neither expect nor encourage individual conferences'. Of the rest, a third schedule two or more with each student, a third schedule one so that students know how they work and can decide for themselves whether to schedule more, and a third invite but don't schedule conferences.

Jill Baumgaertner (2004), who said she makes 'heavy use of conferences', schedules three tutorials with each student during the three weeks before the final week of the term, when students are revising their best writing. She finds those meetings to be 'the most valuable use of my time and theirs'. Because students don't know the hard work of revising, 'They need to have a space of time when we don't have class when all they are doing is working on their writing.' At the first conference, each student sets an agenda for their concluding work. By the final conference they have formed 'a healthy respect for writers'.

In an advanced course I might try Baumgaertner's approach, but in introductory courses I prefer to require a conference early. One reason is that I realized during the second half of a recent poetry class that students who were having a hard time getting themselves into the different modes of seeing, thinking and writing that poetry requires hadn't learned enough about those from written responses. The breakthroughs came about through the give and take of a conference.

So why don't I do more response that way? Although I enjoy occasional conferences, more than five or six a day wear me down and I lose concentration. So after scheduling one conference for all students, I let them decide whether a conference or written response will serve them best. About three-quarters of the way through a recent course, at a chance meeting in the hallway, Kayli told me, 'I think my story is about at the point where I'd like your response.'

'Are we meeting, or am I writing?'

'I think I want you to write first, and then I'll decide if I want to talk about what you have written.'

'Okay. Attach a good memo.'

I took her request to mean that group response had been encouraging, she thought the story worked and she hoped my written response would confirm that; but if I found problems, she would ask for a conference. I like it that she does the deciding. One thing writers should learn from a course is what kind of response they need, from whom and at what stage.

Conference or written response?

I've also noticed that some students usually prefer written comments. They may feel pressured by a conference and find that written response gives them space to think things through. One said, 'I lose track of all that we talked about in a conference, but when I have written comments I can go back and read them again and think about what they mean.'

Students are more likely to prefer written comments if they are typed. Bly (2001: 193) writes, 'When a writer's teachers attach a typed, separate note to a paper being returned, he or she feels more respected than if there were only marginal notes on the paper itself and a sentence or two at the end.' In addition, typing a note 'tends to make you, the teacher, contain and summarize your feelings about the work'. In my experience, typed comments are also more likely to address the writer rather than just offer fixes for the text, and in this case they tend to have something of the dialogic quality of a good conference.

A response printed out is likely to be read more carefully than one read from a computer screen. It's easier to mark up printed comments. And students tend to bring to the screen their habits of reading web pages – sampling here and there rather than reading sentence by sentence.

At least part of the time, some teachers may prefer to record their response in an audio file and attach it to email or upload it to the student via the campus course management program. This would work well for a lengthy reader-response that is aided by reading aloud from the student's writing.

Two Issues in Response Practice

Negotiating the personal in our response practice includes thinking through two issues: when and how much to praise; and whether it is wise to offer an interpretation that goes beyond the writer's awareness of what a piece is about.

The question of praise

Nearly 80% of those responding to my survey indicated they are highly likely to 'find a way to praise or encourage the writer'. Probably some of us believe that writers *need* praise to keep them going on a difficult journey. We know, too, that revision should be driven by a sense of what is strong or alive, and that praise might help them find that.

But we also know that when praise becomes predictable it loses effect. And to some it may give the impression that our standards are low.

Praise can also be manipulative. When Stafford (1986: 65) rejects 'encouragement', he appears to mean praise:

> Encouragement signifies that someone has a program that they have already arrived at for doing something for you. I try to get away from that in my teaching. A lot of teachers become that encouragement machine. That is deadly, I would rather be envious of my students than encouraging them ...

I think that praise is 'deadly' when it fixes the writer's attention on pleasing those who have the power to dispense praise. Stafford prefers an 'interiorized' satisfaction from writing. He also (1978: 78) warns, 'You can become a lost soul in literature just as surely as you can in any activity where you abandon yourself to the decisions of others.' Students who have been socialized to seek approval are at great risk of adopting what we say is good, and on our say-so, not because they see and feel that goodness for themselves. Another way to say this is that approval junkies are at great risk of forming a false consciousness.

Public praise has dangers too. Teacher-heroes from TV or movies commonly praise one or a few students. The impression viewers are expected to form is that other students will then admire and emulate those students. In creative writing, the more likely consequence is that other students will become jealous and envious – and feel pressured to write like the ones who are praised.

And yet, expressing delight at what pleases us is such a natural reaction to artistic performance that Lerman (2003) believes the response session needs to begin with praise.

What's crucial, I think, is that praise be specific. Especially early in the course, I avoid writing 'Nice job' on a draft, though I do look for particular choices to admire. Toward the end of a course I am more likely to acknowledge a strong piece of writing as a whole, especially when my pleasure in reading joins the writer's pleasure in having written. A former student, Jessica Laaveg (2004/2005), now a high school teacher, recalled my response to a piece whose writing she had experienced as a course-culminating triumph:

> I remember you walking by with a twinkle in your eye as you handed it back, but I also remember reading a list of open-ended questions you wrote in response to things that perhaps were confusing to you or needed clarification/improvement. You mentioned what 'worked' in the piece, too. It was specific. I try to do the same in my own teaching – the 'this works because ...' is important so students can begin their own self-analysis. Specifics are tedious and time-consuming and altogether lost by some teachers who have given up, but writers need them to improve.

When Stafford says that he 'would rather be envious' of a writer than offer praise, he must mean that he prefers to respond as a fellow writer who wishes *he* had thought of something he encounters in a work-in-progress, a particular phrase or idea, perhaps, or an image or figure.

Liking doesn't mean lowering standards. Just the opposite. Bishop (1994a: 290) agrees with Elbow that 'liking work allows us to be more demanding of the writer', and as a result 'the work improves. Liking creates a positive chain reaction'.

Praise of what's working easily leads to consideration of what's not yet working. Nancy Sommers (2006: 251), commenting on an extensive study of writing development over four years at Harvard, writes that 'a key finding is that constructive criticism, more than encouraging praise, often pushes students forward in their writing; constructive criticism more than praise reveals instructors' investments in their students' untapped potential'.

Is interpretation helpful?

Asked how likely they are to 'speculate on what the writer seems to want to do in the piece but hasn't yet done', 62% of those responding to my survey said they are highly likely or likely to do so, and only 10% chose either of the two 'unlikely' responses.

Many of us will go a step further. When my survey asked how likely respondents were to 'offer an interpretation of what the piece seems to be about that probably goes beyond the writer's awareness of what it's about', 56% said 'highly likely' or 'likely', and 19% checked either of the two choices at the opposite end of the scale. Joey Horstman (2005) said that Kurt Vonnegut remarked that his job as a teacher is reading the story and saying how he understood it, so that if the writer didn't want it read that way, she could change it. Horstman said, 'I tried it and it worked less miserably than everything else I was doing. It helps the students edit their own stuff.' Ann Townsend (2005) explained why she thinks an interpretive response is generally useful to writers:

> It's not unusual for a poem or story to reveal more to the reader than to the writer. And I don't think it's a requirement for a writer to be fully cognizant, at first, of all his or her motives or gestures. But I do think that revision requires some self-awareness. If my interpretation surprises or startles the writer, it also enlarges his or her ability to think about the piece.

That has been my position too. So I was surprised when Martin Cockroft (2005) told me he does not believe a writer needs to know what a poem is about in order to revise. 'Writers often don't know what their poems are about. The process for me is not about knowing what I'm writing. I'm not sure if I need to know. I ask what a poem is becoming.' He added that the *way* it becomes 'is not necessarily controlled by what the writer thinks about what it's saying next, but more about what would come next'.

He also worried that writers who rely on interpretation for revising might reduce the poem to cliché – a little message they think the piece should get across. This is also Katherine Haake's (2000: 110–11) reason why she 'almost never' presents what she thinks is the meaning of her students' stories:

despite the insightful readings of my students (which they learn to produce in literature classes), I've never been convinced interpretation is very good for writing. Where there's interpretation, there's an equal sign that functions for the most part to reduce the pure necessity of text. And we should be opposed to this, to anything at all that reduces textuality; we should focus our attention instead not on *what* but on *how* texts mean, trusting that meaning will take care of itself, as surely it will, with the reader.

I agree that we should not *emphasize* what a text means over how it means, but I believe we can do both, each in relation to the other. Even though he resists interpretation, Cockroft could recall a time when it helped him revise. When he showed his wife a group of his poems, 'she said they were about journeys'. It was something he hadn't noticed that he found helpful to notice.

It's also worth noting that Cockroft's more intuitive approach to revising fits experienced writers better than beginners. Learning to listen to and be guided by the inner voices of intuition may require an initial period of more deliberate composing, when readers' interpretations may help the writer grasp how a poem means.

One reason I'll continue to interpret some student writing – albeit cautiously – is that a motive for making art is to be deeply understood. How can artists know that they have succeeded without hearing from readers what they understand a piece to be doing and meaning? My wife, Amy Fichter, a professor of life drawing, recalled a graduate professor in art 'telling me point blank that my drawings were about relationships, period'. She explained that she 'had started making images that were dealing more with things like violence, sex, struggle', and this professor 'knew they weren't about real (as in really enacted) violence'. She recalled, 'I didn't say much in response, but on the inside I was beaming. Someone finally gets it! That may have been the first time someone said out loud what I knew inside all along.'

When interpretation is intrusive

We also need to remind ourselves that interpreting students' writing can be risky.

When coming from an authority, one danger is appropriation. T. J. Rivard (2004) chose 'very unlikely' in response to whether he would 'speculate on what the writer seems to want to do in the piece but hasn't yet done'. He explained that his goal 'is to help students develop their imaginative voice', so he tries 'not to cloud it with my own'. He worries that students would 'take my speculation as the direction they should go' and push aside their own intuitions. This suggests that teachers who do offer interpretations also need to encourage writers to resist them.

To a writer, interpretation can bring revelation, but not all revelation is welcome. Lad Tobin (2004: 44) remarks about 'the striking differences between what students mean to say – about their families, their feelings, and themselves – and what actually comes out'. He adds, 'I've gotten used to these gaps, and I usually find these moments of unself-awareness absurdly and poignantly endearing.' Yet, even more than essays that disclose experiences of shame or trauma, these essays disturb him:

> because they seem to contain a large troubling gap between the student's conscious understanding and unconscious emotion. This kind of contradiction or discontinuity in a student's personal narrative – it usually occurs at the end of the piece – is familiar to writing teachers as a retreat, a summing up, a resolution ... The gap is the denial of something I know the writer knows but won't let herself say or even feel. I am, of course, unsettled when one of my students describes an eating disorder or admits to resenting a parent. But I am far more unsettled when they deny what they have just confessed.

In such instances, Tobin writes, 'I am constantly aware of how the text reveals more to me about them than they realize about themselves – and constantly aware that it would [be] awkward and painful for me to tell them so' (p. 45).

I have been more cautious about telling writers more than they know about their writing since a conference several years ago that for a time disrupted a good relationship. Lisa Percy (2004) came in to talk about a new poem that fascinated but also mystified her. She had written it in a local nature reserve, which supplied the images. My recollection was that she told me that the poem had come to her something like a dream, that it was different from anything she had written and she wasn't sure what to make of it. After she read her poem, I observed casually – without first learning how ready she was to hear the interpretation – that it might have a sexual meaning. The suggestion obviously disturbed her. The conference ended soon after, with her still upset.

We did eventually restore a good working relationship. She went on to teach high school and occasionally wrote back about her experiences.

Later she married a teacher of creative writing, which piqued her interest in the personal side of this teaching. So recently I asked her about that conference. Neither of us could recall details, but in an email to me she offered this account:

> At the time I felt you had crossed a line because I was not looking for the kind of feedback you were giving me. I, like most people, I hope, have my dark secrets that I would rather not share in certain circles, and although I think my writing may have been touching on a difficult experience, I think your interpretation was not on target and so my reaction was to be offended. For much of my life, and still to a degree, I've cared sometimes too much what people thought of me and how they viewed me. I guard myself and any bad experiences I've had from the public eye.

She also recalled that the incident 'hindered my class experience thereafter. I imagine I was probably more unwilling to participate actively and was dreading the next conference. I do believe that writing is an emotional release in many ways and through the class I know I thought a lot about my childhood and experiences'. She added that even though she thinks of writing as 'a healing experience and a celebration of memories and life's experiences', she avoids writing about some experiences because 'perhaps I'm scared to face some of the darkness lurking in the back of my mind as well'.

Limiting the risk of interpretation

In becoming readers and writers of literary genres, we learn to find and interpret gaps, apparent contradictions, patterns of imagery and symbols. When we focus this capability upon student writing and say what we think we understand, we risk telling some writers more than they are ready to hear. So it's worth considering ways to limit the risk.

Obviously, the least risk comes with keeping the interpretation to ourselves. Martin Cockroft (2005) said that when he recently read a poem with an apparent sexual meaning, he mentioned it to his wife. But when the writer in a conference 'didn't show any indication that it might be taken sexually – she was talking about fish in a river –' he said that he 'didn't draw any attention' to the passage.

Having the writer set much of the agenda for response also reduces the risk of intrusion. If I had drawn more questions from Lisa first, I would have gained a better sense for what she did understand – and learned whether she was ready to hear what I told her.

I could also have asked more questions myself, especially reader-oriented questions. James Plath (2004a) described his approach to me:

> I usually get around the 'sexual reading' in personal conferences by having the student (with my door wide open) answer this simple question: 'What were you hoping the reader would think or feel in response to this set of images or this phrase?' That's an offshoot of one of my first conference statements: 'Tell me about what you were trying to accomplish with this poem/story.'

Such questioning invites the writer to interpret her own poem. It echoes Lerman's practice of asking responders to phrase reactions as questions.

When we do offer interpretation, another way to limit intrusiveness is with reader-responses that suggest how a poem *might* be read. Todd Davis (2005) told me, 'I'll say something silly like, "Don't think I've got a dirty mind here..."' and then he'll describe how he responded to a part of a poem. If the writer is female, though, he reminds himself that 'as a male, you're in a power position' and such an interpretation 'might be heard as a come-on'. So then he might say, 'I read this poem to my wife and this is what the images are evoking for us.'

Tobin's (2004: 54) experience with seeing therapists led him to add free-association to reader-response. He writes that he may tell a student, 'As I read your essay, I had this image in my mind ...' or, 'This may be way off but I just connected what you're saying to ...'. Due to the influence of psychoanalysis, he is also more likely to rely on metaphorical language. He recognizes the risk, though, and adds these cautions: that we should never 'insist that our students confront and reveal material they have repressed'; that we remember that 'people can only go as far as their own defenses will allow'; and that we need to understand 'that a writer, like a patient, might not be ready to write the narrative that we think or hope is lurking just beneath the surface'. Yet, because 'it can be valuable to help students gain access to and control over unconscious material', he concludes that 'we shouldn't be afraid or reluctant to provide support and opportunity to students ready and eager to engage in that process' (pp. 54–5).

Tobin adds that the *perception* of a gap in student writing could have more to do with 'the teacher's own unresolved issues' (p. 47), a possibility I'll explore in Chapter 7.

Chapter 6
Negotiating Authority as Teachers, Models, Mentors

> *When we analyze a case of some pronounced influence, our question is not why the one person had the power to influence the other, but rather what tendencies were there in the mind of the other, probably in his unconscious, which made him so ready to be influenced. There must exist some unconscious readiness to believe, some predisposition toward the influence.*
>
> Rollo May (1939: 96)

The central theme of Anna Leahy's (2005) collection, *Power and Identity in the Creative Writing Classroom: The Authority Project*, is that we who teach artistic practice need an *authority-conscious* pedagogy. At the least, this means being aware of our different kinds of authority and knowing why and when we might want to either limit or extend each kind.

Our most obvious kind of authority is our institutional authority to set expectations, make assignments and give grades. Related is our pedagogical authority to create a setting, plan provocative learning experiences and help students to process that experience and to set and meet goals – in a word, to be a mentor. Like other writing teachers, we also have authority as practitioners who know writing from the inside and who can thus respond insightfully to students and their drafts. Most mysterious is the authority based on the image students may form of us as a person who lives the life of an artist; students seeking models may develop a fascination with us that is difficult to negotiate – or even to acknowledge.

The main reason to distinguish these kinds of authority is to recognize that they can interact with each other in surprising ways. For one instance, gaining authority as mentor or as model may elevate our institutional authority as grade-giver, even if that is not our intention. Even a deliberate attempt to downplay institutional authority in order to better *accompany* students as a mentor may have the paradoxical effect of making our judgments and our grades matter more to them.

Students' Stereotypes and Authority

In another sense, however, authority is simple – a way of naming the ethos we have with students that persuades them to take us seriously enough to follow our guidelines, work with our suggestions, accept our judgments. 'Having authority' in this sense depends partly upon factors beyond our control – especially our students' stereotypes.

Gender stereotypes in particular have more impact on the authority students ascribe to teachers than most of us (at least most men) realize. Leahy (2005: 17) cites studies showing that male teachers score lower on 'authority' portions of student evaluations when they become more personal and supportive, apparently because such behavior departs from masculine stereotypes. More significantly, she found that female teachers face a no-win situation: if they adopt traditional signs of authority such as distancing, students tend to perceive them as 'too masculine', but if they are more personal, nurturing and receptive, students are more likely to challenge them – over a grade, for example. This is a provocative finding. I earlier cited Mary Swander's (2005: 169) identification of the typical critique-based workshop as 'the established male model'. When she rejected it, she noticed that although 'most male students welcomed the kinder, gentler approach', female students were more likely to challenge her authority. 'In the tangled web of interiorized inferiority,' writes Swander, 'women expected a woman in authority to act more like a man than a man.' But Leahy's findings suggest an alternate explanation: perhaps the women were upset with Swander because they felt they had lost a needed model of female *authority* – they already had female models for being nurturers. And male students may have welcomed the kinder and gentler approach because that was what they expected from a woman.

Rachel Hall's (2005: 87) 'The pregnant muse: Assumptions, authority, and accessibility' presents her surprising discovery that her authority as professor declined when her pregnancy marked her as Mother: 'Becoming a mother is an empowering creative act, but instead of inspiring respect, I was often dismissed, treated with a mixture of boredom and condescension. When a friend mentioned that television sitcoms suffer a drop in ratings after an infant is introduced into the story line, I had a moment of recognition. My ratings were dropping.' Students preferring traditional gender roles may have perceived contradiction between the roles of mother and professor; and students who hoped to be taught by a Mysterious Artist were apparently led by their stereotypes to see instead 'just a mom'.

Age is a variable factor in the authority a typical class will grant us. Younger professors may dress formally or ask students to address them formally in order to increase authoritative distance and demonstrate seriousness about their role and their work, but older professors often dispense with such trappings in order to reduce authoritative distance, the better to accompany students. Other marks of difference such as race and ethnicity also factor into a teacher's negotiation of authority with a particular class.

Negotiating our Formal Authority

When students cut class, skip assignments or offer lackluster response, we sometimes think we ought to ramp up our formal authority – buy power suits, get tough on slackers, give pop quizzes. Those are the kinds of things colleagues suggest.

The problem is that such actions contradict moves to limit our power in order to reduce authoritative distance. Bizzaro (1994: 234) says that teachers who offer reader-response instead of telling students how to fix writing to suit teacher expectations 'must relinquish power in the classroom, abdicate authority granted them through tradition and privilege'. He adds, 'The liberation of students begins with the teacher's willingness to undermine his or her authority in the classroom by using that very authority to do so.' We also reduce authority when we ask for writers' memos to guide our response or when we ask students to set an agenda for a conference.

Jeffrey Sommers (1989: 177) argues that 'the most effective role for the writing instructor' with such a pedagogy is that of 'guide or fellow explorer or editor'. But Sommers also acknowledges that this role can feel 'risky and troubling, especially for instructors who have grown used to the comfortable and powerful role of judge, or for young teachers insecure about their own authority in the classroom'. He remarks, 'It is quite easy to feel "dumb".' Bizzaro (1993: 7) makes the disquieting observation that 'early efforts at decentralizing authority in the classroom will be problematic'.

Personal or formal dress and address

Caught in the contradiction of needing some kinds of authority some of the time while at other times needing to come across as more of a fellow explorer or supportive responder, we clearly ought to be reflective about how we negotiate authority. Consider, for starters, ways we choose to *express* authority – our typical appearance, manner and tone and the way we expect students to address us.

Tobin (2004: 97) observes that new teachers 'are hyperaware of the choices they are making – what to be called, what to wear, how to arrange the desks, what tone to take in the syllabus'. Little wonder, then, if these new teachers, in his words, 'often end up resorting to demonstrations of authority that only mystify their students'.

We don't get much help from our context – few colleges and universities offer standards for such things as 'proper dress', and many professors with advanced degrees prefer the garb of the working class – blue jeans. We can trace some of the shift toward informality to the distrust of authority that arose in the Sixties. Jerry Farber (1990: 139), speaking out of that milieu, questions even the title *teacher*. He will accept it as a 'a relatively straightforward job description' but prefers to jettison 'the Brahmin claptrap, the mystification, those stupid nostalgia-for-feudalism titles that we hide behind – none of that helps us teach; it gets in the way; it is to be outgrown'. He prefers to say that 'we are all students, some of whom have made a career out of helping others learn'. Disdain for formality was also brought to academia by professors with blue-collar backgrounds. As John Wylam (2004) said, 'Life as the son of a millworker means you don't take titles and airs seriously at all.' Jim Heynen (2004) said he noticed a 'democratizing of the setting – we don't even have faculty johns any more'.

Teacher-artists in particular seem to prefer that their authority be located in what they know rather than in their title. Heynen said that when students ask what they should call him, he tells them that it's not an issue for him, that 'authority is a relationship between knowledge and ignorance. If I know things you need to know, we know who the authority is'. (He sometimes adds that if they wish they may address him as his wife does. 'Honey?' they ask. 'No,' he says, 'Your Excellency'. Jokes gather at sites of unease.) One indication from my survey that creative writing teachers construct an informal teaching persona is the way their students address them: 62% by first name and another 5% by 'an abbreviated name, nickname, or pseudonym'. That's two-thirds who are addressed informally. I don't know the percentage in disciplines outside the arts, but I suspect it is much lower. Ben Yagoda (2003) did some informal research and found first-name basis more common in smaller colleges, among younger faculty, in the humanities and related disciplines, and in certain parts of the country, especially in California and the North East.

He also writes that especially in larger colleges, the preferred term of formal address is 'Doctor' rather than 'Professor'. Thus one factor limiting formal address in classes in the arts is the higher percentage of teachers whose terminal degree is not a doctorate – just over half the creative writing teachers responding to my survey. One told me that he begins the first class saying, 'This is English 109, and I'm Phil Hey. Please don't call me *Professor*; and don't call me *Doctor*.' His follow-up, 'You may call me *Master*', must nudge them toward the other choice. Barbara Bogue (2004b) said she gives students choices. 'I tell them, "I'm not a doctor. Call me Barb or Professor".'

However, 44% of creative writing faculty *with* a doctorate also said their students typically addressed them by first name.

Several respondents confirmed my sense that we deliberately reduce authoritative distance in order to be more effective in the parts of our teaching that depend upon working alongside the learner. Kim Peterson (2004) mentioned 'warmth, ease of conversing, rapport with my future colleagues'. Jessica Farquhar (2004) had a full-time tenured professor who went by his first name, 'and I really appreciated it a lot as a student. It breaks down communication barriers, as far as I'm concerned, and this is really important in a workshop environment'. Laura Apol (2004) told me she prefers first-name address as a matter of reciprocation: in a good creative writing course 'students are crossing a boundary, being not just a student but risking an authentic self, and if as receiver, you only occupy your classroom self, you are dishonoring that'.

As might be expected, the disadvantages of informality appear when greater authoritative distance seems desirable. Peterson wrote that 'occasionally a student takes too many liberties in assuming I'm their best friend instead of their instructor', but she added that this happened only 'two or three times in 11 years'. Mary Swander (2004) told me she wouldn't mind if students addressed her by first name now, but she started teaching when she was young and *looked* young. 'I could tell right away that it was too familiar. In my first teaching job, students asked me if I wanted to snort cocaine with them. I thought, "They've got to start calling me Professor Swander".' She added, 'It was good to have that distance.' Elizabeth Swingrover (2004b) also began asking students to address her formally when she was 'a young lecturer in the department and also female'. She explained, 'I teach many other courses besides creative writing, and like to maintain a certain professional distance, since I grade them. It seems silly to pretend I'm their best bud.' She added, 'I've been to workshops where the (famous male) teacher puts his arms around people and buys them beer.' Clearly, one risk of reduced authoritative distance is loss of confidence among students that they are regarded equally and will be treated fairly.

Like Bogue, I let students choose – 'Professor Vandermeulen' or 'Carl'. One reason I do not insist on first-name address is that students from some backgrounds and cultures are uncomfortable addressing a teacher informally (so I also avoid dressing so casually that such students might wonder whether I take seriously the work we do together).

A factor I did not consider is that especially in smaller colleges, students tend to generalize such expectations, so what I thought of as my own decision to allow personal address made it harder for my female colleagues to expect formal address and in this way help first-generation college students learn to regard women as authority figures.

All things considered, a teacher new to a school should ask around before making decisions about dress and address.

Transcending the ordinary

As writers, we're aware that the kind of work a piece of writing can do depends partly upon its tone. Consider what Mary Oliver (1995: 105) writes about gains and losses that resulted from the move in poetry toward the ordinary:

> There was, in the tone of the old poems, a certainty, an authority which was implied and fortified through its elevated diction ... I am talking about a diction and a tone that was *other* than the daily, the usual, the ordinary. In and of itself, apart from the content of the poem, this tone suggested to the reader that something of import was on the page – was contained within the occasion of the poem. Since, as I see it, the work of the poem is to transcend the ordinary instance, to establish itself on a second, metaphysical level, this tone was important, and useful. It served, in the old poem, as a steeple serves a church; even in the distance it says: Here is holy ground. Here is something different from the everyday.

The kind of work that a class can accomplish also depends upon the tone that is set, partly through our own decisions about dress, address and other aspects of our teaching persona. Because a course is an opportunity for doing fine work, even for constructing a new self, it needs to offer a space that, if not quite holy ground, at least rises above the mundane.

Teacher as Mentor

Elizabeth Swingrover (2004a) begins her 'Introduction to Creative Writing' syllabus by emphasizing the authority she brings to teaching from her practice as an artist; then she relates this authority to students' learning:

> As a creative writer myself, and someone who has been *thinking literature* for a long time, I know how poems, short stories, plays and novels actually work, what makes them tick. My job is to get you to first of all *appreciate the craft* that goes into writing literary works (not genre, not formula, not slick stuff); to get you to acknowledge the *forms* (a sonnet vs. a villanelle); **and** our rather ultimate purpose – trying to get you who are someone else so entirely different from me, with different habits, reading background, expectations, to *produce a fine poem, short story, etc.*

Her experience clearly gives her authority as a teacher. She has developed a writer's sense of craft and awareness of form. We also hear in 'not genre, not formula, not slick stuff' that she knows what the literary community values so she can help students learn to evaluate their work. And although she begins with her experience, her focus is on the students and on the work she is 'trying to get' them to produce. She talks about knowledge, skill, habits – and assumes these do make a difference, especially in getting students to a place where they can keep moving forward on their own.

To put all this another way, she's capable of being a mentor. Of teachers responding to my survey, 82% indicated they served as 'Mentor for at least one person – student, colleague, community member'. A mentor helps a learner move forward on a journey of becoming, and whether the journey is vocational, personal or spiritual, the mentor is one who has traveled that road. Mentoring is also interpersonal teaching.

Sometimes mentoring is built into the curriculum. Keith Ratzlaff (2004) described working each year with six students, some poets, some essayists, on year-long senior honors projects. 'The one thing a year-long project does is put pressure on a student to see themselves as, at last, *a writer*. Almost all of them get writer's block for the first month or so, then, like most of us, they find a way out and *become* writers. That sort of thing almost never happens during a semester.' Because of the honors project, Ratzlaff has learned to look beyond an individual course to 'see the development of writers as a larger process that spans their entire college careers'.

Andrew Scott (2004) said he mentors several students each semester who 'seek additional guidance along their path as fiction writers':

> Sometimes, this means students want me to validate their desire, to say that becoming a fiction writer is really an 'acceptable' thing to do with one's life. One student said he wanted to do what I do (meaning:

write and teach creative writing), and after I told him how sorry I was to hear that, we discussed graduate programs, the life of a writer, and general notions of suffering.

Even his tone reveals how personal mentoring is. Scott added that he also serves as something of a mentor to colleagues and hopes to do so with community members. This aspiration, he said, 'comes from my model teachers, too. All of them served their various communities as writers. It's something instilled in me by the graduate program at New Mexico State University'. Teachers of the arts are more likely to say what Scott also said: 'I serve as a mentor for all of my students.' I don't think he means that he develops an intensive one-to-one relationship with each writer but rather that he takes a mentoring *approach* – teaches through an attentiveness to what is alive in a student that might be made to flourish.

A word that sets a student on a journey

Part of mentoring is pointing to potential. Many of us have become artists and teachers because we had a teacher who saw something in us that at the time we could not see on our own. Nicole Mazzarella (2004) told me she realized that 'very small comments' from teachers have shaped her experience and her journey as a writer. She added, 'I don't know if we always remember that.' As a college freshman, she was a journalism major doing creative writing 'on the side'. An adjunct professor read some of her writing, looked at her and said, 'You are going to consider going on for an MFA, aren't you?'. Mazzarella said that the question 'set me on a journey'. It told her – and let her tell herself – 'You could do this'. Carolyn Holbrook (2004b/2005) told me, 'I was always in trouble as a teenager, but an 8th grade teacher believed in me. I wrote a sweet little poem, and she said I should consider writing. I just never forgot that. Everyone else called me incorrigible.' In carrying on that practice of acknowledging talent, Holbrook has learned that 'sometimes things happen much later because of something you said'. One of her students had been chemically dependent at the age of 12. 'She wrote one little passage in a larger piece, and I said, "That's a story to tell".' The student 'developed it into a publishable book' and went on to pursue a PhD.

Theresa Williams (2004) helps students name and know themselves by discovering their personality type via the Myers-Briggs Personality Type Indicator, often available through career centers. She said that the indicator makes concrete for students how differences in personality lead to differences in reading and writing. She invites them 'to explore how their temperament affects what they are interested in writing, their philosophy about life, and even how they might construct their sentences'.

We too easily assume that students' talents and potential are evident to them; we ought to assume that they need people they trust to tell them who they are and what they are capable of becoming. Halfway through a course, one of my graduate literature professors, Les Whipp, wrote each student a letter mentioning capabilities and qualities he or she brought to the classroom community. My letter describing me as a 'peacemaker' surprised me – but then helped me claim that side of myself.

Teacher as Model

No one seems to doubt that a writing teacher should teach out of the *experience* of being a writer. Bizzaro (1994: 15) observes, 'Certainly, teachers of poetry writing classes who do not write *should*,' partly so that they 'experience first-hand what their students will experience.' Should the teacher also present himself or herself as an embodiment of 'writer'? Bizarro cites David St. John: 'It is crucial that the students sense their teacher's excitement and involvement not only with their writing but also with his or her *own* writing.' Yet we also perceive the risk of making the course too much about ourselves. Most of us want to avoid a 'cult of personality' but we may not realize that we might nevertheless have students who become fascinated with us and take us as a model of the person and artist they hope to become.

Writing and revising with students

Bishop (1999: 9) says that in composition, part of the established 'figure' of 'the writer-teacher or teacher-writer' is 'one who advocates that teachers write with and for their writing students as well as with and for their colleagues'. Among creative writing teachers, the practice of writing with students appears less common. Nearly half of the respondents to my survey said they never do it or give it little emphasis; however, the rest said they make some or even significant use of the practice. Barbara Bogue (2004b) writes with students to reduce formality as well as build trust. 'We are seated in a circle,' she told me, so 'I write with them and share my prewriting with them.' Student evaluations show her that this practice 'gives me more credibility, because I work in the art form that I teach'. Ryan Futrell (2004) said he writes with classes, primarily to position himself as a fellow writer. He also tries 'to bring in particular problems I'm working through' in order to ask for help, and he finds students receptive. He added, 'What I don't want to do is bring something in with a "this is how you do it" mentality.' Jim Heynen (2004) said that while working as an artist in the schools he noticed that 'the most successful writing was done in classrooms where the teacher participated with the students. It's a great equalizer'. Consequently, he announces to his own students two expectations for in-class writing: 'Whatever we write doesn't have to be good'; and 'I'll do it too'. Although he rarely reads his published work to a class, he will read these exercises 'because often it's much like theirs'.

James Plath (2004b) told me he quit writing with students for this very reason. He began doing assignments with students 'when it was the mood to decentralize the classroom', but he said it 'proved disastrous' because seeing that his first draft wasn't clearly better than some of theirs 'helped their ego, but it took too much away from my authority'. He found that students were 'reinforced in their belief that their opinion is worth as much as the instructor's, so suddenly they became more defensive of their own work'; the experience, he felt, 'allowed them to retreat to the defense system that it's just anyone's opinion'.

Perhaps one solution is to use writing with students as a way to teach revision. Heynen said that Robert Bly came to his class with an exercise involving 'a bag of stuff from nature, including twigs and rocks. He has everybody find something interesting, and the first step is to describe it: feel it and smell it and become acquainted with it. The next step is to compare this object to your mother'. (Heynen noted that students often chose an object that had 'a bizarre relevance to their relationship with their mother'.) Later, when they read their drafts, Heynen said, Bly's own writing 'was not half as good as some done by the students'. But a week later, Bly sent him a revision, and 'that became the real lesson' because it was amazingly better: 'If the writing is important and a person works on it – applies the discipline and the craft – then this is what can happen.' Pat Emile (2004b) told me she enjoys writing her own piece on the board while students are writing. 'They see me changing things, then ask why I did this or that.' Gina Franco (2004) has a poem with drafts going back 10 years. 'In the beginning you can't see the final draft. It had many lives. I use it to convince them that the work can be in flux.' Natasha Sajé (2005) goes a step further, showing students frank comments from a friend such as 'not worth keeping' and 'I don't know what you're doing here' to illustrate how writers can benefit from frank exchanges with trusted readers.

Presentation of the teacher's finished or published writing

Because we value the presence of authors performing their own work we bring writers to campus, and some of us require students to attend readings. Yet one writer whose works students may never encounter is the one who teaches their class. Asked about the emphasis placed on 'giving your own finished or published writing to the class, in writing or in oral performance', nearly a third of teachers responding to my survey said this practice was 'not used' in their teaching and another 28% gave it only a little emphasis. Only about 20% chose either of two levels at the 'much emphasis' end of the scale.

One reason teachers avoid bringing in their own work is the conscious or unconscious assumption that the classroom is a place of critique and evaluation. As Gina Franco said, students are 'used to evaluating, and they don't feel comfortable doing that with a teacher's writing'. Thom Tammaro (2004) emailed that although he will use his own work to demonstrate revision, he otherwise tries to keep it out, 'especially when there's some kind of evaluative process involved'. He explained, 'It's not fair to them. There's undue pressure on them to respond favorably, even if I tell them to be critical. Bottom line: I'm still the guy giving the grade.' He said that if students are 'curious about my work – and they are – they can buy my books or check them out of the library – which they often do'. Donald Platt (2004) was unequivocal. 'I *never* use my own writing in courses that I teach.' His feeling is that 'teaching my own work would be in poor taste' because students 'would feel constrained to be "appreciative" and/or "complimentary" about the work, given the presence of the author in the room as their teacher, who also happens to be grading them'.

Another reason teachers are reluctant to present their own work is to avoid suggesting that students ought to imitate it. Some teachers are willing to share their work with interested *individuals*. Matthew Roberson (2004) wrote in email that he knows students are interested in his writing because every term 'at least three students present me with a copy of my book'. However, he hesitates to bring his work to class because he doesn't want to lead students in the directions he writes 'and it's been my experience that it's easy for that to happen'. He wants them 'to know what's possible out there and make their own decisions'. He added, 'If they search out my interests by themselves, that's another matter. I'll talk to those students about my stuff.' Chris Maier (2004) described a similar practice, though he sometimes gives copies to individual students. 'Now that I think of it, the students that I tend to slip my stories to are usually the ones who've become most engaged in their own writing – who seem least susceptible to infection.'

Teachers were also concerned about the ethics of placing themselves in the center. A reason Franco gave for keeping her own writing out of the class is that she doesn't want it to compete with students' writing for time and attention. 'Their time is valuable to them. They don't like to see it wasted, that workshop time.' She also suggested that the practice might place the teacher in competition with students, coming across as, 'Look at what I'm doing. I'm the *writer*'. She added, 'It works better in the community college. There they want to see it. They don't feel that way here' (at Knox College, which offers a major in creative writing). Bill Davis (2004) admitted that he had been 'getting pressure from advanced students' to bring in his own work, but his feeling was that 'it's criminal with a captive audience to force it down their throats'. When he was a student he had a professor who read his own work, and that bothered him. The professor said, 'Let's talk about this', but Davis saw that as façade. 'We were expected to admire it.' Matthew Roberson said, 'Right or wrong, I feel like there's something awfully self-important about the writing professor who says, "Look at me!"'

So it's interesting that Michael Frizell (2004) said that 'the main advantage' he sees in using his own writing is 'to show them me'. He asked his students if they saw the use of his writing as an advantage 'and they said, overwhelmingly, "Yes!" The main reason cited was that I came across more human to them'. His conclusion is confirmed by bell hooks, who writes that when professors 'bring narratives of their experiences into classroom discussions it eliminates the possibility that we can function as all-knowing, silent interrogators' (in Berman, 2001: 54). In other words, in some circumstances, offering our own work to our students is an act of humility rather than pride.

Kim Peterson (2004), who uses both her published and unpublished work in class, listed three benefits: students 'see that someone like themselves can be published. They help me improve my work. Their improved editing skills strengthen their writing'. She added, 'I hope I don't come across as stuck on what I've accomplished. To balance that I also use student work that gets published.'

Other teachers who present their own work also try to find a balance. Jill Baumgaertner (2004) doesn't have students talk about her writing because 'that puts them on the spot', but if she has something published, 'I'll make copies and pass them out, so they know I'm working as a writer. Sometimes they'll come with questions individually'. Mary Biddinger (2004b) said she hands out 'a little packet of my poems' at the beginning of the semester, without inviting students to discuss it. However, if they ask her to read some she will. 'I tell classes that I want to share some of my own writing because they will be sharing so much with me over the semester, but I also remind them the course is aimed at their own aesthetic goals, and their own plans for their poetry.' James Plath said he will read some of his work 'because students deserve to know where your own criticisms are coming from. It's not fair to students if you don't give them some of your work'. Laura Apol told me she reached this conclusion from experience as a student: 'I know when I've been in workshops myself that I wanted to see who was giving me advice. That was a huge part of things. If I didn't resonate with their writing, I wasn't sure that I wanted their fingerprints on my work or that I trusted their help with the kind of work I was trying to do.' But she could also recall workshops where she felt about the teacher, 'A little less of you would be fine'. Joey Horstman (2005) will read his work to class 'but let them skip that day'. He'll also 'pick something with a flaw' that he can discuss 'and talk about my frustration with it or say how I'd do it differently now. Or I'll say, I don't know how to solve that problem yet, and then I'll show them how I've tried to hide it'.

Frizell mentioned a particular risk of sharing work with students: 'Every now and then, things are revealed about me, my personal life, that I would prefer not to discuss.' LeAnn Mortensen's (2004) syllabus for 'Creative Process and Imaginative Writing' has a link with this caveat: 'Click here to read my sometimes upsetting, angry, funny, four-letter-word work (that means it isn't everything for everyone).'

Clearly we have good reason to limit attention to our own writing but also good reason at some times and in some ways to make it available to students. If one constraint is the assumption that the classroom is a place of critique, then that may be another reason to emphasize other kinds of response instead.

When students try to be like their teacher

If you want a fascinating conversation – once the embarrassment passes – just ask creative writing teachers about the ways their students have tried to be *like* them. When I asked Patrick Hicks (2004b), he quickly said, 'I haven't noticed students' imitation – God knows there are better role models than me out there'. But then he did recall a former student, then in an MFA program, whose decision he knew he had influenced, though only, he had thought, through encouragement. 'He's there because of our conversations but not really because of *me*.' After considering further, he admitted, 'It's uncomfortable to think of them learning through being like me, maybe because I want them to find out who *they* are.' He wondered aloud, 'If they are emulating you as a professor, is that a disservice?'

Yet Hicks had no difficulty recalling his emulation of his own teachers, J.F. Powers, for one: 'After studying under him, I was more gruff with people because he was that way with me.' Hicks also recalled a powerful need: 'You're 22 and you want a role model that's not your father.' After our interview, Hicks emailed to say, 'The more I think about it, the more I think that perhaps students do try to emulate how we approach the act of writing' (2004a). Jim Heynen (2004) told me about a similar experience with students imitating him:

> I notice it happening. It's always a curveball to me. Rather than feeling comfortable, I feel uneasy, but I battle with my discomfort. I found it funny when a student started wearing the kinds of shoes I wore – totally unstylish. I certainly have noticed with students who have taken a couple of my classes that by the time they are in a second class, when it comes to workshopping, they beat me to my own comments. They have learned to read like me.

It's hard to get used to the idea of being a hero for some of our students – to imagine that they could view us as having triumphed over the self-doubt and other insecurities that plague them to attain self-knowledge, wisdom and prowess as artists. Yet were our own models all that *we* imagined them to be?

Jill Baumgaertner laughed when I asked whether students have said they want to be like her. 'I had a student several years ago who said he wanted to marry someone like me!' Then she considered the question more seriously. 'I guess I have, but not in the past decade, because I think that there's a point at which the age barrier comes in. When I was first teaching and in my thirties, it was easier for them to imagine themselves as me.' She reflected further. 'It's a strange question. You don't quite know what it is.' She recalled an article by a former student, now writing screenplays. 'He talked about my influence on his writing, but I had no memory of it, and what he quoted didn't sound like something I would say. I thought he had created those memories. You have no idea how the students will take the person you are and the things you have said and use that.'

If our students *create* memories of us and of our influence, that at least says something about their need for models. Baumgaertner added, 'I've had women students in particular talk to me about how it is that I can have a family, be a writer, be a scholar.' She said, 'They take it all in with great curiosity.' But she could also identify: 'I was the same when I was a college student. I had two female professors, and I memorized everything about their hair, their clothes, how they would speak. I glommed onto these things, and they were so important for me because I had no other models.' Jim Heynen told me, 'We make assumptions that what matters is what we're doing rather than what we are. But what we are is a big part of how they are learning.' Katharine Haake (1994: 78) is among few creative writing teachers who have written about students' desire to imitate a teacher. She says about her first students:

> Many became personal friends. And, I must confess, I loved the adoration. Isn't that what writers want? Well, I don't really know about that, but I do know from experience that if you become a successful mentor to your students, they will in fact adore you and they will want, oh they will want, to be like you.

Psychologist and counselor Rollo May (1939: 93) discusses a 'general influence of personality' which occurs 'when one individual assumes to some extent the personality pattern or role of another. The student, for example, will take on the tone of voice or peculiar manner of gesturing of his favorite professor'. My own most striking experience of this kind came several years after college, when I took some of my high school students to a conference at a nearby college, telling them to find the room where my most influential college literature teacher, Stanley Wiersma, was leading a session. They told me later, 'We knew right away we were at the right room because he sounded just like you.' That perception astonished me. I had admired his willingness to be surprised by a literary work, but his teaching voice had seemed theatrical to me. I never supposed it had tuned and toned my own.

May's way of accounting for such imitative behavior focuses on the learner's goal: the learner 'sees other individuals succeeding in their movement toward the goal he has picked for himself, and he adopts their behavior patterns by unconscious or partially conscious imitation' (p. 94). However, cultural theorist Rene Girard (1972: 146) emphasizes instead a tendency to imitate and *then* form goals. In contrast with Freud, who made *desire* primary for growth and change, Girard makes imitation primary. He says that people seek out and identify with a model who seems to them to possess a 'plenitude'. They assume that this plenitude derives from what the model *has*, so they want it too. In this way, desires are *formed* through imitation. Both May and Girard help us understand why students can become fascinated with a teacher who seems to them to 'have something', either something they have wanted or something they could not know they wanted until they met someone whose possession of it awakened in them a desire to claim it for themselves.

May explains that this 'general influence of personality' operates mostly *outside* the conscious awareness of both model and subject:

> It is as though the unconscious minds of the one doing the influencing and the one influenced were carrying on a conversation of which their conscious minds did not know. This brings home the eternal truism that it is what the counselor really is which exerts the influence, not the relatively superficial matter of the words he utters. 'What you are speaks so loudly that I cannot hear what you say'. (pp. 96–7)

He says that teachers resist conscious awareness of this influence because teachers *'bear a tremendous responsibility.* We shall be influencing others whether they or we wish it or not'. He adds that 'we had best frankly recognize' this influence because 'lines of force' go out from the teacher 'much farther than he ever imagines', so that if the teacher 'is especially neurotic in tendency, he will be like the bearer of a contagious disease' (p. 97). Girard (1978: 7) agrees that the power of imitation eludes awareness, but he attributes this to culture: 'In the science of man and culture today there is a unilateral swerve away from anything that could be called mimicry, imitation, or mimesis.' He challenges this prejudice, arguing that 'there is nothing, or next to nothing, in human behavior that is not learned, and all learning is based on imitation' – a truth he says we resist because we fear 'that insisting on the role of imitation would unduly emphasize the gregarious aspects of humanity, all that transforms us into herds'; thus, if we 'give a leading role to imitation, perhaps we will make ourselves accomplices of the forces of subjugation and uniformity'.

Shortening the Time Span of Master-Apprentice Relationships

If at least some of our most serious students seek to become writers by identifying with and even imitating us, how do we respond to Patrick Hicks' comment, 'It's uncomfortable to think of them learning through being like me, maybe because I want them to find out who *they* are'? His worry can be summed up in a word: an *epigone* is a follower, usually of a significant artist or philosopher, who remained *merely* an imitator. John Glavin in 'The intimacies of instruction' (1997: 13) remarks, 'All teaching, all successful teaching, falls into one of two kinds: abusive and seductive. The rest is merely instruction: tedious, safe, unlikely to make a difference.

Both abusive and seductive teaching are, of course, inevitably corrupting.' One way they corrupt, it seems to me, is that both tend to produce clones, epigones.

I've questioned teaching practices that lean toward what Glavin calls abusive, particularly the workshop in its more critique-focused and agonistic versions. However, in affirming modeling, at least when it takes the forms of writing with and sharing our writing with students and performing our own fascination with good writing, I may *seem* to endorse what he calls a seductive teacher, the kind of 'good teacher' who is 'the superior narcissist, whatever his or her mastery of a field, someone who can enthrall, overpower ...' (p. 12).

Many students seem to believe that only through such a teacher can they find their way. Consider Robert Brooke's (1987: 682) account of the teacher idealized by the learner as the Subject Supposed to Know: 'The mentor, the priest, the therapist, the lover, the guru, the martial arts master ... helps us "find ourselves", helps us "unlock our true feelings", helps us know ourselves as we can't on our own.' One teacher I interviewed said she heard that a former student referred to her as a 'witch' (meaning, I assume, a woman with mysterious powers for healing and transforming). It's easy to see how our students' desire for teachers with mysterious powers could lead them to imagine that they have found in us what they seek – and then induce us to play that guru.

The danger with such teaching, writes Glavin, is that 'the student is always being called on primarily to witness only the teacher whatever the ostensible subject'. Such teaching he calls 'inevitably corrupting' partly because the impressionable students know only indirectly, through the teacher's knowing rather than through their own apprehension. As a result, writes Glavin, 'the student's witness can only be false'. He concludes, 'The more effective the teacher, the more likely he – or she – is to make the student bear false witness: the more engaging, the more memorable, the more lastingly impressive the teacher, the more profoundly perjured the student' (p. 14). Evidence supports Glavin's observation that male teachers are more inclined toward narcissistic teaching. Leahy (2005: 17) cites Basow's study, which finds: 'Women tended to focus more on the student as the locus of learning; men on themselves.'

Stephanie Vanderslice (2008: 70) reminds us that American creative writing programs are particularly susceptible to narcissistic teaching because they are characterized by 'a firmly entrenched star system' – that is, teachers are hired more because they have gained fame as writers than because of evidence that they have the desire and capability to *teach*. This system, she writes, 'results in a pedagogy characterized by an anti-intellectual cult of personality', anti-intellectual because such teachers have not established a culture for thinking about teaching and learning – one that would help them, for instance, to design a sequence of learning experiences that will take students to a place they can claim as their own, safely beyond the aura of the guru.

Even if we manage to avoid the extreme of narcissistic teaching, at least some of our students will identify with us, place us on a pedestal, even imitate us. Then how do we help them to define their own artistic identity? I believe that the best way to do this is first to acknowledge, with Bizarro (1994: 234), that students do come into artistic knowing through master-apprentice relationships, in which students' witness of the teacher can be transforming – and then to build in ways to 'shorten the time span' of those relationships.

Helping students learn from their own experience

One way to shorten the time span of master-apprentice relationships is to design the course so that students learn 'through their own experience', in Glavin's words, and not 'only through the teacher'.

A few years ago a former student, then in an MFA program, complained that he was 'suffering through an intolerably bad poetry class'. He diagnosed the problem as 'a lack of direction in the guise of openness'. What he *wanted* was a sequence of assignments that would take him on a journey that he could not construct on his own. It's a reasonable expectation of a *course*. Guest writers are often asked about their process – how they know which subjects are theirs to work with, how they find ideas, when and where they write, how they revise. Prospective teachers of writing ought to be able to give a similar accounting of their process for helping students become writers. Said another way, they ought to acquire authority not only as writers but also as those who help students compose themselves as writers.

In *Teaching Poetry Writing: A Five-Canon Approach,* Tom C. Hunley (2007) argues, as I have, that for beginning writers the dominant workshop approach falls short, requiring them to do critique before they are ready to do it or to learn from it, and leaving them little time to develop a process for coming up with ideas, seeking and using response and revising. His response is two-fold: he moves peer response from class to a listserv; and his students use the freed-up class time to write together, with exercises inspired by the five canons of rhetoric. He reasons that if these canons have for centuries enabled teachers to help students to become writers, they should work for poetry as well, and also give students a language for discussing each other's writing. That's how students learn 'through their own experience' in his classes. I also assign comparable – though fewer – exercises, but my own emphasis has been upon the experience of dialogue with responders that reflective writing makes possible, enabling teachers and peer responders to offer more useful response, which writers then *internalize* and bring to bear on subsequent episodes of writing and reflection.

I admit that at the start of a course the task of bringing students who have never written a poem or a story to the point where most of them can write a good one does seem impossible. Shoshana Felman (1989) best explains to me how the impossible in this teaching becomes possible. Drawing upon her study of Freud and Lacan, Felman describes how the teacher must operate through the student's *ignorance*, just as the analyst is 'taught by the analysand's unconscious' (p. 604). Like the analyst, the teacher 'cannot in turn be, alone, a master of the knowledge which he teaches'. Instead, 'he attempts to learn from the students his own knowledge' (p. 605). Dawn M. Skorczewski (2005: 67), in *Teaching One Moment at a Time: Disruption and Repair in the Classroom*, also cites this passage from Felman, observing that it 'suggests that she believes students have much to teach their teachers about the knowledge that is produced in their classrooms'. Skorczewski responds skeptically, 'How is a teacher to learn about "his own knowledge" from his students?' The specifics of this process, she says, 'remain largely uncharted in the literature'.

My own attempt to chart that process appears in the previous four chapters: students write, and they reflect about and publicly question that writing to solicit response, and I and the members of their writers' group respond, primarily to let them know how readers are likely to *experience* the writing. We also try to answer the writer's questions and ask a few of our own. Rather than fixing writing, we help writers understand their writing, consider where it is coming from and discover where it seems to need to go. All the while, writers find new models, become better readers, and learn about other students' ways of reading alongside my ways of reading, and they summarize in writers' memos how such response has influenced revision. Through this dialogic process, writers gain experience and learn to ask better questions. Sometimes a better question enables them to find their own answer. Other times it enables me to know what I need to say or ask that could help them move toward a breakthrough – something I cannot know until our dialogue brings me to the point of knowing. This how I 'learn from the students [my] own knowledge'.

These are also ways that students learn from experience and not just from witnessing an admired teacher and model artist.

Helping students to resist our textual authority

Another way to shorten the time span of the master-to-apprentice relationship is to encourage students to resist our influence as they develop their own authority. Jim Heynen (2004) illustrated this thinking in talking about his habit of reading articles on creative writing pedagogy but then pushing away in order to come up with 'an alternative of my own that I think is better'. He remarked that a Jungian thinker 'said this had to do with the authority of mentors. We need within us the authority of a mentor, and if we've never had that, we're always searching for a voice to help us work out the relationship between authority and response'. Even while affirming that our students need us to be the kind of authority that they must contend with, he also acknowledged that accepting this role can be difficult. 'There are situations in which I find myself being looked at as the authority, and my temptation is to resist it. I'm uncomfortable with it, but a voice tapping me on the shoulder says, "You are the authority, be it".'

My own thinking about the need for our students to struggle against authority comes from Mikhail Bakhtin (1981: 342), who sees human change as occurring in a kind of 'place', an inner 'contact zone' where the internally persuasive voices of the self not only 'interanimate' with the internally persuasive discourse of others, but also struggle with and partly appropriate more distanced *authoritative* discourse. This authoritative discourse may be 'religious, political, moral; the word of a father, of adults and of teachers'. He even asserts that the main way a person is transformed is through *appropriating* this authoritative discourse, an active process that must be driven by his or her own internally persuasive word engaged in a *struggle* with the authoritative word. The implication is that good teaching offers authoritative discourse but also challenges learners to push back, so that what they make of the encounter is truly their own.

Apparently quite a few of us have not imagined that *some* student resistance is a good thing. The statement on my survey that most mystified teachers reads, 'Students in creative writing courses need to learn to resist the influence of the teacher and to find their own way to write'. Maureen Dunphy (2004) first offered clarification. 'I obviously don't want my students to "resist my influence" when it comes to the basics of writing a narrative, such as the need for conflict in a story or being consistent in how one formats dialogue.' A little less than half chose the neutral response, but overall a few more did agree than disagree.

Randy VanderMey (2004) was one who strongly agreed:

> I'm responding here to the much wider culture of students in which they cynically calculate what it will take to 'get through' college and gauge their teacher's expectations in light of that alone. The moment when they can finally say, alertly and with conviction, 'you want me to do this, but I want to do that – and here's why ...' is a big moment in teaching and learning as far as I'm concerned.

He added, 'I operate from the premise that my students begin with something already better than anything anyone could give them, though neither they nor I may know exactly what that is.' So his method is to 'look past an initial success and ask them to push their project to another level. I'll keep pushing until I see something that I can't recognize as an echo of my own sensibility'. Dunphy also looks closely for that 'something better' in a student; her commitment is 'to encourage any shred of individual voice I sense, regardless of how I might feel about the "results" of that voice'.

One way I encourage resistance is to assign an imitative project for the second half of the course: ask students to find a writer they can learn from, describe that writer's technique, especially aspects they want to try themselves, and then do an imitative piece. They turn in with it a writer's memo that includes an account of what they picked up from the model but also of how their own writing resists and departs from that of their model. My intent is that they learn that the pushing back matters as much as the taking from.

Late in the course, I also tell students that I like to find in a portfolio writer's memo good reasons the writer has found to resist suggestions I've made. I can tell that they take notice; some smile, valuing the permission to disagree. Quite a few accept the invitation.

Mary Swander (2004) told me that Marvin Bell as a workshop teacher 'was good at encouraging everybody to choose their own style and subject matter and not to be writing like him. He'd comment on the variety of poems before him. He kept reinforcing that so we wouldn't all collapse into the workshop poem'. She commented, 'When you're young, you instinctively learn by imitation. Then it's time to find your own voice.' Nicole Mazzarella (2004), explaining why she prefers to discuss student writing in conferences, said that she can help writers 'to see that they can question me. If they disagree with my comments, we can process it'. And if she feels that the student is too much shaping a story to her expectations, she will sometimes try 'to bring them back to their original impulse for the story'. She added, 'I wouldn't want them to look at their writing in a few years and feel I have turned them into me.'

Mazzarella also tries 'to read as much as possible so I see how other writers are doing things different from what I'm doing'. And she encourages students to take creative writing classes from other teachers so that they experience a variety of influences.

Some teachers help students find alternative models – for example, along with their responses to writing, they give a student pieces by published writers that do something comparable to what the writer is doing.

Another way to encourage students to resist a teacher's influence is to create a classroom that honors oppositional voices. Joy Ritchie and Kate Ronald (1998: 219–220) explore how their 'attempts to teach rhetoric as feminists' changed their rhetorical choices as teachers. 'Our conception of audience, the appeals we use to persuade, and the ethos of our voices become part of the rhetoric we and our students examine.' One practice they adopted as a result was writing a regular 'journal' for the class in which they engaged in dialogue with journals written by members of the class.

> This practice of writing to and with our students is a key element in our teaching, and we have adopted it as a feminist practice in all our classes. Our journals and students' journals combine public exploration and public demonstration of our knowledge about the course materials with private analysis of connections between the rhetoric we are studying and personal lives and issues. These dialogues, between us and our students and among all of us and the rhetoric we're studying, help us avoid some of the single-voiced thinking in our classrooms, enhance the possibilities for reexamination of students' and teachers' ideas, loosen the moorings on what is marginal and what is central, and call into question whose coattails we're riding.

This practice can also work in a creative writing class. Paying this kind of close attention to what students write or say fosters their agency in creating the event we call a course.

The comic corrective

A further way teachers can encourage dialogue and cohesion among students while helping them to push back against authority is by creating a space in which students can laugh at each other, at themselves and especially at the teacher.

I'll mention a personal example. I have sometimes assigned a 'list poem' to teach students that a pattern of concrete details can make an impression without need for generalization. I suggested that they work with contents of their 'miscellaneous' drawer. When my daughter was in the class (another kind of negotiation of the personal), she took delight in doing the assignment with the contents of *my* desk drawer and in reading the result to the class:

In My Father's Desk Drawer

Film mailers, paperclips,
Senior pictures, his and ours and others, unnamed.
Whiteboard markers, conference nametags,
Lenscaps, pencils, photos, tape,
Button – We're **Proud** to be Canadian!
Automatic pencil leads, decomposing rubber bands,
Sandpaper. Old watch.
Staples, slides, labels, tapes, postcard –
Sadak in Search of the Waters of Oblivion, 1812.
Dust, receipts, and stains.

– *Lynae Vandermeulen*

Since then I've included the poem in my journals to the class that coincide with an assignment to try a list poem.

Another of my journals for the class includes the following poem, written to help students negotiate some of the paradoxes of the course – including the risk of turnabouts in relationships that are explored in the next chapter:

Proverbs for Poetry Class

If you are given an assignment to write a poem
you will succeed when the poem wriggles free
from the assignment.

If you write a poem for a grade
your stanzas will be lashed by strings
like those from which your arms and legs dangle.

If you write while desiring this woman's art
and that man's scope,
your poems, too, will reject you.

> If you write in fear, poems
> that might have leaped into your lap
> will smell fear, shrink back, and show their teeth,
>
> and if you shape effigies from your fears,
> others here will likewise shape their own,
> and this pack of masks
>
> may consort in shadows,
> begetting offspring none will reckon
> as their own.
>
> Follow instructions and advice,
> knowing that instructions
> and advice do not write poems.
>
> You cannot catch a cat by chasing it,
> but if you wait it will come to you
> and let you hold in your hands
> what you wanted to learn about poems.

One further idea: if my creative writing courses met just once a week I'd use a practice I learned from Robert Brooke – having a different student each time (or pair of students) begin each class with 'minutes' of the previous class. When I do this in a course in rhetorical theory, I tell students that these minutes may take any form. The only requirement is that they help us recall aspects of the previous class. Students have written songs, poems, raps, letters to Mom; they've created games and puzzles, made videos, made and explained sculptures, performed comedy sketches. Besides putting us back in touch with the previous class, these minutes provide a space for carnival and for gentle mockery of authority, so that every so often, guru gets refigured as bozo.

Chapter 7
Problems and Crises in Relationships

> *A mentor or teacher has such tremendous power! And he or she has no trouble finding prey. Wanting a mentor at all, any kind of mentor, is a major, elegant passion of life. What's more, this wanting mentors is a passion that knows no sociological barriers ...*
>
> Carol Bly (2001: 16)
>
> *[A]s teachers we may be the direct target of ... latent content, the object of transference as needy, intense, erotic, and/or disruptive as anything uncovered by psychotherapy.*
>
> Mark Bracher (1999: 3)

I argued in the previous chapter that we should model for students the life of a writer and reader but also deliberately help students resist us and our ways of thinking and writing so that they are free to become the artist they need to become. That's a tricky negotiation, complicated by our academic setting, where a few students worry more about good grades than good writing, where those who most want to be writers may fear and envy other writers, and where some students want too desperately to write well, especially if they like and admire the teacher. Add that the teacher must switch between accompanying and supporting writers on the one hand and articulating high expectations and judging results on the other. Such shifting relationships are susceptible to miscues and misunderstandings that trigger doubts and then accusations, perhaps leading to breakdowns in relationships. And in a highly collaborative class, one or a few angry or wounded students can infect others, including teachers. As Jeri Kroll (2004: 90) quips, if her students 'didn't like the feedback they were receiving', she could easily become 'the wicked witch of the west with her own jealous agenda'.

I don't want to raise *too* much concern about breakdowns, because that could lead to the opposite problem – a classroom so emotionless and controlled that little really happens. The reason we need to understand the peculiar risks in our teaching is not to avoid taking them but to take them with, as Jim Heynen (2005) put it, an informed attentiveness. He wrote that to him 'a class is an organic entity whose shape is not fully predictable at the beginning of the semester'. Consequently, the 'productive shaping and dynamics of the class require attentiveness and flexibility from me as instructor. I try to see how the individuals and entire class are evolving and to align my teaching with what I see happening or potentially happening'.

Tribulations and Attributions

My survey *appears* to reveal relatively few relationship problems in creative writing. 'A close relationship with a student deteriorated, for no obvious reason, into resistance and suspicion' was reported as seldom or never a problem by 83% of respondents and as only 'occasionally' a problem by most of the rest. Similarly, 'Instead of decreasing, the anxiety level of a class increased during the course' was reported as seldom or never a problem by a little over 80%, with 14% experiencing the problem 'occasionally' and 3% a little more often. Such problems *should* be infrequent or we would look for another way to make a living.

One problem we might expect with master-apprentice teaching *appears* uncommon. A total of 70% reported that students seldom or never 'accused you of expecting them to write the same way that you write'. Of course, it's hard to know how many such accusations never reach the teacher.

To what extent have you encountered each of the following problems in your teaching of your typical introductory-level course during the last five years? (Frequently = 5; occasionally = 3; never = 1):	5	4	3	2	1
A close relationship with a student deteriorated, for no obvious reason, into resistance and suspicion	1, 1%	0, 0%	21, 13%	30, 19%	102, 64%
Instead of decreasing, the anxiety level of a class increased during the course	0, 0%	4, 3%	22, 14%	40, 25%	89, 56%
Students who resisted revision, apparently feeling that their original inspiration was what mattered	30, 19%	38, 24%	49, 31%	27, 17%	11, 7%
Students who accused you of expecting them to write the same way that you write	5, 3%	5, 3%	18, 11%	35, 22%	92, 58%
Students whose prose seemed labored or blocked, as if they were trying much too hard	20, 13%	34, 22%	53, 33%	30, 19%	17, 11%

Yet respondents also reported a surprisingly high incidence of problems that may be *symptoms* of troubled relationships: 'Students who resisted revision, apparently feeling that their original inspiration was what mattered' was frequently a problem for 19% and more than 'occasionally' a problem for another 24%. Writers who won't change when others indicate directly or indirectly that change is needed may not trust their ability to improve upon their first inspiration, but neither do they appear to trust their readers, including teachers.

Even more significantly, 'Students whose prose seemed labored or blocked, as if they were trying much too hard' was frequently a problem for 13%, more than occasionally a problem for 22%, occasionally for 33%, seldom for 19%, and never a problem for only 11%. Further, I think we get even more labored or blocked writing than we realize because labored writing often reads like poor writing, so unless we know that its writer *can* write well, we are likely to infer that the writer invested little effort, cannot thread cohesive sentences or thinks in muddled ways.

Even when we recognize labored writing or encounter students who feel blocked, our tendency is to blame internal psychological causes, because that's the familiar explanation – but also because it rescues us from the painful question, 'What is it about me or this student's relationship with me or the class that is silencing him or her?' If we view ourselves as helpful and encouraging we are even less likely to ask that question, and yet those qualities may make some students want to write so well for us that they can hardly write at all.

Another reason why I think we have more relationship problems than we realize is that we lack a common discourse to name and explain them, so that if we do notice signs of discord we view them as anomalies to dismiss rather than as problems to solve.

Breakdowns in relationships with individuals

Since our teaching depends heavily upon relationships, we can hardly avoid feeling deeply troubled when a good relationship turns difficult and distant.

Sometimes departmental divisions infect teachers' relationships with students. One respondent wrote that students with whom he had good relationships were later sometimes swayed against him by a colleague who 'distrusts creative writing and imagination, any efforts to help students pay attention to their inner lives'. These students 'drifted over to the other side (worshipping more in the church of reason than art)'.

Sometimes we make worse a problem that started elsewhere. Andy Mozina (2004), who uses writers' groups of six led by a teaching assistant, told me that in one group a member 'had had her work joked about in a way that made her cry', but the teaching assistant didn't report this to him. Mozina only noticed that the student's work declined, and that his conference with her did not help. 'I think she thought I was also too hard on her work.' He said that if he had realized what had happened in the group, he would have worked with her differently.

Laurie MacDiarmid (2004), in the context of saying that she has usually been able to turn relationship problems around, mentioned causes of them that she has observed:

> Actually, I've had more reversals in the opposite direction. That is, fraught relationships that I thought were hostile (like the mulish student who doesn't talk and just glowers in class, usually male, refusing to revise) become quite productive (that mulish student is now in his own MFA program, teaching composition, and emailing me about how it's difficult to get students to talk during class discussions, read the material, and write anything intelligent in response). Sometimes it's a matter of personality or style. I'm quite extroverted and open; shy students can make me paranoid. With students who seem to be having trouble expressing themselves in class, who glower and sometimes stomp out of the room during discussions or workshop, I usually ask them in conference if there's any way I can make the classroom a better place for them. Then they open up. Usually.

MacDiarmid illustrates the value of Tobin's (2004: 130) advice that we should 'learn to read the complex of interpersonal relationships' that 'shapes all academic work'. She also considers how her own personality enters and responds to the mix of relationships.

When a class takes a wrong turn

Chris Matthews (2005) was among the relatively few who indicated on the survey that occasionally 'Instead of decreasing, the anxiety level of a class increased during the course' but he saw such a turn as expected, given the thoroughgoing change we try to bring about:

> Anxiety may increase in my courses for a couple of reasons. One is that the term is short and so, right about the time the students are acclimating to one genre, we switch genres. Two, and related to this, is the fact that students anticipate, I think, becoming better and more

comfortable as writers, when really the process is one of thoroughly rethinking their assumptions about writing. In this case a certain anxious uncertainty is a sign of their learning. Both of these are productive anxieties, I think.

This is a helpful insight, that we should hope for and expect a degree of productive uncertainty. At the same time, we need to stay alert for signs that uncertainty is arousing anxiety and threatening to turn destructive.

Because we teach high-stakes classes that are highly interactive, even a minor departure from ideal conditions can have repercussions. Juliana Spahr (2004) sent me a list:

> Sometimes it can be as specific as a certain student insisting on the discussion going a certain way. Sometimes though that certain grumpy student can be a great presence in the class. Sometimes I think this can also have a lot to do with me. If I'm overworked in other parts of my academic life, sometimes I don't have the time to get my head into the right space and cultivate community as I should. If I have to blow off the class because I've got a thousand meetings, then they can pick up on this really quick.

Spahr added, 'Sometimes I don't deal well with the grumpy or dismissive student and then the other students don't feel protected by me.' Liza Ann Acosta (2005) described such a situation – an older male, auditing the course, whose presence threatened others:

> He kept turning in papers that were fiction instead of non-fiction and that had nothing to do with the prompts. He also had issues with my teaching of the class (young Latina woman) so he sent me long letters telling me what/how to teach. The students were extremely anxious as the class progressed (so was I), worried about whether he was going to be in their small workshop next.

(Her experience suggests that we should refuse requests to audit, except from those who agree to participate fully in the work of the community.) Jack Ridl (2004) mentioned a black student who would preface reading a piece with some variant of 'You aren't going to understand this because you haven't been through what I have'. Viewing this behavior as a defense mechanism, he finally responded by having 'an open discussion one day in class that got things aired out'. He asked students, 'Has anybody had experiences that are not the same as hers, but comparable?' One woman said, 'about three or four times a day. Nobody knows what's going on. Unlike you, I'm invisible. I'm white and I'm lesbian, and I can barely stand it here anymore'. That exchange helped the group recognize that people can feel isolated and misunderstood for a variety of reasons. Ridl realized that such a crisis could either pull people apart or bring them together. He concluded, 'I lucked out'.

Differences or perceived differences, especially in moral standards, can set students against each other. Jim Heynen mentioned that a class with students who write stories close to pornographic or with despicable characters, may also include 'indignant people who slice them to shreds on moral grounds'. He doesn't encounter this problem in a beginning class though. Conflict within a class can also result from external events to which students respond in opposing ways. After September 11, Heynen's class almost erupted because some students were militaristic, others pacifist.

The teacher's perceived stance on a controversial issue can also trigger a reaction in students who identify with the opposing position. Mary Swander (2004) told me that she brought into a creative nonfiction class an essay about a nurse who worked in an abortion unit. Her intent was 'to demonstrate technique: framing, scene summary, natural voice', and she took no stand on abortion itself. It was a weekend course with mostly women, all 'very tight', and they decided she was anti-abortion. Swander remarked, 'Group dynamics, on a roll, can get really strange.' She said she expected students to see that 'I bring in essays all the time that don't represent my point of view', but she also realizes that students often make the opposite assumption.

Competitiveness can also lead to conflict. Heynen gave the example, 'two good writers pair off, two cats at each other's throats'. Or students begin a workshop with comments that 'are stupidly vicious because it's a kind of writing so different than their own' – a response that seems to say, 'let's make sure this kind of writing doesn't stand without challenge'. At that point, he said, students are 'breaking all my rules, so I end up reprimanding'. He's learned that the reprimand may clear the air – or do its own damage.

Another cause of conflict he's noticed is 'maybe a couple of students demonstrate a familiarity with me that irritates other students'. Such a problem is more likely to occur when the teacher is an adviser or mentor for those students. Others notice the closeness and suspect favoritism. One solution is to remind students we work with closely to avoid giving that impression. Occasionally, though, when a writer I was mentoring was so much stronger that the others were intimidated, I've simply told the class that they were not competing with the writer. This seemed to help the others appreciate the gifts of the writer rather than feeling threatened. A similar option is giving an outstanding writer a teaching assistant role in the class.

It takes passion to write well or teach well, but passion can also carry us away. Andy Mozina recalled an incident from grad school when his over-reaction to a student triggered a reversal in his relationship with a class. A story that a student brought to the workshop so appalled him that he 'did not give a neutral response'. He told me that he 'was repelled by the sensibility' in the writing and that he 'used strong language' in responding. 'The class just looked at me. It was the worst moment of my teaching life.' Later, overhearing a few of his students 'going on about that scene in an amazed voice', he realized that he 'had kind of flown off the handle'. He knew what he had *intended* – 'to exhort the students that this is not what writing is about' – but he also knew that his response was over the top. 'I don't think I could have made it any harsher.' He could understand how it came about – 'I tend to be quite hard on myself as a writer, and I transferred that to students'. The incident taught him that he 'needed to have a procedure for filtering myself so I never hurt a student again'. Since that time he has 'come to the position that I will never lie to a student, but I will say the truth as softly as I can. When we workshop in small groups, we will always start with what's strong. It could be the only grammatical sentence or the only image that's not off the shelf. That buys me much good will'. In addition, instead of just pointing to weaknesses, he tries to suggest 'the next thing to try'. He added, 'I don't think you have to break them to get them to take the next step'.

Probably the best action a teacher can take when a class does take a wrong turn is, as MacDiarmid suggested, to confer with the students who seem most involved, get their sense of how the class might be better for them, and ask how they think they might be better for the class. If the problem is with the student rather than the class and if the conversation fails to incline the student to work with rather than against the others, the teacher may have to insist upon changes in behavior in order for the student to remain a part of the class. Some teachers might hesitate to make that move, but we are authorized. We teach an interdependent community and we are its primary defender.

Madly Kind and Gentle – and Standing in Their Way

Often when a relationship breaks down or a class takes a wrong turn, we can identify the causes and respond in appropriate ways, but other times no cause is apparent. David Malone (2005) wrote about breakdowns, 'I wonder if they're not unavoidable consequences of the writing student/teacher relationship'. He said he has posted on his door this sentence from a course evaluation for a composition class he taught his first year: 'I didn't learn much in this class, but I did learn a little bit about how to destroy a paper ... and the human spirit'. Malone offered this analysis of why students sometimes react so strongly to response:

> Students present us with work that many of them think sums up who they are: they hope this story will make us bow down and worship them as the next Shakespeare, and they're desperately afraid we'll tell them they're flawed and worthless and mundane.
> And what we do is say that these places in the piece are promising, but the story needs to have most of its bones broken and reset, plus several organ transplants. Even if we're madly kind and gentle, they still see us as standing in their way.

Malone, like Matthews, makes a good case that some tension and even anger are unavoidable in a course where students are highly invested in their work. Thus, as Jim Heynen also observed, a class can go wrong 'even if all have taken the class because they've heard I'm wonderful'.

I would add that a class may be *more* likely to go wrong in such a case because it's even harder to take the kind of critical response Malone summarizes – let alone a grade – from a 'wonderful' teacher, *especially* if he or she is 'madly kind and gentle'. That's the conclusion I reached studying the most baffling class I've ever taught. It was the fall of the year 2000, so I call it my Y2K poetry class. Beforehand I expected it to be one of my best classes because I knew most of the students and also knew that many of them also had high expectations for the course. So I was baffled when, in its first few weeks, it became hushed and apparently fearful. The problems cataloged in the survey questions that begin this chapter all showed up: increasing anxiety, accusations that I expected students to write like I do, resistance to revision, blocked and labored prose and breakdowns in relationships. Before that class, I rarely experienced any of these problems. Why should they happen with the class I expected to go better than most?

Teacher as stumbling block

When a class goes awry for no discernible reason, we tend to vaguely blame 'chemistry'. Teachers involved in master-apprentice relationships might instead turn to Rene Girard's provocative theory of the 'stumbling block'. A stumbling block is an admired *person*, a model – for example a teacher of the arts who is herself or himself an artist. Because at least some of our students want, perhaps desperately, what they think we possess, we can trip them up without realizing it, and a reason we would not realize it is a self-identification as 'madly kind and gentle', one who avoids being a cause of another's anxiety or pain. When relationships begin to break down, that kind of teacher claims innocence – and thus tends to assume that someone else must be to blame. But if the injured students also see themselves as innocent, they too look for someone else to blame, and who could that be but a teacher from whom so much was expected? Once mutual blaming starts, it's hard to say where the trouble will end.

My approach to teaching the course followed the practice I recommend in this book: writers' groups rather than workshop, reader-response rather than critique early in the course, writers' memos to let the writer set an agenda for peer and teacher response, and an emphasis on a close and supportive classroom community. The first few classes seemed to go well, and the first set of poem drafts submitted for my response were promising though uneven – about what I expect early in the course. I offered mostly reader-response to help writers understand how their poems could be read, and I responded to the writer's understanding of the writing as presented in their memos. I tried to nurture potential, and I praised particular aspects of their writing, but seldom praised a poem as a whole.

Class sessions were disappointing, even though students knew each other well. By about the third week, discussion questions that students should have been able to answer were met with silence or brief tentative response, as though many were afraid to speak. I talked about this with a colleague sitting in on the class, Joonna Trapp (2005), and she said she wondered if students were preparing well enough. To check that out, I gave a quiz on which several students received a grade that, while confirming Joonna's analysis, must also have heightened fears of a low grade. (I should have known better – quizzes to check up on students clash with a pedagogy that claims to trust them.) I couldn't understand why a class of good students with whom I had good individual relationships appeared not to be taking the course seriously. It didn't occur to me that some might be too panicked to suppose that studying the text was going to offer any help at all in what was looking to them like impending disaster.

As we approached the first significant grade of the course, the midterm portfolio, I could sense increasing anxiety, so I invited students with concerns about their work to schedule a conference. I mentioned that they might ask me to do a non-judgmental 'movie of the reader's mind' response – say what I was noticing and connecting and how I was thinking as I worked through the poem in the role of its reader. After class I asked Joonna whether I should demonstrate this mode of response, and she said she had a poem that needed response, so we agreed that I would respond to hers. So in the next class, Joonna read her poem and then I worked through it again slowly, primarily observing that the first part created certain expectations and that I couldn't yet see how the last part met those expectations – that instead it appeared to move in a new direction. I said she might think about whether it was one poem or two and, if one, consider what might bridge the two parts.

All the while, Joonna took notes, which confirmed to me that she was finding value in my response. But when I turned to the class to invite further comments, what I saw astounded me: over half the faces had an expression of shock, as though I had said something deeply painful. I was so taken aback I didn't know what to say, so we moved earlier than I had planned into writers' groups.

After class Joonna emailed to thank me for the response but added that she could not make sense of something else that was happening: students from class were coming to her office and offering sympathy for having had her poem 'torn to shreds' in front of class. It was clear to both of us that that had not happened. So why did at least half the class simultaneously perceive it that way?

A couple of the students (urged by Joonna I later learned) came separately to talk to me about their concerns. The first said that my written responses had seemed so critical that she had lost confidence in her writing. She thought her poems were getting worse instead of better. Naomi, my advisee, said class discussion was limited because students had the impression that I was looking for a particular 'right answer'. Both comments ran counter to what I usually heard from students or read in course evaluations. I couldn't understand how students, especially an advisee who I thought *knew* me, had formed such a distorted impression.

Later I realized that I had also been questioning whether some of them were who I thought they were. When the class had early on become tense, my response was the typically human one of wondering who was responsible. I didn't suppose that *I* was contributing to the problem – I had taught previous classes the same way, and nothing like this had happened before. I began suspecting that one or two students I did not yet know well were saying things to turn others against me. At the time, I would have said that I was trying to get at the cause of the problem. Looking back later, I realized I was looking for a scapegoat.

The double bind

None of the teachers who said in my survey that they preferred that students address them formally gave as their reason 'to avoid putting students in a double bind', but Elizabeth Swingrover (2004b) came close when she explained that she prefers 'to maintain a certain professional distance, since I grade them'. Girard (1972: 147) defines a double bind as a 'contradictory double imperative'. When we are sometimes warm and encouraging, at other times distant and impersonal, we place students in a double bind. Jessica Farquhar (2004) provided an illustration. She recalled that when she began teaching as a student in graduate school, her students 'expected that I would understand their lax attitudes because I was a student myself and because I really set myself up as an equal. Of course, then students are surprised when I show any kind of authority; I think it makes them feel betrayed'.

If closer relationships increase the likelihood that students will be caught in a troubling double bind, then a paradox of our teaching is that deliberate moves to make a class safe *can* make it more dangerous. We would *expect* that such moves toward being 'madly kind and gentle' would move us closer to the ideal expressed in O'Reilley's title, *The Peaceable Classroom* (1993), and would make us seem like less 'the Authority' to students. However, as Lad Tobin (1993: 20) explains:

> ... from a student's perspective a writing teacher is an authority figure, even – or especially – in process classrooms. In fact, the teacher in composition classes in which students are asked to write about their personal feelings and to meet in one-to-one conferences actually holds more authority, because the stakes are higher.

In other words, even though this book recommends that teachers limit their authority in order to accompany students, listen to them and encourage them (i.e. nurture their writing self), these moves, by raising the stakes, may make the teacher *more* of an authority figure to students. Thus, such a teacher is more likely to place students in a double bind than he or she realizes.

We are seldom as reflective as we should be about the double binds in which we place students, perhaps because these are always part of teaching: we accept students as they are – but at the same time we expect them to become more, different, better. Students realize that this is how a course works – and yet they may feel confused or even betrayed if they also have a close relationship with the professor. My most profound discovery when I later studied my Y2K poetry class was that the source of the problem was not the students I suspected – the ones I did not know well – but the students with whom I had previously formed a close relationship as faculty advisor. I thought that our good relationship would make it easier for them to do well in my course, but I failed to see how it also made things harder: as advisor, I was their advocate, but becoming their teacher meant also having high expectations for them and, with that, avoiding being too accepting of their first drafts. Students who had known me as an advisor who was sensitive to their concerns now encountered me as a teacher who seemed oblivious to their feelings – more like a nemesis. Naomi said in an interview after the course was over, 'I knew Carl beforehand. I get along with Carl outside of class really well. But it is hard for me to connect with him in class. Carl is very much concerned with your academics. He always wants to push you a little harder.' When I first read this, I wanted to protest that Naomi had told me before she came to college that she wanted a real education. Wasn't I just doing all I could to help her get one? But when I *listen* to her I can hear her confusion about who I really was.

Most students who know us well do understand that we need to take on a different persona as a teacher. Jeannine had been my advisee, my student assistant, my peer teacher for a freshman seminar, and a student in classes other than creative writing before she took my course in Reading and Writing Poetry. Afterwards, she agreed to write about how our prior relationship made it both easier and harder to take a class with me:

> I am more comfortable in your classes because I know you so well, but also feel much more responsible for participating in the class discussion and supplying 'right' answers. I can't slack off in your class without feeling guilty. If the class hour doesn't go well, I feel personally responsible. I tend to work harder in your classes because, to be truthful, I don't want to let you down. I also think, however, that I am more in tune to what you're looking for, so I'm better equipped to respond. You also understand me better and are more likely to understand what I'm trying to say.

A student from another college also told me that because she liked her creative writing teacher and knew him well, she 'wanted to show him my best work, so I tried harder.' She also felt that she 'couldn't slack off, because he would be able to tell'. We can hear a hint of threat there, especially in her belief that he would *know* if her work fell short. Such a student, from both admiration and apprehension, may try too hard, and if the work then does fall short, the teacher probably will wonder why the student seems to be slacking off. Then the student may perceive the suspicion and feel hurt and even anger, because she knows she has done just the opposite. Unless the teacher recognizes that such a problem often arises from *too much* effort, both may feel betrayed.

Close relationships influence a teacher's desires and perceptions too. My three advisees, Naomi, Beth and Brina, were among the reasons I wanted to teach their course as well as I could. In other words, their presence raised the stakes for me as well. At the same time, I assumed that our having established a good relationship would make the course easier for them. Now when I read their letters written at the start of the course, I find real concerns that, at the time, I took lightly. Because I knew them to be good writers, I assumed that they would know themselves that way, and I thought that they knew me well enough to trust that I would help them through whatever difficulties the course posed. So I failed to suppose that they and a few others in the class so much needed to hear praise and reassurance from me that when they found only limited praise of particular aspects of their work along with quite neutral description of my attempt to respond as the reader evoked by the poem, they read my lack of praise as disappointment and imagined that my descriptive response must be criticism. I seemed to have become a very different person from the one they thought they knew.

Double binds resulting from prior close relationships must be more common in small colleges, where students and faculty often have a relationship before a class begins. Thus, I asked in my survey, 'At the start of a typical introductory creative writing class, with what percentage of the students are you likely to have already formed a relationship (student in a previous class, advisee, student assistant, member of organization you advise etc.)?' Only 17% of teachers responding indicated that they had formed a prior relationship with more than a quarter of the class, and most of those teach in smaller colleges. I teach in a residential college of 1200 students, so I typically know more than half the students on the first day of a creative writing course, and perhaps a quarter of them will also be advisees.

Some might conclude that if double binds can cause such problems, then teachers should avoid them by staying distant. But given my belief that good writing teachers are multiple, playing different roles at different distances from learners, I don't see how double binds can be avoided. In studying my Y2K class (see Vandermeulen, 2005), I did conclude that teachers who closely *accompany* students, as persons and as writers, need to identify the students for whom the stakes are high and be ready to help them negotiate the inevitable double binds. This includes students for whom the course is such a profound experience that they become obsessive about perfecting final projects or portfolios. I am now more likely to tell highly capable but over-anxious students that they'll wind up with an A in the course, so they can quit worrying about the grade and just enjoy learning all they can. Otherwise they may produce labored or blocked writing, which I'll discuss a little later.

Mimetic contagion

Natasha Sajé (2004b) told me that she sometimes experienced increasing anxiety during a course, finding that 'It often shifts when students are resistant and defensive and try to create allies in the class'. As a result, 'Someone becomes a scapegoat, usually the teacher'. That was my assumption in my Y2K course too. My surprise was that the ally-creating and scapegoating takes place through a mostly unconscious process: first, I didn't realize that I had placed students closest to me in a double bind, increasing their need for my reassurance, a need that made them read my neutral comments as criticism. What happened next is that members of their writers' group noticed their disappointment, so they naturally offered support and sympathy, along with reassurance that the writing deserved better. This reassurance gave credence to the belief that my comments must have been harsh, since the writer was so hurt by them. Consequently, the next time I returned response to drafts, all members of the group *expected* my comments to be highly critical, so that was the only way they could read them. Rene Girard (1978: 21) gives this process a telling name, 'mimetic contagion'. A group of people unconsciously pick up from each other a feeling or belief – and then feel that it *must* be true because everyone says it is. No one set out to persuade others that my comments were harsh; they imitated each other into this shared conviction. That's also how over half the class came to the point where they could simultaneously perceive that I was 'ripping to shreds' Joonna's poem. The students who were later interviewed by Joonna confirmed that much of the talk in their groups was about me and about how harsh my comments seemed.

I have since warned students not to use groups to vent. As I explained in Chapter 5, I do ask students to summarize my response to their writing for their group members, but to summarize actual response, not translate into 'I don't think he liked it' because that can morph into 'He hates everything we write'.

Mimetic contagion might be described as a collective false consciousness. Like the double bind, it must be more common in small colleges and where people know and trust each other – or hold back from challenging each other's opinions.

And it must be a much more significant factor in collaborative classes where students develop supportive relationships, especially where the stakes are high. One implication is that student evaluations in highly collaborative courses are likely to vary more than usual from class to class because collaboration gives the perceptions of influential members more opportunity to be unconsciously imitated by others. We – and tenure and promotion committees – typically assume that what students write on evaluations are individual judgments, so we lend them more credibility when many students say the same thing. But in a course where students have many personal interactions, a more likely explanation is that in the process of trying to account for something that has troubled them, each is retelling a story they have collectively but unconsciously composed – a story that likely obscures the real problem. Like other texts, course evaluations require interpretation.

Pretentious and Blocked Writing

One of the ways we know that an introductory creative writing course has worked is that the final portfolios are wonderfully various, but each has pieces that seem to suit and express the writer. We tend to say that such writers have found their subject matter, have discovered what they have to say, have found their voice. It's also writing in which readers experience *presence*.

Yet sometimes, from students who seem capable of writing well, we get writing that is pretentious (the writer trying to be someone else) or blocked (the writer trying so hard to say so much that the sentences collapse under the pressure). Sometimes we get writers who are stopped, who cannot write at all.

Pretentious writing

Sometimes highly intelligent students indulge in stylistic excess. Keith Ratzlaff (2004) thought of 'essay writers who take the excesses of someone like Dave Barry as models'. They:

> think they're being smart and ironic (and they are, in some ways) when really they are overwriting their material in a way that keeps them from actually thinking about the issues they're writing about. There are certainly more men who do this than women. Why? It's an aggressive style, I guess, but that's probably too easy. Overwriting of

any kind seems to me a failure of the ear on one level, and a failure to find an audience to help hold the voice together on another.

Matt Guenette (2004) found, too, that students whose writing was pretentious were 'usually the smarter ones' and more frequently males. 'In a class where I might label an equal number of men and women as exceptionally bright, men typically write a more romantically stylized, overwrought prose than the women.'

Writing that might be described as defensive rather than aggressive sometimes comes from students who lack confidence or who are inexperienced in reading the genre. Monica Berlin (2004) observed:

> ... students at the intro level (usually students taking the course for fun rather than towards a major/minor and without any previous background) believe there's a particular 'voice' associated with creative work. It is heavy handed. They cling to words like *abyss*. They spend more time using their thesaurus than necessary. They use a lot of words and somehow manage to say nothing. They create semantic circles of nonsense. They want to sound formal, they're full of pretension, and as a result they silence their true voices.

Joey Horstman (2005) said of such writers, 'They have no idea what they've gotten themselves into. There's a kind of image they have of what it is to be a writer. They want to fit into that image. Or they've been affected by writing that they think is interesting.' He is most likely to encounter this in poetry class, where he calls the problem 'Tontospeak' because 'they take out all the articles'. He usually responds in conference by saying, 'Tell me what you were trying to say', and then he'll often 'hear the line they need to start with'.

In identifying why students do this kind of writing, Berlin pointed to lack of reading experience. Students who produce such writing:

> tend to not be very good critical writers. They don't read for pleasure, nor do they see any reason to read outside of an assignment. They took creative writing as part of a unit in high school English and thought it was easy. They've never developed their critical skills beyond the high school classroom and as a result, they often claim 'writer's block'. They cannot read critically and thus they struggle to write critically. They cannot read a poem for anything beyond 'how it makes them feel' and how it reminds them of something that happened in their past ... They tend to ignore the context of the work, the work itself, and the fact that very few things were created in the world with them, personally, in mind. Everything is not about them.

Her response is to 'work very hard to ask them to stay inside the poem or the story. To refer directly to the reading. To learn to perform close readings. I must teach them to ignore "symbols" and instead to read for more general meaning'. She added, 'rarely does the student take another such class'. Patrick Hicks (2004b) told me he suspected that much pretentious writing 'comes from the fear of having a class read your work'. He explained, 'Many of my students don't want to write about what they know, so I often get stories about lives and experiences that are far beyond the pale of their understanding. No matter how often I say, "Write what you know, write from the gut and not the head", they don't listen, in part because it's hard to share your dark fears with a class.'

Blocked writing

The pretentious writing that I have just described is most likely to be produced early in the course by students who feel a need to create the impression that they are strong writers. The kind of writing I call blocked often comes later in the course from students who have become desperate. Patrick Hicks told me he could think of a specific example where a student 'was trying way too hard'. He told the student, 'I can tell you've spent a long time at this, but, paradoxically, it's worse for it. You're not telling me a story. You're using fancy words. Writing is not dumping a thesaurus onto the page.' Laurie MacDiarmid (2004) offered the valuable insight that such writers may care too much – or too much need to impress an authority:

> Mostly, I think students put all the same pressures on themselves that we put on ourselves. They want to please us, they want to be recognized as valuable by us and their peers, they want to be 'famous' in whatever ponds they find themselves in, and all this pressure to be perfect makes them procrastinate and overblow and drink and sleep or not sleep too much, etc. The kind of student who's blocked (rather than just stopped) is generally a very intelligent, type A personality, highly invested in outside approval, can be male or female, tends to be female (here), and finds him/herself mostly in opposition to some outside authority which must be a) courted, b) challenged. Impossible task, hence the concrete effect.

Sometimes the writer is 'invested in outside approval' because he or she is replaying a relationship with a parent who was impossible to please (see the discussion of transference later in this chapter). Writers trying to impress authority or live up to some internalized standard of perfection can create unreadable prose. For example, one of my students praised the poet she studied for a descriptive paper, arguing that the poet's 'ability to use metaphor to essentially highlight a target concept from which she creates an original view provides the reader both an opportunity to interpret the poem through bilateral balance of her subject matter as well as a means from which an aspiring poet can survey how "metaphors work in an amazing variety of ways" ...'. Before she turned that paper in, she told me several times how much she was learning from the study and how hard she was working on the paper. Returning it ungraded, I told her that I thought she had worked *too* hard on it, packing so much into sentences like this that the reader could not unpack them. She took a few days to relax and refocus, then turned in a much more readable paper.

As MacDiarmid suggests, in such a case a better question for teachers than What's this writer's problem? is this one: How is my course or my relationship with this writer making it impossible for her to write? Unless we ask this question, we may urge such a student to try harder, which will deepen frustration and likely stir resentment.

This was another lesson I learned from my Y2K poetry class. I had known Beth since she visited the school, and she came as the first to declare the new writing major that I had had a lead role in designing. I was her adviser, and we talked often, sometimes about the directions her interests might take her, sometimes about more personal concerns, sometimes just to talk. She was capable of experiencing wonder and enjoying life, and her writing often expressed this pleasure. I failed to see the power of another motive – her need for me to have a good impression of her and a nagging fear that she was not a good enough writer to deserve it. I was committed to helping her become the best writer she was capable of being, and I think she came to read my offers of help as indication that she *needed* a great deal of help. I didn't realize that she also imagined my assignments to be much harder than they were so that she worked harder on them, making them seem impossible.

We can address the problem of blocked writing on two levels. On the level of the class as a whole, we can set a tone that encourages exploration and playfulness. Michael VanderWeele (2004) mentioned play: 'When we care too much, the play goes out of it. To write well, we need a kind of engaged eagerness, and too much seriousness or intent can get in the way.' He said he also drew from game theory 'the notion of form, of playing by an external set of rules. These help objectify'. Joey Horstman said he tries to calm students with humor. For instance, the first day he reads Barthelme's 'The School' (1982), a story in which all the little pets in an elementary classroom die during the school year, one after another.

The other level on which to address the problem of blocked writing is that of our own relationship with our most responsive students. Asking whether they are trying so hard that it is impossible for them to succeed includes asking whether *we* are trying so hard to teach them that we are making things worse for them.

We also need to consider whether our relationship with them has become subject to one of the subtle and powerful mechanisms that haunt master-apprentice relationships.

Three Mechanisms of Master-Apprentice Relationships

When a student's writing seems strangely blocked or when our relationship with a student or a class changes for the worse and we cannot identify a cause, rather than looking for a scapegoat, I have argued that we ought to consider whether we have become a stumbling block for one or more students. That means asking, 'What have I done – or failed to do – that tripped people up?' That question not only helps halt the mutual blaming, it also helps us become more aware of subtle dynamics that I call mechanisms because they seem to operate on their own, outside of anyone's awareness or intention.

Mimetic rivalry

The previous chapter presented Rene Girard's (1972) position that humans are basically imitative and that even our desires are largely discovered through imitation. That is, our primary mode of becoming is to identify people who seem to us to possess a fullness or plenitude, to assume that they are what they are because of something they *have*, and thus to want that object for ourselves (p. 146). When this object they possess is a capability, we also assume that they can enable us to claim that capability for ourselves, particularly when they are *teachers*.

According to Girard, the subject's desire for the object encounters no resistance from the model as long as the object is plentiful because then the model is not diminished by helping the subject attain it. Teachers, for example, gain satisfaction from helping their students become stronger writers. However, in school, the capability to write well is symbolized by an A, and a 'good teacher' isn't supposed to give many As; but a good student may feel rebuffed by a lesser grade.

In addition, teachers may feel vaguely threatened by outstanding writers. What happens to a teacher's ethos if he or she does an invention exercise with the class and a few of them produce more impressive writing?

Such tensions reveal a risk for what Girard calls *mimetic rivalry*: the model, instead of helping the subject gain access to the object, seems to become an obstacle, actively *preventing* access. Such a rivalry might begin to develop when a teacher is critical of a writer, and the writer interprets that response as a put-down rather than an attempt to help. The subject infers that the model now desires after all to keep the desired object for himself and, perceiving rebuff, begins to draw back; the model, sensing suspicion but not its cause, feels betrayed and likewise draws back, inadvertently confirming the subject's suspicions. Neither subject nor model perceives his *own* contribution to the rivalry that is beginning to develop. As Girard explains, 'The model considers himself too far above the disciple, the disciple considers himself too far below the model, for either of them even fleetingly to entertain the notion that their desires are identical – in short, that they might indeed be rivals' (pp. 146–7).

We might expect the subject to simply turn away, lose interest. Yet, paradoxically, the subject may instead become *more* fascinated, imagining the model as a godlike being who thus has good reason to despise a lowly subject (and who of us is free of inner voices that tell us we deserve to be despised?). At the same time, a part of the subject desires all the more to be as godlike and invincible as the model appears to be. Desire for the object may also increase. Girard (1978) writes, 'Since the model obstinately bars access to it, the possession of this object must make all the difference between the self-sufficiency of the model and the imitator's lack of sufficiency, the model's fullness of being and the imitator's nothingness' (p. 296). We can see why Girard calls the model a 'stumbling block', which he describes as a 'special form of temptation, causing attraction to the extent that it is an obstacle and forming an obstacle to the extent that it can attract' (p. 416).

Although I did not imagine it at the time, I now believe that such a mimetic rivalry developed between me and members of my Y2K poetry class, at least Beth and Brina. Both wanted to write well, and both heard my responses to them as highly critical, a barrier to their success. According to Girard (1972: 146), it is not through words but 'by the example of his own desire that the model conveys to the subject the supreme desirability of the object'. Like my own best teachers, I teach poetry writing partly through the example of my own desire. Sometimes I recite poems, and I often include my own poems in daily journals I distribute to class. Beth, Brina and others did perceive me early on as a model who could help them become poets; and then later they perceived me as a distant and critical teacher who would 'tear apart' their poems, apparently in order to frustrate their desire to become writers.

One reason I did not recognize that we had become rivals was my obliviousness to its cause – the double bind they were in because they had previously known me as advocate and advisor and now encountered me in a course in which I distanced myself from them, partly to keep them from being too easily satisfied with their early efforts.

In addition, our prior relationship, besides raising the stakes on both sides, also led me to respond more frankly to their writing because I assumed they knew that I believed in them as writers. Thus, my reader-response, while much less critical than it seemed to Beth and Brina, offered little of the praise they sought. So they read it as criticism. When they and others told each other in their groups that I seemed unimpressed with their work, mimetic contagion engendered a shared impression that I was too critical, and that in turn deepened the rivalry.

It makes sense that one consequence of the double bind, according to Girard (1978: 292), is loss of 'faith in the capacity of language'. How do we address someone whom we thought we knew but who – some of the time – seems to be a different person entirely? Our attempts to speak to such a person are reduced to stammering. Where blocked language was most evident was in Beth and Brina's prose. Late in the course, students chose a poet, identified aspects of technique or approach, described these in a paper and demonstrated some of what they had found in a partially imitative poem of their own. The paper called only for description, and yet Beth and Brina seemed to believe that it also demanded profound interpretation. Supposing the assignment to be more difficult than it was, they worked harder. Girard (1978: 298) points to the paradox that operates in such a case: 'Desire has its own logic, and it is a logic of gambling. Once past a certain level of bad luck, the luckless player does not give up; as the odds get worse, he plays for higher stakes.' Beth insisted months later that this was one of the most difficult papers she had ever written. She even brought a draft to a conference with me, and we talked about it for at least a half hour. Since she still seemed unsure, I followed up with a page of written response, urging her to simplify. She was using vague categories like 'creative description', so I recommended simply 'description' or 'use of detail'. Yet the final paper used the even muddier 'descriptive perspective'. Even worse, some sequences of sentences repeated themselves, as though stuck in a loop:

> As a writer, Sandburg must continually keep his reader in mind. If they cannot understand his work through the tools he has chosen to convey meaning, then he has failed as a writer. Reader-writer relationship is imperative, without it, no work can hold meaning.

Text has meaning only when it is read and understood. Sandburg places himself in the shoes of his readers to better ensure his own clarity and sense of seeing or understanding.

What no one would suppose is that the paragraph is supposed to be about Sandburg's use of visual detail. Only when I looked back at this writing after the course was over did I notice that every sentence is about getting in touch with one's reader – something Beth felt was 'imperative' but found impossible because she imagined me as a reader who insisted on her best while expecting far worse.

I knew Beth could write well – and I found confirmation in her accompanying writer's memo about her imitation of Sandburg. There, instead of trying to impress, she simply wrote what she noticed as one writer trying to learn from another. She began by announcing clear main points: 'In my poem I paid most attention to his subject matter, use of cliché, repetition of phrasing, and alliteration of certain words for the sake of emphasis and the attention of the reader.' Then she explained these points clearly, in paragraphs that moved forward instead of looping back. Aware by then that her trying too hard was somehow getting in the way, I graded her partly on the writer's memo instead of the paper.

According to Girard, when mimetic rivalry develops, the subject responds in either of two contrasting ways: with accusation focused upon the self; or with anger focused upon the model/rival. Beth responded in the first way: believing she deserved all the criticism I could give her, she blamed herself for failing to learn from it. Girard (1978: 296) observes that in such a case:

> Even if he holds himself to be persecuted, the subject will necessarily ask himself if the model has not got perfectly good reasons for denying him the object. An increasingly weighty part of himself will carry on imitating the model and, by virtue of this fact, will take the model's side, secretly justifying the hostile treatment he believes he is undergoing at the hands of the model and interpreting it as a special condemnation that he probably deserves.

My colleague Joonna later asked Beth in an interview whether the course had been hard for her. Beth replied, 'It killed me. In a good way'. She explained, 'I love Carl, I wanted him to think I can write, I wanted to please. Then I hated Carl. I was frustrated with myself, with being a poor writer. Then, I realized I wasn't willing to be critical of my own work.' But her blocked writing reveals that she had become *too* critical.

Brina reacted the opposite way: feeling belittled and attacked, she counterattacked, especially in a note included with her final portfolio that ridiculed my failure to appreciate her 'heart-work'. The note appears in the excerpt from her article at the end of this chapter; in her words from its title, she 'pushed back'.

In my interviews with other creative writing teachers, I found few who were aware of relationships that had deteriorated due to mimetic rivalry, perhaps partly because its dynamics stay hidden until we have a name by which to know it. Elliot Khalil Wilson (2004) did describe a relationship with a student he mentored that turned into what sounds like mimetic rivalry. He met her – I'll call her Jennifer – when she was one of the students who helped interview him for his position. She asked him then whether – assuming he was hired – he would work with her on a directed study in advanced poetry. He agreed, and after he was hired, they went ahead with the plan. Things went well at first, but he told me that his training is in criticism rather than in creative writing, so he believed his gifts were best suited to helping students become aware of weaknesses that impeded them. Thus, one thing he told Jennifer was that her poems were 'turgid and murky', and later he even jokingly introduced her to a colleague by saying, 'This is Jennifer, and she writes turgid and murky poems'. From that point, their relationship became strained – and required considerable effort to restore.

Clearly, at the beginning, Jennifer was eager to work with him, but she also must have felt unworthy to work with a poet she deeply admired. The quip he hoped would joke her out of a bad practice must have seemed to her to expose her folly in ever hoping to claim the name of *writer*.

Wilson said he had met similar resistance from a class. He thought that as strong writers, they would welcome and benefit from the kind of incisive criticism an excellent editor provides, but instead they withdrew and became suspicious. He joked that his 'moniker' as teacher seemed to be 'clumsy sadist', but I could hear pain behind the joke. He had offered what he perceived as his gifts and felt that they had been rejected. I told him that his students probably had a parallel reaction: they brought work they thought reflected their gifts and concluded from his response that they would never write well enough to suit him.

The story illustrates what can go wrong when a teacher of creative writing tries to do what most of his colleagues would admire: articulate lofty expectations and be diligent in showing students where their work fails to measure up.

As teachers of the arts, once we know that such rivalries can develop, and recognize our role in the process, then we can respond with empathy, usually preventing more serious problems. Recall Laurie MacDiarmid's response to resistance in a class: 'I usually ask them in conference if there's any way I can make the classroom a better place for them.' That's a disarming question. Empathy also pulls us out of the pain *we* feel when we encounter disappointment or anger in students we've done our best to teach.

Transference

My colleagues Karen (2004) and Jeff Barker (2004b) teach theater courses and direct plays, so they both work closely with many of the same students. In addition, they host these students at gatherings in their home and stay in touch with some for years after graduation. They thus become for many students a kind of second family, so they can observe how close and complicated relationships change through college and beyond. When I asked if they encountered reversals in those relationships, Karen said, 'I don't have many problems like that, but some of them have completely stopped speaking to Jeff for as long as a year or two.' She explained the difference this way: 'Most students in college have their relationship with their mother pretty well worked out, but maybe not their relationship with their father.'

That explanation illustrates *transference*. It says that for the students who stopped speaking to Jeff, the *real* issue was an unresolved problem with their father that they transferred to Jeff. Terry Eagleton (1983: 160) usefully explains transference as a *repetition* of an original psychical conflict: 'We repeat, sometimes compulsively, what we cannot properly remember, and we cannot remember it because it is unpleasant.' The repetition of the conflict is one of the subject's 'unconscious ways of avoiding having to come to terms with it'. Analysts expect transference and may even use it to experience a patient's psychic life so that they can intervene in a way that helps the patient stop replaying old conflicts. However, teachers who are unaware of the dynamic of transference would probably wonder what *they* did to cause the student to turn against them. They would also be too likely to respond by playing the role the subject projects onto them, in this way sustaining or perhaps even deepening the underlying conflict.

How should we respond to such students? Not, says Tobin (2004: 48), by telling them that they are being driven by their unconscious:

> There is no moment when I would ever say to a student, 'I notice that there is always a mother figure hovering in the background of your essays; why do you think that is?' or 'To improve this essay, you

need to confront the transference emotions that are obviously being stirred up in our relationship.' But, as a writing teacher who firmly believes that we ought to allow students to write autobiographically and that we ought to pay more attention to the role of the unconscious in the composing process, there are plenty of moments when I sense that I am being pulled into the role of parent, confidante, therapist.

A teacher who, like Jeff Barker, recognizes that the conflict isn't really *about* him or her might observe to such students that they are responding with unusual emotion or intensity and ask them if they know what's going on or where it's coming from. If they recognize that they are overreacting and do not understand why, they may be open to suggestion that they get help to get to the root. At other times, a teacher needs to be patient while the student works through the problem or comes to the point where he or she is ready to seek help.

We also need to remind ourselves that not only powerful resistance to a teacher but also strong identification with a teacher may reflect transference from a prior relationship.

Counter-transference

With counter-transference, it is the analyst's (or in our case, the teacher's) psychic conflicts from a prior relationship that are transferred. Whenever we have inexplicably strong feelings of attraction or repulsion toward a student or group of students, we ought to ask ourselves whether we are unconsciously replaying a prior relationship. Again, Tobin (1991: 342) is helpful:

> As teachers, we also can go no further than our own complexes and internal resistances permit, and thus we, too, need to begin with self-analysis. We, too, need to identify the extent to which our responses to our students and their writing are not neutral or objective, the extent to which counter-transference responses interfere with our ability to help students improve their writing.

I've realized that a powerful motive in my own teaching has potential to become obsessive. When I was a child and youth, my father verbally abused my mother – harangues that sometimes went on for days. I remember wishing she could find strength to stand up for herself, talk back to him. I also fantasized speaking for her. But I was a child. I could imagine the words but lacked the courage to speak them to my father. Confusing me further was the fact that outside these spells, my father was kind, thoughtful, wise – a local leader in soil and wildlife conservation. Growing up caught between the two sides of my father as well as between my mother and my father formed my imagination first as a way to escape, later as means to effect transformation and reconciliation. That early experience is a reason for writing this book. It is also a reason I care about helping students, especially female students, to overcome self-doubt and find a voice for talking back to what oppresses. Now, knowing this about myself helps me recognize when I am trying too hard on behalf of such students.

When our emotions are more intense than we can account for, or when our behavior becomes obsessive, we need to ask whether the impetus might be an unresolved psychic conflict. If so, unless we get help to recognize and resolve it, we are too likely to create problems for ourselves and others. Payne (2000: 92) observes, for example, that teachers who are unaware of their counter-transference are more likely to revictimize students who have been abused. She writes that 'survivors of physical or sexual abuse often don't have the ability to distinguish what is appropriate and safe to disclose because the very abuse is their primary education in transgressing boundaries'; she adds that such students 'may not fully realize the potential for professors to abuse their power'.

Like Tobin, Mark Bracher, in *The Writing Cure: Psychoanalysis, Composition, and the Aims of Education* (1999: 3), makes the case that writing teachers ought to know more of what psychoanalysts know because of similarities in our work. Citing Ann Murphy (1989), Bracher argues:

> [O]ur work helping students to find their voices frequently brings us face to face with a dense array of demons – fears, resistances, angers, and traumas – in our students and in ourselves. Indeed, the sub-text or latent content of a composition classroom often threatens utterly to overthrow the more cognitive dimensions of our work. In encouraging our students to unlock and express their ideas, feelings, and beliefs more effectively, we are, like psychoanalysts, insisting that they confront lost or denied elements of themselves.

That our own journey into the classroom is also likely to be haunted by 'lost or denied elements' in our students and in ourselves is something we need to acknowledge in order to teach responsibly. Nancy Welch (1997: 61) worries that otherwise students may get caught in a never-ending apprenticeship, moving from one 'master' to the next, since the transference likely to accompany such a relationship 'traps students and teachers in relationships of allegiance and unexamined admiration'.

This means that we need to scrutinize not only conflicts with students but also attractions, felt on either side.

Intellectual, Artistic and Personal Attraction

Mary Biddinger (2004b) mentioned on my survey a relationship problem it didn't broach: 'More often in poetry writing classes, I experience students having a "crush" on their instructor. I've often wondered why this is so (but then again, I idolized my own undergrad profs).' It's not hard to see why 'crushes' would develop in our teaching. Any kind of teaching is likely to nurture strong relationships between teachers and those students who most want to learn what they teach, but the creative writing class, as Biddinger observed, is especially close:

> I've found that the creative writing classroom seems to be more intimate than, say, a freshman composition class, and perhaps that's why crushes are more likely. I completely understand, and in fact I encourage students to stop by during office hours, contact me via email, attend local readings, keep in touch once the semester is over, ask for letters of recommendation, and so on. I have even established friendships with many students after the term finishes, especially with my nontraditional students.

One reason creative writing is more intimate is that artistic persons often feel 'different', marginalized, so they are gratified to be among those who share a love of words and of beautiful things made out of words. We tend to identify with our most interesting students as they do with us. Add what Regina Barreca and Deborah Denenholz Morse (1997: viii) observe – 'that acts of learning and teaching are acts of desire and passion' – and consider whether this is anywhere more true than with acts of learning in the arts.

A factor too is the tendency Girard described for a subject to seek out a model who seems to possess a fullness or plenitude. Mark Coggins (2011), in 'The Singer Affair: How a Crush On a Teacher Landed Me a Role in Her Novel', describes the teacher in a way that shows how easily one kind of desire transmutes into another:

> Although she was only a few years older than me, she seemed bohemian, worldly-wise and alluring in an European or – at the very least – East of the Mississippi kind of way. She graduated from Vassar. She had long straight hair and gamine-like good looks. She toted her cigarettes around in the front waist band of her skirt, and nothing was more provocative than seeing her pull one out and light up.

Recall, too, that we teach in a way that is highly interpersonal. Many of us meet students in one-to-one conferences, partly to understand the thinking and feeling behind a piece of writing, which is also likely to be in several senses personal. We develop mentoring relationships, at least with those most serious about becoming writers, attending not just to what they write but also to the person and writer they are and might become. Thus, for many of our students, we fit May's (1939) description of the 'true counselor', one who 'seeks to understand people from the standpoint of appreciation'. He observes that students 'prize this kind of understanding' because it helps give them a sense of worth. But the understanding that helps writers to break down inner barriers, freeing them to write or revise, also closes the distance between teacher and student:

> ... it draws the other human being for a moment out of the loneliness of his individual existence and welcomes him into community with another soul ... Such understanding, it is not too much to say, is the most objective form of love. That is why there is always a tendency on the part of the counselee to feel some love toward the counselor, this person 'who understands me'. (p. 119)

May adds, 'Significant teaching requires empathy, for only thus does the professor's mind meet the student's in a fructifying intellectual experience.' But the way he describes this meeting of minds sounds more than Platonic:

> Knowledge may go from mind to mind through relatively impersonal means; but we should all admit that the more significant kind of knowledge is that in which there is a mutual participation, a partial identification of the minds of teacher and student. Then truth is made a living force passed from one to another, and education becomes truly a 'leading out' of the highest creative potentialities of the student's mind through inspiring contact and participation in the creative actualities of the teacher's mind. (p. 123)

A related reason why 'crushes' might develop is the tendency of students who want to become artists to view their writer-teacher as a model. Biddinger confirmed that in her experience, sharing her own writing with her classes 'relates very much' to the problem. This is audible in her language: she 'idolized' her own undergraduate profs – which must have been partly because they lived a life of reading and writing that she wanted for herself. Remember that Girard says that we are always on the lookout for those who seem to have what we might want because they can also be our means of becoming.

One more reason for 'crushes': even if we do not give our writing to our students, some will find it, and it is likely to reveal our own desire, usually through personas more intimate and more passionate than our teaching persona. Thus some students – who already tend to identify the speaker or the central character with the writer – may imagine that they encounter there the person we *really* are. We shouldn't be surprised if imagination carries them farther.

Maintaining boundaries

Barreca (1997), while observing that a teacher is an object of desire, also emphasizes that he or she should be an unattainable object:

> Professors retain, for students, the magical quality of being both available and distant at the same time. The relationship resembles a courtly romance; desire is ritualized into a series of intellectual curtsies and bows which, while always flavored by the sexual, were never meant to be translated into the physical ... Teachers were taboo – or should have been – since there was a sort of intellectual incest at work, a prohibition which meant that the student was free to love and want, while the teacher was required to remain disinterested, distinguished, and practically disembodied. (Shaw's Henry Higgins protests that a pupil is 'sacred', declaring that 'teaching would be impossible if students were not sacred'.) A student felt – rightly or wrongly – that the teacher, like a parent, was a safe object of desire, since it was necessarily one-way .... (p. 3)

That is one reason for teachers to avoid responding to signs of attraction in students – to give them freedom to love what they have taken the course to pursue.

Another reason is that the teacher-student relationship is unequal in power. Some or much of the time, then, it is subject to complex motives. Barreca writes that 'instead of sex sublimated as ambition', in the cases of students falling in love with teachers, 'what we're dealing with is ambition sublimated as sex'. That is, what such students want is 'to be the teacher and not sleep with the teacher' (p. 2).

And a third reason is the double bind. If a class is a poor place to conduct therapy, it's also a poor place for a student and teacher to carry on a relationship rife with conflicts of interest.

It's worth adding that partly because of the move on the part of teachers toward informal dress and address and toward relationships that are more like accompaniment, teachers now seem less distant. And recently, personal technology – email, instant messaging, social networking, cell phones and texting – have further blurred boundaries between formal and informal as well as between public and private. For example, many teachers are Facebook friends with some of their students, and even if the teacher uses Facebook primarily to encourage intellectual and artistic connections, the relationship of 'friend' gives to each unusual access to images and personal messages of the other, and it gives the students an apparent 'in' with the teacher. Being in the same social network can make a romantic relationship between a teacher and student more imaginable – as well as easier for either to initiate.

Cultural shifts have also made students more likely to violate taboos. Already at a time in their lives for pushing back the boundaries, students are further encouraged by media images idealizing no limits, extreme actions. Thus many creative writing teachers can relate to Biddinger's feeling troubled about 'one aspect of creative writing', namely that 'certain students have pushed these limits beyond what is acceptable'.

Her email to me mentioned a further reason students cross the line, the persona that teacher-artists sometimes adopt:

> Perhaps this is gender related (though I've heard instances of the reverse from my friends), but as a woman instructor I feel rather uncomfortable being seen as 'the embodiment and messenger of poetic mystery and beauty' in the classroom. Sure, I idolized my professors and the visiting writers that I met as an undergraduate ... but I would never have dreamed of asking them out to dinner, sending incoherent, alcohol-addled midnight email messages, or inviting them to a party in my home where no other faculty would be present. I also would never have mentioned 'cuteness' or 'hotness' on English department student evaluations. To me, these behaviors cross the line between mentoring and harassment. I like to excite students about poetry, but if they're excited enough to follow me (a wife and mother) around campus, then perhaps I'm selling the poetry thing a bit too heavily.

That the 'Rate My Professors' (2011) site includes 'hot' as its ultimate rating increases the likelihood that students will add that rating to an 'official' course evaluation. The presence of a 'hotness' scale for professors also adds credence to Glavin's (1997: 12) charge that in students' eyes, the 'good' teacher 'need be no more than, and is never less than, the superior narcissist, ... someone who can enthrall, overpower, subject the enormous force of culturally-enforced adolescent self-admiration'. This charge gives us added reason to question the kind of teaching that is too centered on the life and person of the artist-teacher. Biddinger said it well when questioning the 'charisma factor' in the creative writing classroom:

> I've had professors who were charismatic, and those who weren't. Both taught me equally well, and in fact I was more prone to consult with instructors with a minimal sexiness quotient, because I felt they'd take writing itself more seriously. I find egocentric teaching very off-putting; for example, when a professor shows favored treatment or gives more positive feedback to a student who is obviously mooning over him (asking for autographs, quoting his works, bringing gifts to class). I don't want my own competence as a workshop leader to be contingent upon personality and charm. I also want students to feel comfortable disagreeing with me, because after all, I'm just one reader.

A Student's Perspective on Resistance

I mentioned that this project began with a class that I had expected to go well because I knew and admired many of the students signed up for it but which instead, partly for that reason, went badly. Brina Wiuff was one of two students who were particularly frustrated by that turn of events, as she explains in her article below. When Brina included with her final portfolio the angry writer's memo she quotes in the article, I called her and we talked. I told her that I and some members of the class seemed to be trying much too hard, but I didn't understand why. I promised her I would study the course until I did understand, which led to an article (Vandermeulen, 2005) and later to this book.

Brina took the course as a sophomore. Two years later, as a senior English major considering graduate school, she joined another senior to study the two sections of the course that I taught the first semester of that year. Their papers, along with my study of Brina's class, composed a panel presented at the Southwest/Texas Popular Culture Association conference early in the second semester. Brina reflects on her experience with my response and then looks at the reactions of students who also resisted my response. Her study of the other students is omitted due to space constraints.

Pushing and Pushing Back in Poetry Class

Brina Wiuff, Northwestern College

When a student enters a creative writing classroom, their expectations of the class, their personal experiences, their personalities, and their emotions enter with them, complicating the process of the classroom. The student's anxieties confuse, complicate, and occasionally even destroy their sometimes-delicate confidence and their opportunity to learn in the classroom setting. A complex tension occurs between the student and the instructor – the instructor pushes and the student succeeds, pushes back, fails, or any combination of the three.

Anxieties creep into the minds of even the most intelligent and creative students, sometimes causing them to become defensive towards the professor and other students, to believe they have failed, or to entirely give up. Why are students who are accustomed to doing well suddenly afraid that they no longer have what it takes to succeed?

My Story: The One Who Pushed Back

Two years ago, I was in Carl Vandermeulen's Reading and Writing Poetry class. In the last writer's memo to the last poem in my last portfolio at the end of the semester, I wrote these words answering a response I had received from Carl about a poem I had written similar to Frost's 'Acquainted with the Night':

> This may not be the best poem ever written, it's probably not even worthy of being called a Frost-copycat, but that was a baseless reason for you to tell me it is worthless. I'm sure you can think of better reasons for ripping my heart-work to pieces ... I don't care how you choose to evaluate this poem; the true values lie in the lessons learned. Maybe it wasn't worth your time, but it's what I have to offer you.

These are harsh words. Two years later, I look at them and try to understand why I thought these words were appropriate to include in a writer's memo intended for my professor. I am not a vicious or angry person, and yet, there the words are – abrasive and emotionally charged – powerful words punctuating the end of the jarring journey of 'Reading and Writing Poetry Class'.

I remember signing up for the class for the first semester of my sophomore year – excited to be able to take a class with Professor Vandermeulen. He was my advisor and I worked closely with him on the staff of the *Beacon*, the college newspaper. His desire and ability to go out of his way for students however he was able to impressed me. We had developed mutual respect, respect that seemed to persevere through late *Beacon* production nights and indecisiveness about my major – but had not been tested by the classroom setting.

My initial comments to Carl about the class reflect my honest initial feelings and ideas about the class, including my fear of it:

> [T]he reason I'm interested in learning how to express myself more creatively with words in poetry is to break through that fear. I'd like to be able to develop an ability to not only write poetry well, but also have the confidence it takes to read it out loud in front of an audience. I've learned that the best way to become comfortable with something that terrifies you is to thrust yourself into it without reservation and let it carry you.

I was afraid. I had never written poetry before and I had very little experience reading or understanding poetry. However, I knew how to overcome my fears – I must try. I had faith that once I tried my hand at poetry, the poetry and the words themselves would carry me. I would become successful. I was a person who was used to succeeding and I had no reason to think this poetry class would be any different.

Then the class began.

Poetry was not easy. Many of my poems were forced – they were created by sheer acts of will, acts motivated only by assignment. Looking back, the forcedness of the poems, the stiff and obscure words, is obvious to any reader. Many of my poems were simply not good – and I knew it. The words did not carry me away as I had wished they might; instead, I felt suffocated by them.

I felt that Professor Vandermeulen reinforced my personal feelings of failure and almost devastated me in the context of the classroom. I received response after response from him – each pointing out where my poems went wrong and sometimes suggesting ways that I might make them right. Because of my inexperience as a poet, and because of the lack of positive response from Carl, I thought I was not doing anything right. I wanted to know what my strengths were, what I could do well – not only because I needed encouragement, but also because I needed to know what I should build on. Carl was trying to teach me how to fix my poems and I was hearing him say that there was nothing worth saving. Furthermore, my respect for him as a person and as an instructor caused me to put even more stock into what I heard him telling me.

I should have walked into his office and made sure I understood him correctly. I didn't. I had three close friends in the class, girls very much like myself, who were having similar experiences with the class. We realized we all felt as if we were failing, for similar reasons and we collectively turned on Professor Vandermeulen. We could not all have failed – so maybe he had partially failed us. We made our case against him and fed off each other's feeling of hurt and frustration.

I was angry and frustrated. I initially wrote the writer's memo to 'Acquainted with the Light' with the intention of changing it. I wrote it because it was an accurate portrayal of how I was feeling. If I wrote it out, maybe I would feel better. Instead, I decided to communicate with Professor Vandermeulen honestly in my anger and frustration – feelings that I am confident would have dissipated if I had been honest with him before the last writer's memo.

I finished the class – buried so far beneath both my words and Carl's response – feeling as if I had failed us both. The harder I tried, the worse my work became. Interestingly, my feelings of failure superseded what my grade for the class reflected.

As I look back and try to understand what happened, some things are clear to me now, but others are still mysterious. My instructor expected me to do well. I expected myself to do well. When I was not meeting my instructor's or my own expectations I believed I failed. Professor Vandermeulen pushed harder – and I eventually pushed back. I was not able to write a line of poetry for over a year and a half.

* * *

A Conclusion of Sorts

The creative writing classroom is a complex game of push between the student and the professor. The professor pushes the student, who may otherwise not have any reason to move. Students either let go of what they think they know and allow themselves to be pushed along the path of learning, or they resist. Resistance is most likely a symptom of a student's anxiety, lack of understanding of how the creative writing classroom functions, and of the connectedness a student feels to their own writing. This anxious resistance can limit what students learn and the work they accomplish.

A creative writing instructor can limit these stressors by:

(1) Acknowledging that the conditions of the course are likely to arouse anxiety – expecting it and not being as threatened by it when it does happen.

(2) Specifically cautioning people against using their groups as a place to vent, and urging them to go to him instead.
(3) Explaining why he responds as he does, so that students are more willing to trust the process and not worry too soon about whether they have arrived.

Chapter 8
Resolving Dilemmas of Grading

A crucial missing element in most writing pedagogy is any experience or instruction in ascertaining the value of one's work.

Brian Huot (2002: 169)

By the time most students arrive in our classes, they have marks all over the texts of who they are. I think this starts in grade school, or before, for certainly some students, even there, are noted for their 'creativity', while others, for example are 'good at math'. For the most part, our response strategies reinforce these perceptions, and the whole grading system feeds into the expectations of students as 'approval junkies'.

Katherine Haake (2000: 108)

The truth is that it did not take me long to feel relatively comfortable, relatively like myself, as a discussion leader. But as a reader and grader of student writing, I responded to my fear and insecurity with hypervigilance. I covered students' work in corrections, explanations, and justifications; the fact that I was the authority, that I knew more about their essays than they did themselves, was never in doubt and never to be questioned.

Lad Tobin (2004: 98)

If we were to re-imagine the creative writing class, starting with our central assumption – that students are a community of apprentices, learning from a master and model – we would imagine a teacher who would offer *response*, eventually including careful evaluation of finished work, but we would find little reason to suppose that this master should announce at the start – as syllabi typically do – that members of the class will be sorted out into who's hot and who's not.

That's what *grading* amounts to.

Incidentally, the preferred term in the UK and Australia is 'assessment'; in the US, 'assessment' usually refers to a college or university's procedures for evaluating the success of their programs.

Grades Impede Learning in the Arts

It's easier to see how grading would impede learning within a community of artists.

Most obviously, it fosters competition, which threatens collaboration. Part of encouraging collaboration is creating a hospitable space, but good hosts don't sort out guests on a single scale of worth. The guests may enjoy limited competitions, with different winners and losers, but all should feel in the end like a contributor, not just a winner or loser. Aurelie Hagstrom (2004), in proposing hospitality as an ideal for the classroom, lists among its obstacles 'arrogance, impatience, lack of respect, lack of humility'. Grading pushes both teachers and ambitious students toward every one of those attitudes: especially early in a course, a student whose work is viewed as *impressive* arouses contradictory responses in other students – admiration, perhaps, but also envy and fear. A couple of weeks into my fiction writing course, Ryan read a stunning response to an exercise – first-draft writing with depth of thought and an engaging complexity of character. A couple of hours later I happened upon a conversation between two members of the class.

Kayli said, 'I am *never* going to be able to write like Ryan.'

I said, 'It's not a competition. I don't measure your writing against Ryan's.'

'I can't help it. I'm competitive.'

Natalie added, 'I was just going to stop by to tell you that I'm hopeless as a fiction writer.'

I said, 'I want to read stories like *you* can write. I don't want you to try to write like Ryan.'

She considered that. 'Well, that makes me feel better. Still, if Ryan's paper is in a stack being handed in, I'm going to put mine at the other end of the stack.'

Such feelings must be common in any class where students witness others' performances. It would also be easy for someone like Ryan, sensing envy and resentment, to in turn become resentful. He's just enjoying writing and presenting his work to others. What's *their* problem?

A second way grading gets in our way is that learning an artistic process calls for playfulness, an attitude of exploration, a willingness to risk. But fear of the grade makes students want control: guidelines for writing the essay, story, poem or play that will nail down an 'A', later a quick fix for drafts that haven't arrived. Thom Tammaro (2004) was eloquent in explaining how grading during the process can interfere with learning:

It's a workshop – in a workshop you learn by making mistakes. I encourage them to make mistakes. Mistakes and failure are the best teachers, especially in an intro class. I'm more interested in productivity and creating good writerly habits. I'm looking for their meeting the objectives of an assignment at a 'satisfactory' level, not a graded level. Imagine trying to distinguish between an 'A' quatrain and a 'C-' or 'D' quatrain when you're trying to teach what a quatrain is! I can't! It's important that they know what it is, that they've tried their hand in writing a few, and that they understand its workings. There's enough judgment ahead for them if they are serious writers and begin sending out their work for publication. I read them Rilke's first 'Letter to a Young Poet'. I hope to train them into reframing the 'Are my poems any good?' question into 'How can I make my poems better?'

And as Theresa Williams (2004) wrote, 'Sometimes when a grade hangs over an assignment, they may try too hard or put too much importance on that one assignment.' In the terms I've used, all these anxieties that come with grading put pressure on the writing self, which seldom responds well to pressure. Martin Cockroft (2005) knew from experience how grading can limit learning. In his undergrad course, individual writings were graded. He recalled that he 'received above-average but not excellent grades in poetry and fiction' and that the professor 'praised some of the same students over and over again, and indeed, they were the best writers in the class'. He told me, 'I spent my workshop with a hunger for the professor's eye. I resented the students I knew he loved. I wondered what I might do differently to become one of those students.' But in grad school he found a difference in the spirit of the class that he called 'striking' because the focus was on poetry rather than on who was best at writing it. 'I learned to write poetry in order to talk about poetry. I learned to trust the other students.' He also 'attempted all sorts of poetic experiments – many of which worked only marginally well'. Had he been receiving grades, he said, 'I probably would have been devastated, and I surely wouldn't have risked as much again.'

Further, in the highly interactive and interpersonal creative writing class, learning depends on a good relationship between the teacher and the students. The teacher/master should be a nurturer of that fragile *writing* self, an empathetic listener when students deal with highly personal matters in their writing, a coach and mentor helping to develop the writer's guide self, even a *model* of the person, artist or teacher students might some day become. Grading can contradict and interfere with all these roles. I'm not surprised that when Payne (2000: xvi) describes the self-disclosures about eating disorders that her students write, teachers often ask her, 'So how did you grade these?' She explains that 'this question isn't really about evaluation, about wanting a rubric or set of assurances about standards. It's about anxiety'. Yes, but a very real anxiety: how can a teacher be empathetic enough to receive such highly personal disclosures – and then objective enough to assign them a grade – without seeming inhuman? And how do we maintain good relationships with students that we place in such a powerful double bind?

The conclusion seems obvious: given everything else we need to be and to do for our students, *we can't at the same time grade them*.

But you know the rest: to keep our jobs and maintain respect for our discipline at academic institutions that sell certification, *we must turn in meaningful grades*.

We're in a double bind too.

Subverting the grading system

Many teachers respond to this dilemma the way Ann C. Hall (2004) does: 'I think these students need to risk, and there is little in the educational system that promotes that, so I try to ease up on the grades.' Carol Bly (2001: 197) eases up all the way. Deciding that it is futile to resist the assumption that 'MFA students must get As', that's what she turns in. She explains that grading induces fear, and 'fear-laden people simply don't think up metaphors' (p. 198). Jack Ridl (2004) also frankly admitted to me, 'I give all A's so I can teach'. In an article called 'Degrading the grade', Ridl (2008) explains how his teaching changed for the better after he realized that grading 'interfered with the value of constructive critique':

> The grade was not an assessment, not even a reward or a punishment. It was a consequence. As soon as I would suggest to students that they could do something else with an ending or a line break or change the tone, all they heard was a grade plummeting. Defenses rose. They refused to see any alternative to the way they had composed the work, and stood firmly for the A grade they deserved. The result was stifled growth, inauthentic work, begrudging changes that took little if any effect, a hostile relationship between what should be a coach/mentor and a growing writer.

Once he removed the pressure of grading, all this changed. Students 'began to discover real value in everything written, successful or not.

We had complex and provocative conversations about the importance of the material'.

The change also freed him to teach better:

> I put away being a tough grader and became a 'tough responder'. All that means is that I was no longer hesitant to make suggestions and corrections for fear I might 'stifle' a sensitive soul. I no longer had to tell them the lie that they needed to develop a tough hide in order to take criticism. They could maintain their vision and voice and sensitivity. They could welcome critical response because it was in their behalf and their poem's behalf. Critical response did not lead to a grade which had led them to play it safe and learn little. Critical response led to growth and the intrinsic joy that comes when beginning artists realize what can be done instead of hiding within what they can already do.

When colleagues and administrators object that students don't produce quality work without the pressure of the grade, he points to results: 'In 15 years since my epiphany, more than 60 students have gone on to the best MFA programs in the country and are publishing.'

Ridl did acknowledge to me that he could get away with giving As because he was tenured – and secure enough in his position to shrug off criticism.

Involving students in deciding their grade

Another way teachers ease the pressure is by negotiating the grade. Realizing that 'worrying about grades on creative writing assignments does not help writers' but that 'nevertheless, a final course grade is necessary', Steve Coyne (2002/2008) meets with each student twice, at midterm and then again during finals week, when they 'arrive at an agreement' about the course grade. He asks them to prepare for these meetings by collecting copies of their work with instructor comments and with student response. Then they look at criteria for grading in the syllabus and talk about how they have performed in relation to those criteria. They also answer two other questions that he considers key: 'Consider which students have produced written and verbal feedback on your work that has been the most useful'; and 'Consider which students' creative writing is among the work you think is the strongest produced this semester'. Coyne remarked, 'It's gratifying to see how much consensus develops among students about who the stronger writers are and about who the best commentators are.' He added that most of these conferences go well, 'and those few which are difficult are still a lot less upsetting and disruptive than disgruntled and disengaged students scowling through class meetings'.

This negotiation approach does seem workable, especially with the self-analysis that applies shared criteria, but I do have concerns. One Coyne mentioned: 'Students, especially the best, tend to low-ball themselves.' Another concern is that a few students have a *higher* self-estimate than their performance merits, and I'd rather avoid that argument. A third is that peers tend to value conventionally good, accessible writing over difficult or original work of greater depth. I'm sure Coyne would agree that the instructor needs to affirm such work, but I'd also worry that students who know that their grade depends partly on the judgment of their peers might too much write to impress peers.

A more serious but less visible concern also comes to mind. In earlier chapters, I asked why we place so much emphasis on critique, both in the workshop and in teacher response to student writing. Perhaps part of the answer is that teachers of the arts so dread judgment that they turn it over to students. Might the workshop be popular with teachers partly because it establishes a pecking order that does the grading for them?

Systemic Confusion

Is anything in academia as intellectually incoherent as the 'system' of grading? All that can be known of a student who receives a B in a course is that in someone's judgment, not even necessarily the teacher's, he worked harder, was better behaved, did better work or improved more in doing it than another student who got a C in the course.

But if a symbol can have so many and such different meanings, does it really have meaning at all?

Confusion about the purpose and meaning of grades

One notion common in elementary schools that lingers in college is that a grade signifies progress or improvement. By this way of thinking, if a student begins the course writing terrible essays, but he works hard and winds up writing quite good ones, then he should get an A. But what about another student who begins as a good writer and improves only a little, though her writing at the end is clearly better than that of the first student?

A quite different notion, that grades 'reinforce' or reward learning, retains its appeal among educators on elementary and secondary levels because it promises a way to control behavior. In this case, a good grade symbolizes compliance. But is that what we want? 'Compliant artist' is an oxymoron. Writers should find satisfaction in the work itself and in the meaning and pleasure it brings to audiences, not become dependent upon approval. A further problem is that when teachers use grades to manipulate behavior, students learn to play the game too, as when they say, 'I made the changes you told me to make, so why didn't I get an A?' Using grades to reward or punish induces much of the behavior that irks teachers: students asking in one way or another what we *want*; students (often female) who have come to view a good grade from a respected authority as a mark of identity and who thus freeze up when that identity seems to be at risk; students (mostly male), who, having learned in earlier schooling to disdain 'brown-nosing', continue in college to hold back from intellectual engagement that could awaken the life of the mind.

It's worth observing that many of our metaphors for grading relate to money. In the early years of schooling, grades as 'payment' for good behavior or achievement are part of the 'hidden curriculum' by which students are socialized into the values and practices of a capitalistic system. One manifestation still present in college is the notion of 'extra credit', which sounds like merit pay.

Coexisting with these is the quite different idea that the purpose of grading is to identify those students who are good enough at doing something that they should keep on doing it – take more courses and even pursue a vocation or avocation that draws upon that talent.

Lack of agreement about what should go into a final grade

Given the confusion about the purpose of grading, I should have been less surprised at the lack of agreement among creative writing teachers about whether a final grade should be based upon the effort invested or the work produced. W.T. Pfefferle's (2006) 'Creative Writing' syllabus is unequivocal:

> Nothing matters as much in this class as the quality, originality, and scope of your poetry. You write continuously during the semester and turn in a portfolio at the end. That portfolio counts for 100% of your grade, so it needs to be clean, professional, interesting, big, exciting, moving, and compelling. If it's not, then you've wasted your time.

At the opposite extreme, a surprising number of teachers go so far as to *exclude* from the final grade their judgment of the quality of a student's writing. According to my survey, at least 10% of the creative writing teachers who collect a final portfolio choose not to evaluate it for the quality of the writing.

One reason they give is the difficulty of judging artistic work. Catherine Wiley's (2004) syllabus announces, 'I will NOT assign a grade to your work, as the notion of grading creativity strikes me as ridiculous'. And Juliana Spahr (2004) wrote, 'I feel that poetry is so diverse right now (and a good thing too!) that for me to say this is a good poem and this not would be absurd.' She added that she has biases that derive 'from sources such as my education, my reading, my friendships with certain groups of poets' and that it 'wouldn't be fair for me to let this enter into my grading'. Similarly, Ann C. Hall (2004) said that she views her emphasis on process rather than products as 'a form of intellectual and creative humility for me – who am I to judge? We all know the stories about famous authors being told by their teachers that their work was awful, then they go on to become a great author. I don't want to become one of those teachers!'

Of course, another reason we resist grading is that much of the writing our students do is personal. Lad Tobin (2004: 108) writes that when teachers say they can't grade personal writing, what they usually mean is 'I can tell whether it's good or bad but I am worried that my students will be unable to understand that my judgment is based not on the quality of their experience but on the quality of their writing'. Even if the *writing* isn't personal, students may be so invested that they *take* evaluation personally. Elizabeth Slattery (2004) remarked, 'What I love about teaching creative writing is coaxing the work out of the students, so that part is relatively easy for me, but then to criticize their babies and stamp a grade on their foreheads, well, it is hard not to second guess myself.'

Other teachers so strongly associate grading with objectivity that they believe they must exclude all judgment. Jessica Farquhar (2004) wrote, 'Any creative writing course I've ever had has not judged the quality of the writing itself. While it is important to discuss the values we place on aspects of writing and why we like what we do, it's really very subjective in the end. Grading, however, should not be subjective.'

If we leave out estimation of the quality of a student's writing, what's left for a grade to represent? Most obviously, effort. When Sam Abrams' (2004) 'Creative Writing/Poetry' syllabus announces that he's going to grade 'by the numbers', those numbers represent only attendance and quantity of on-time work completed:

> I am going to try to do it by the numbers this quarter. You are to hand in a minimum of two poems each week ... and attend every class.

If you hand in 20 poems, on time, none late – certainly no big bunch at the end! – and attend every class you will earn an A, even if your poems are less than great and your comments less than wise. If you miss more than 10% of the classes and hand-ins without very good excuses, you get a B, more than 20% misses a C, and so on. Got it?

Matthew Roberson's (2004) 'grading contract' approach also emphasizes effort, and he said that this does cause him some worry:

I'm sure some administrator will at some point find some excuse to give me grief about the grading contract. But I feel it's important to make sure that students feel unafraid to take risks in class, and the contract lets them know that they can still get a high grade even if they write about strange things in strange ways. Yes, some mediocre students end up with an A. But, and this is something I make a big deal of in class, there is a 'good faith' clause in the contract. If students turn in sloppy, ill-conceived, or incomplete work, there's no way they'll get an A. At the end of the term, I have a lot of As, but a lot of Bs and Cs, too. Some students will shoot themselves in the foot no matter what.

Many other creative writing teachers apparently tolerate this same drawback, since they also appear to grade less on quality of writing than on various kinds of effort. In my survey, 'Attendance and participation in class discussion/workshopping' was rated highly important or important for determining a final grade by 83% of faculty. 'Consistency, persistence and care in reading, generating ideas, and revising, and completing a certain quantity of work' was rated highly important or important by 85%. These came in ahead of 'Your evaluation of the quality of a portfolio of finished writing submitted at the end of the course', which was rated highly important or important by 76%.

If the course is graded, indicate the importance of each of the following for determining a student's final grade (highly important = 5; not important = 1):	5	4	3	2	1
Attendance and participation in class discussion/workshopping	92, 58%	38, 24%	18, 11%	3, 2%	0, 0.00%
Consistency, persistence and care in reading, generating ideas and revising, and completing a certain quantity of work.	107, 67%	27, 17%	14, 9%	1, 1%	1, 1%

Writing about the process of generating ideas, getting response, revising	17, 11%	23, 14%	33, 21%	32, 20%	44, 28%
Journal responses to assigned reading	11, 7%	28, 18%	31, 20%	26, 17%	54, 34%
Formal critical or descriptive writing on literary works	6, 4%	25, 16%	26, 16%	31, 20%	60, 38%
Students' self-evaluation of their finished writing	20, 13%	25, 16%	29, 18%	29, 18%	48, 30%
Students self-evaluation of their engagement, progress and learning over the span of the course	21, 13%	25, 16%	25, 16%	26, 16%	52, 33%
Your evaluation of the quality of individual works completed as the course goes along	51, 32%	32, 20%	31, 20%	16, 10%	21, 13%
Your evaluation of the quality of a portfolio of finished writing submitted at the end of the course	87, 55%	33, 21%	10, 6%	7, 4%	15, 10%

I doubt that Roberson's remark that some administrator may 'give me grief' about his system indicates a serious worry. Most administrators expect a syllabus to include a clear and specific account of the means by which the final grade is determined, but they rarely ask what the resulting grade actually means and to whom. However, once you've turned in grades, just try to get the registrar's office to change a B+ to an A−. You'll have to give reasons and sign documents. The registrar plans to put that grade into a transcript and impress it with the official seal of the institution, certifying that grades are *important*. Then why so little concern about what a grade *says*? Is this just a lapse, or does the confusion conveniently hide contradictions that we would rather not confront or serve purposes we aren't supposed to scrutinize? As teachers, we ought to live that question.

Putting Grading in its Place

For working through the confusion about the purpose of grading and arriving at greater agreement about the kinds of performances that should go into a grade, I like Brian Huot's (2002: 168) observation that we are *accountable* to our institutions to report grades that accurately and usefully describe students' performances in a course; but at the same time we are also *responsible* to our students to establish conditions that enable real learning. The tension between these two goals is acknowledged. I think that when creative writing teachers say they can't grade writing, they usually mean what Jack Ridl frankly admitted − that he couldn't figure out a way to grade *writers* while preserving the close relationships needed for real learning. So I appreciate his honesty – and I agree that being responsible to our students matters more than being accountable to our institutions.

But I would prefer to give each its due.

First, giving all As is not an option for most of us because administrators and committees reviewing for tenure or promotion are unlikely to be impressed by a teacher who flouts a commonplace of education, namely, that the work students do ought to be able to be evaluated.

Giving all As has consequences for our departments too. Barbara Bogue (2004b) told me that, at her university, the creative writing program has been warned about grade inflation. 'If all students receive A's, we're scrutinized about whether this is a discipline.' Not only at her university. And programs that lack credibility lose funding when budgets tighten.

One apparent solution would be to make our courses pass/fail (presumably an exception built into the system for courses where grading conflicts with learning). But either that exception is rarely granted or else few creative writing teachers have sought it. Of those responding to my survey, nearly 94% said that their introductory creative writing course was graded. Scott Geisel (2004), one of the few respondents whose course is pass/fail, wrote that this gives students 'the freedom to perform something new that they're really afraid of not doing well'. But he is also aware that the stigma of 'low standards' attaches to pass/fail courses, which may be why few teachers go that route. In addition, a few students intent on doing just enough to earn their 'pass' can dampen aspirations others have to write something amazing.

Grades mean what their audience takes them to mean

For most of us, a better way to be both responsible and accountable is to put grading in its place – and make that a small place. I like how William Stafford (1986: 75) says it:

> The teaching part I would keep as far as possible from reminding them they are in this area where there are minefields to cross in which they might ruin their grade. So as much as possible I would postpone, dilute, avoid, play down the idea of evaluation. They would, I suppose, always know that sooner or later I'd have to grade them. But that's not part of our daily life; that's not part of the learning.

To 'dilute' and to 'play down' evaluation, we could begin by asking who is the primary audience for grades. I'd say that it's those who might request from us a letter recommending a student for a job or for advanced study. I think we feel accountable to that audience. A society that aspires to choose candidates based on merit rather than on class, nepotism or some other favoritism needs to have fair and reliable ways of determining who is most deserving. Tests cannot do the job. Samples of work have value but also limitations. Only teachers who have observed a student's performance over time and in different situations can speak with authority about the character, desire, habits and talents that were demonstrated. The grade sums that up, indicating how strongly we would recommend that the student be invited to do more of the kind of work that was done in the course.

One implication is that a teacher's informed judgments become a legitimate component. I agree that a grade should emphasize what was actually demonstrated in the course, while in a written recommendation we are more free to speculate about a student's potential. Nevertheless, we need to stop disparaging judgments that are, in part, subjective. Consider the extent to which letters of recommendation call for subjective judgments. The most important decisions humans make involve subjective judgments, and part of the point of an education in the arts and humanities is to become better at making them.

A second implication is that a grade for a writing course should significantly reflect a student's demonstrated talent as a writer. That's the main thing members of admission committees look for in applicants' portfolios. Consider this statement from Indiana University (2011):

> Committee members read the applications carefully, with a decided emphasis on the manuscript portion. We look for talent that genuinely excites us and that we feel we can work with and develop. The manuscript portion of the application is, by far, the most important part of the application and the main criterion on which decisions of acceptance are based.

If such an admissions committee also looks at an applicant's grades in creative writing, it is reasonable to assume that they will read those as in part the *teacher's* judgment of the student's talent.

A fringe benefit of defining grades as meaning what their primary audiences take them to mean is getting past tiresome arguments about grade inflation. A graduate admissions committee would read a B in a creative writing course as indication that the student was faithful and did work that was good – but not good enough to persuade the teacher that the student ought to study it at an advanced level. Only the A indicates a high level of talent along with the desire and discipline to develop that talent. Thus I question one online syllabus that defines a B as 'Very Good; better than what can be expected from the majority of students in a beginning writing class.' This is saying that most students in that class will receive a C or lower – a prospect likely to panic many of the students, even those taking the course for general studies credit. I doubt that the statement is even true; it sounds like one of those things teachers say to sound 'rigorous' – or to make students feel better about the grade they actually get.

If the A and the B are defined by strength of recommendation for further study or for work as a writer, I would say that the grade of C is defined by a different audience – the institution. A 2.0 is typically the minimum GPA for graduation, which means that a C as a final grade indicates that the student performed just well enough to be considered on-track for a degree. The reputation of the institution depends upon the capabilities demonstrated by its graduates and since we do have a stake in maintaining that reputation, we should assign grades below C to students whose performance does not merit a degree.

Grade levels are often named with comparative terms such as 'superior' and 'average' but these are meaningless without reference to a comparison *group*. For example, we hear the mantra, 'C is average', but that cannot mean 'average among college students' because at the undergraduate level, a 2.0 is typically the *minimum* GPA for receiving a diploma. If C really were average, half the students would be denied a diploma.

An important benefit of defining grades as meaning what their primary audiences take them to mean is that the grade is no longer a vague – and thus powerful – symbol of human worth. Instead, grades help answer a question students ask: Am I good at this? One reason some of them take a course, especially in the arts, is to discover the nature and extent of their talents. That's something they expect that a good teacher can tell them, in words but also with a grade that indicates relative standing among those who take the course. They deserve a credible judgment, since they make important choices based on what they believe to be their most significant talents. I tell students that I don't want to hear back from them in two or three years that my estimate of their strengths and weaknesses – in words or in a grade – led them to a bad decision, either to take up a pursuit that defeated them or to forgo a challenge they were capable of meeting.

Students understand that telling useful truth about their potential is only hindered by games teachers play with grades. So I will not 'award points' or talk of 'earning' anything, especially 'extra credit'. With Stafford, I prefer to play grades down, not talk them up.

Delaying the grading of writing

We're more familiar with the other way Stafford would limit grading – postponing it. Teachers who pursue this way of thinking avoid grading works-in-progress (where quality is hardest to judge) and instead collect for grading at the end of the course – and sometimes at midterm – a portfolio of the best pieces written and revised during the course. Over 75% of teachers responding to my survey said that a portfolio makes a significant contribution to their students' final grade.

However, many of these teachers apparently also give grades as they go along. On my survey, the importance for the final grade of 'Your evaluation of the quality of individual works completed as the course goes along' ran the gamut, but with more teachers placing it on the 'important' than on the 'not important' side of the scale. This surprises me, but I can also understand how they might have been persuaded to follow this practice. For one thing, students get regular grades in most other courses. For another, some students have become hooked on knowing 'how they are doing' by course-delivery systems that frequently update course grades. Promoters like to call this 'monitoring progress', but at least for the learning of an artistic practice, 'progress' is not easily monitored. Real growth may, for a time, take the form of one failed attempt after another. A colleague who teaches acting, Karen Barker (2004), put it memorably: 'Anyone who wants to learn to act has to be prepared to suck for a long time.' Some writers do strong work right from the start, but others, equally talented, may struggle for some time before they break through, after which nearly everything about their writing becomes dramatically better. These happy surprises are likely to be prevented by regular grading because it limits the risks that enable learning.

What makes more sense for our courses is structuring them in two distinct movements – a long one focused on learning, then a short one for finishing and evaluating the best products of that learning. Teachers who are required to turn in midterm grades might work through this sequence twice, although some just turn in the same grade for everyone at midterm. One respondent wrote that he and his students 'agree that in a poetry writing workshop, grades are essentially beside the point, and midterm grades meaningless'. So he turns in a B for everyone, feeling that his students agree 'that a B is encouraging, but not wildly so'. My own choice is to collect a midterm portfolio and return grades with extensive comments aimed at helping writers think about what they've accomplished and what remains to be accomplished. I assure them that I feel no compunction to 'average' these grades into the final grade. If a writer, especially in an introductory course, makes a late breakthrough that leads to a strong final portfolio (as frequently happens), then an uneven midterm portfolio no longer says anything meaningful about the writer's talent or potential.

Giving tentative grades at midterm also has other advantages: first, some students who worry unnecessarily about grades (thousands of dollars in scholarships may be at stake) can relax and go on to do their best writing once fear of a low grade is set aside. Second, 'final portfolio' sounds like less of a threat after they've done one. Third, a few students need a reminder that the course is half gone and they have accomplished little (imaginative people can excel at delay and denial). Others may need to hear that a direction they've taken looks unproductive (talented writers are sometimes drawn toward kinds of fiction that only devotees read, or toward poetry that is too sentimental – or inaccessible). In addition, I find that my students become better evaluators of their own and others' work during the rest of the course after they have examined criteria for judgment, applied them to their own work in self-critique and considered my own evaluation of their work.

But in spite of what I've just said, if I were teaching in a school that did not require midterm grades, I would not collect and grade a midterm portfolio, because students need a longer period of learning before evaluation begins. If a few individual students appeared in danger of ending the course with a disappointingly low grade, I'd let them know earlier while they still had time for remedy.

If I am required to grade at midterm, during the second half, I grade any analytical or descriptive papers assigned but continue to avoid putting grades on artistic works-in-progress.

I invite students to include pieces from the midterm portfolio in their final portfolio, but they are also free to make the final one entirely new. Typically three-quarters of the work in final portfolios is new or extensively revised.

Evaluating Artistic Writing

The difficulty of evaluating writing in the artistic genres increases when we know the writer and know how much the writing means to the writer – and when the writing is highly personal. Yet in all but extreme cases, evaluation is possible. Lad Tobin (2004: 108) says that the claim that personal writing *cannot* be graded 'makes little logical sense' – that just as we can establish criteria to evaluate other kinds of writing, we can construct criteria for evaluating the more personal genres, and if we are worried that students might misunderstand our criteria, 'then we need to work harder to make those criteria clear'. Such clarity is often lacking, according to Katharine Haake (1994: 88), because we treat criteria as 'obvious' or 'natural' and judge students' success or failure 'by how "good" their work is, without adequately defining what's "good"'. To give an example, I've seen an A defined in a syllabus as 'a maturity of ideas and craft'. An expert reader may be able to recognize 'maturity', but a student told that his writing lacks it will feel belittled more than enlightened.

Evaluating for qualities rather than quality

What many creative writing teachers have settled upon is to avoid judging the quality of any individual piece of writing and instead to look for the *qualities of good writing in the genre* demonstrated in a portfolio of writing.

Writers and critics mostly agree on these qualities. Paul Willis (2004) observed that 'most student poems fail for basic, objective reasons. The most common kind of failure is to neglect the particular, evocative image for empty, emotive generalization'. Steve Coyne (2002/2008), who makes evaluation of a writer's work a significant part of the grade, listed positive qualities that students as well as teachers can recognize in good writing:

> Effective imaginative writing emphasizes specifics. It tends to show rather than tell. It strives for a strong and original voice. It avoids clichés. It values striking and appropriate metaphor. It is organized around poignant conflict. It develops characters who are convincing and interesting. It is cast in effective sentences. In the case of poetry, it reveals a control of sound devices other than just rhyme.

Writers who learn how their writing measures up against criteria like those know something about what they've accomplished and what they still need to learn.

Even the more subjective criteria can be explained. Although Catherine Wiley (2005) questions grading 'creativity', her syllabus does mention as criteria 'originality and boldness'. She said she explains to students, 'I would rather have you "fail" while attempting something really difficult (like a sestina) than get too comfortable repeating something you already do well.' Then she further defines originality as 'a lack of cliché, a lack of predictability, and a real attempt at fresh language'.

Many teachers grade primarily on aspects of craft that the course has emphasized. One online syllabus made clear that no one needed to write a terrific *play* to get an A:

> Your in-class writing and final plays will not be judged as 'good' or 'bad' or whether they make great theatre. Instead they will be assessed on how well you demonstrate your knowledge of and ability to execute the skills learned in class through your writing. If I can see that you understand how a character is created and developed, how conflict is used to propel a plot, and how action is used onstage, it doesn't matter whether your play is 'liked'.

This emphasis also gives students breathing space in courses where the time devoted to a given genre is too short to finish a significant piece.

Avoiding bias

Emphasizing qualities over quality does have some limits. In drawing attention to craft, we may slight other ways of valuing literary art. Natasha Sajé (2004a: 25), in 'The politics of literary evaluation', provides a 'framework' for acts of literary evaluation that is drawn from the four theories of art described by M.H. Abrams: the mimetic theory, which presumes that art should 'show us the world'; the pragmatic theory, which 'presumes that art has a social purpose'; the expressive theory, which 'posits that art transports us to a better or higher realm'; and the objective theory, which 'focuses on *the work itself*, judging it on the basis of unity, probability, progression, balance, contrast, coherence, and selection'. Because the mimetic and objective theories address much of what is most teachable, we have good reason to emphasize them in evaluation, but we might also draw criteria from the others. Including originality reflects the expressive theory. And is evaluation complete without *some* attention to social purpose? One reason pieces win awards is that they matter, give readers something that changes their seeing, thinking, feeling. From the experience of writing an MA in creative writing to meet assessment expectations in the UK, Amanda Boulter (2004) reached similar conclusions – not only that 'the magic lies in clear criteria' (p. 134) but also that the criteria need to consider not just the goodness of the work itself but also who or what the work is good *for* (p. 136).

It's also worth reminding ourselves that focusing on craft does not guarantee that our evaluation will be free from bias. Bizzaro (1993: 54), in his study of his own prior responses to his students' writing, noticed that in his desire to be 'objective and fair in commenting on my students' poems', he had carefully defined good writing, but then he found that 'in the process of clarifying what would eventually be rewarded in their poems, I seem to have required my students to write one kind of poem – the kind I write – in spite of the fact that I could see a much wider range of texts called poems in recently published magazines than I was willing to permit my students to write'.

Biases related to gender can be difficult to recognize. Bizzaro, citing Linda Peterson's conclusion that women tend to choose relational subjects while men more often focus on the self alone or the self as distinct from others, draws three implications:

> First, teachers should not 'unwittingly privilege one mode of self-understanding over another' in the assignments they devise. Second, 'the readings suggested as models for the assignment should include examples by and about both masculine and feminine subjects'. And third, 'evaluation of personal essays should not privilege certain gender-specific modes of self-representation, nor penalize others'. (p. 137)

A valuable exercise for reducing bias is for two or several colleagues to collectively evaluate several pieces of student writing in a given genre and then explain their judgments. In my experience, teachers are surprised at how differently two teachers can estimate the same piece, even when they believe they hold similar literary values. Even when they agree on the level of quality, their reasons may differ. The committee that selects submissions for our literary magazine has two or three faculty and five to seven students. We typically find broad agreement on which pieces are the strongest and which are the weakest, but in the middle of the range, ratings can run the gamut, so we talk about why we judged them as we did. The student members are surprised at how much teachers can disagree in their judgments. I take away reasons to look again at kinds of writing I have tended to dismiss as well as reasons to question kinds of writing I have admired.

If increasing the number of readers reduces bias, then another reason to value writers' memos is that they give us the writer's perspective on the work – and perhaps that of other responders – which we can then place beside our own.

Explaining criteria and simplifying grade levels

Percentage grading can work for objective tests, but I can't imagine what a number like '92' might mean as an evaluation of a portfolio. And can anybody tell the difference between a 92% portfolio and a 90% one? I am persuaded by Peter Elbow (1993) that we should reduce discrimination to a *minimum* number of levels. Then the process of judgment is simplified and the difference between levels is clear to students. I use a set of numbers already familiar to my students, the four-point scale in which A = 4, B = 3, and so on. For a portfolio or paper, I describe from four to six criteria, assigning to each a 4, 3, 2, or 0 (I don't bother with 1 – why distinguish levels of no-pass?). Typically the criteria are of about equal importance, so to come up with a midterm grade estimate, all I have to do is scan a row of numbers.

For work not turned in, I record a minus 4 (comparable to a zero on a percentage scale).

Some teachers seek to add definition by working their criteria into a rubric which describes each of the levels. Here, for instance, is Matt Guenette's (2007) rubric from his syllabus for 'Writing Fiction and Poetry':

	3	2	1
Voice	Original, Credible perspective	Fairly credible perspective	Lacks an original, credible perspective
Development	Clear progress of thought; Strong characterization and use of language; Thoughtful resolution	Usually clear progress of thought; Fair characterization and use of language; Fair resolution	Lacks progression of thought; Lacks a strong use of language; Weak resolution
Mechanics Conventions	Correct and appropriate	Usually correct and appropriate	Lack of correct and appropriate choices

A lawyer or assessment officer might approve such attempts to define each level of performance for each criterion (and Guenette's rubric is less complex than most), but for me the redundancy impedes readability.

A way to simplify is to define each criterion at either an A level or a B level, and let students infer the remaining levels. Probably the logical choice is the B level, since competence is easier to define than excellence. Nevertheless, I've preferred to define the A level because mere competence is not something to *aim* for. Below are criteria I have used for the midterm portfolio for Reading and Writing Poetry. A lecture I play for students by Seamus Heaney (1996) is the source of 'groundedness' and 'skyedness' – terms more poetic than 'concreteness' and 'meaning':

- **Groundedness.** Reading the poems offers experience – stuff real enough to taste, touch, smell, hear, see. Word sounds and rhythms help put us in touch with the real.
- **Skyedness.** That real stuff, rubbed together, strikes sparks (or stirs ripples) – meaning, feeling, transcendence, or some combination.
- **Situation and Form.** We can construct a consistent speaker and situation and a believable motivation for utterance – perhaps even an addressee; tone works; poetic form is handled well (intelligent lineation, consistent within a poem); parts work together and come together to form an aesthetic whole.
- **Style.** Language is fresh, alive, inviting attentiveness, giving pleasure through sounds. Poem sentences are structured and punctuated so that they are readable. Figures of speech escape cliché and work with each other.
- **Value/substance.** In at least some of the poems, we encounter deep respect for truth, firm convictions, productive ideas, provocative insights, compelling ways of seeing, an attitude that dances well.

I realize that some of these criteria, especially 'situation and form', encompass several aspects of writing. If a grade reflects just one or two of those, I briefly explain. I also notice that although I primarily evaluate *qualities* of the poems rather than overall *quality*, I tend to define these qualities by the responses they evoke in their readers. And the last criterion moves beyond craft to consider social value.

Each criterion gets a grade (4, 3, 2 or 0), and I don't average these out because I want to focus students' attention on particular strengths and weaknesses, not give them a quick answer to the 'What did I get?' question.

Having students do self-critique prior to evaluation

Boulter (2004: 137) urges that in addition to judging the work itself, 'we must also make a judgment about the writer's own critical relationship to their work', his or her awareness of what they have made and how it works, as represented in 'an accompanying piece, a Critical Rationale, exegesis, essay etc.' One way we can do this is to ask for a writer's memo with a portfolio, discussing where the pieces came from, how they arrived and how satisfied the writer is with the current version.

But to really get at their 'awareness of what they have made', they should do some critique. I ask writers to follow this guideline with one of their portfolio pieces: using criteria from the text, argue that one of the pieces is terrible and then argue that it's terrific. This idea comes from Yancey (1998: 32), who describes her intent this way:

> First, I wanted students to think about their text quite explicitly from diverse perspectives. Second, I wanted to begin to de-mystify how I go about reading and evaluating a text; I wanted to bring some awareness of my reading process into their thinking, again in some explicit way. I was convinced that *if asked*, students could in fact perform a teacher-like reading themselves; and that performing such a reading and putting it in dialogue with their own thinking about their text would be a good means of seeing *possibility* within that text.

A related move she also suggests is to ask students to predict the teacher's take on the piece and agree or disagree with that. This could suit a final portfolio, especially if students are also invited to argue with what they think the teacher's take will be. Either move lets us see how students understand and apply to their own writing the criteria articulated in the course.

I explained earlier that the writer's memo needs to have a personal voice, an authentic voice. Thus, as long as such arguments are just brief moves to aid reflection, I find that they work within the memo, but if I plan to *evaluate* this argument for how effectively it applies appropriate criteria, then I ask students to do it as a separate piece of writing. Here is most of Kayli's:

> The success of the story 'Broken' depends upon the effectiveness of its symbols and motifs ... The work does not function well when the references to communion are too prevalent or forced. As Burroway notes, 'A symbolic object, situation, or event may err because it seems to have been imposed upon the story, existing for its own sake rather than emanating naturally from the characters' lives' (336). The end of the story has symbols that may be too strong and obvious – what Burroway might refer to as 'heavy handed' writing. A casserole filled with communion wafers seems a bit dramatic. However, Jamie's bringing her Bible for Dell to read at the end of the story to perform a pseudo-communion is downright melodramatic. It almost makes the whole work read like a junior high Sunday school lesson.
>
> 'Broken' is, however, unquestionably successful at integrating odd characters and symbols. The story is artistic in the sense Burroway

refers to when she states, 'Pleasure in the artistry comes precisely when the illusion rings true without destroying the knowledge that it is an illusion' (325). Dell is a very developed character and just odd enough to be the type of person who would eat communion wafers for fun; furthermore, her odd lifestyle of writing recipes and memorizing Shakespeare fits the lighter mood at the beginning of the story. Most importantly, the motif of food and sacred eating is woven subtly and effectively throughout the story.

Kayli demonstrates that she has learned to use perspectives from the course to think about how and how well her story works. As Yancey says, doing this kind self-critique demystifies evaluation. It also prepares the writer to hear what others have to say about the work.

Evaluating Effort and Process

If, as one graduate school puts it, letters of recommendation should attest to the applicant's 'ability to persevere and to do well in the writing program', then a final grade should also reflect what we often sum up as 'effort': whether students do assignments, meet commitments, show up for class and engage in its discourse.

Evaluating class participation

Catherine Wiley (2005) makes 'citizenship' a third of the final grade, noting parenthetically that it 'includes attendance, attentiveness, participation, workshops ... all the fuzzy stuff that makes a class work'. Some teachers add an option attractive to introverts – contributing in writing to a class listserv.

Especially where participation is a significant part of the grade, teachers ought to explain how the grade is derived. Elizabeth Swingrover's (2004a) 'Introduction to Creative Writing' syllabus includes this rubric:

> A range: The student is fully engaged and highly motivated. This student is well prepared, having read the texts and completed craft assignments, and has thought carefully about the texts' relation to their writing and the writing of others. This student's ideas and questions are productive (either constructive or critical); they stimulate class discussions. This student listens and responds to the contributions of other students in workshop.
>
> B range: The student attends class regularly, is well prepared for discussion, and participates consistently. This student contributes

productively to the discussion and workshops by sharing thoughts and questions that demonstrate familiarity with the material. This student refers to the materials and shows interest in other students' contributions.

C range: The student meets the basic requirements of participation: preparedness and regular attendance. This student participates rarely in class discussion/workshop. This student may offer a few interesting or insightful ideas from time to time, but these ideas do not connect well to the general discussion: they do not help to build a coherent and productive discussion.

A simpler approach would be to describe the A and C level and let students infer the B level – or even describe only the B level.

I ask students to evaluate their own class participation, partly because I want them to observe how their own contributions connect with and relate to those of others, including their contributions to their writers' groups, which I do not directly observe. I generally ask them to suggest a grade too, since this is one place where they can compare their performance to that of others. Since I'm required to turn in midterm grades, I also have students evaluate their class participation at that time, when they still have time to change; then at the end of the course, I simply ask them to compare:

- Compared to first half, did your role in class change? Was your involvement in class discussions less, greater, or about the same?
- Compared to first half, did your role in your writers' group change? Did the nature or extent of your participation there change?

Here is what April wrote at the end of the course:

I don't know if it was an obvious change, but I know that I made a more conscious effort to be even more involved in the class discussion. I probably ended up participating at about the same level, but I felt more engaged and felt as though my comments were more clear and meaningful when I did have something to say.

As far as groups are concerned, I feel that I had much more constructive things to say during this half of the semester. I used the terminology that I learned more often when writing or verbalizing a response to someone's poetry. I think that overall, my response during group meetings was much more useful to the person that I was responding to during the second half of the semester.

She is able to describe changes in her own contribution in relation to benefits to others – an awareness that will also serve her well, not only as a writer but as a person able to reflect upon her *presence* within any kind of group.

Self-evaluation of process through reflective writing

The likelihood that students will persevere and do well beyond the course also depends upon whether they have developed a good writing process: can read the ways writers read, have some grasp of the subject matter that is theirs to write about, know something about conditions they require to do their best writing, and are able to get good response and do revision. The reflective writing that helps them gain awareness of their process also enables a teacher to evaluate their process. I don't grade memos turned in with works-in-progress, but I do respond to them which helps students write better reflections. I also grade in a limited way the writer's memo that is turned in with the portfolio. One of several grades is usually for 'process', and that includes 'Writer's memo is thoughtful and focused'. I don't like to evaluate writers' memos more closely than that because reflective writing needs an expressive voice, which can be stifled by writing to *impress*.

The other kind of reflection that makes it possible to evaluate process and effort is a *constructive reflection*, which I have preferred to call a journey journal. It's a story about what the writer has learned and how the writer has changed by means of the course. I do grade this story, using criteria such as these:

- Language and style show respect for words, sounds, meanings – and the self of the writer. Voice is believable.
- The journal includes enough particulars of the course and productive actions of the writer to indicate faithfulness, attentiveness.
- The journal makes believable connections among particulars and between the self and the experiences of the course, and it uses the connecting to get somewhere.

I include the first criterion mainly because the aesthetic quality of a story of becoming is a reliable indicator of how much the story means to the writer. The best journals are artfully formed: they may have a memorable title, some have a unifying metaphor, well-crafted language and palpable *desire*. According to Morson and Emerson (1990: 72) Bakhtin would say that what I've called the guide self is responsible for content, but the ideal self (he sometimes said *hero* self) is responsible for attention to form.

Thus, this criterion gets at whether the writing self, the ideal self and the guide self are working together.

The other two criteria are more obvious and objective ways to evaluate a story of learning. The second one says that I expect these stories to include convincing detail from the readings and conversations of the course. As Yancey (1998: 63) says, 'To be meaningful, reflection must be *situated*: the writer creates meaning in context, in community.' Another way I've explained the third criterion is that 'the best journey journals usually begin by defining the writer's main focus or desire in the course and then go on to explain how the writer has accomplished this desire'.

Evaluating learning by the quality of the story the student tells about it certainly is subjective – but no more so than evaluating a personal statement in a grad school application. (And a student who has written a good constructive reflection is better prepared to write a personal statement because she knows better the writer she is and might become.)

Only a minority of creative writing teachers make significant use of students' accounts of their learning as part of evaluation. In my survey, 'students' self-evaluation of their finished writing', and 'students' self-evaluation of their engagement, progress and learning over the span of the course' were considered not important or only slightly important contributors to the final grade by about half the respondents. At the other extreme roughly a quarter rated these as highly important or important contributors. This suggests that once teachers discover that students can write with authority about their own learning, teachers draw upon that authority to evaluate a student's performance and potential.

A further account of constructive reflection concludes the next and final chapter.

Chapter 9
Constructing the Practice and Identity of 'Writer'

> *What is forgotten in our universal condemnation of hypocrisy is that a kind of play-acting with characters, or characteristics, a kind of faking of characters, is one of the main ways that we build what becomes our character.*
> Wayne Booth (1988: 252)

> *We live only by fictions, which are our projects, hopes, memories, regrets, etc., and we are no more than a perpetual invention ... Our hopes, our grudges, all this is a direct, instantaneous product of the conflict between what is and what is not.*
> Paul Valery (1958: 226–7)

Students in creative writing do more than learn the craft of writing; many or most should also come to see themselves as writers – not necessarily as people who write for a living but as those who use artistic genres as ways of seeing, thinking and feeling and as forms of action in their lives and within their relationships.

The main way they construct the identity of writer is by taking responsibility for questioning their work, seeking response and revising, and then by producing finished work that gives them and others pleasure and meaning. Other ways they come to feel like a writer by acting like a writer are explored in this chapter: habits and disciplines of observation and journaling; invention activities such as learning to see, remember and gather information as writers do; identification with and imitation of practicing writers; and constructive reflection – telling the story of what they made of themselves during the course.

The Habit of Art

Flannery O'Connor (1969: 101) writes that the teaching of writing 'is largely a matter of helping the student develop the habit of art'. She sees this habit as 'more than just a discipline, although it is that; I think it is a way of looking at the created world and of using the senses so as to make them find as much meaning as possible in things'. Some teachers allow this discipline and way of looking to develop through the practice of writing, others try more directly to teach them.

Developing 'the habit of art' even benefits students who will never attempt to publish. A former student, now a pastor, told me that Reading and Writing Poetry was the college course he now finds most valuable for carrying on the tasks of ministry. His explanation had nothing to do with sprinkling sermons with poetry or even with improving their rhythm or imagery. It had to do with paying the kind of attention that lets him find moments, images and other story material in the everyday lives of members of his community, enabling him to show them to themselves in telling ways. Particularly since our introductory courses often include students who are meeting general studies requirements, we should view 'becoming a writer' and developing 'the habit of art' in this broader sense.

The journal

Ambitious students in creative writing often equate 'being a writer' with having that mysterious something that confers star quality. David Malone (2005) said that in his experience dedication and persistence matter more. He reminds students:

> The people I know from my creative writing classes who are publishing today weren't the stars of the workshop – they were committed to writing and dedicated to becoming better writers, and they kept writing no matter what anybody said about their work. I can contribute a little, but ultimately you're the one who's going to make yourself into the writer you want to be.

One form this dedication takes in working writers is journal keeping, so it's not surprising that this practice is urged or assigned in many of our courses. When I visited her fiction class at Knox College, Gina Franco, was explaining the journal assignment. Whether students kept a private journal or a public blog (an option she had just decided to add), she stressed that they needed to make *daily* entries. 'You have to stay tuned-in to the idea, "I am a *writer*"'.

Because writers can never predict events worth recording or know when an idea will arise, teachers often stress portability. Mary Biddinger's (2004a) syllabus for 'Introduction to Writing Poetry' strongly recommends an 'itsy bitsy notebook to take with you wherever you go. Excellent for recording ideas when you're on the run!' Michael VanderWeele (2004) said that one rule for his class was that 'I could not see them without having their journal on them'. He followed the rule himself, explaining that he had read that 'about half the task of becoming a writer was imagining yourself as one. That's about setting work habits'.

John Wylam (2004) thinks of journals less as a discipline than as a site of pleasure. The point he makes to students 'is simply that when we talk about "the work of imagination", we don't mean *just* imagination; we also mean work, but a joyful, necessary variety of work'. He said that much of the poetry he sees in magazines 'doesn't strike me as having been a terribly joyful experience for the writer. Maybe the acceptance notice was, but not the poem itself'. He wants his students 'to have more than that, and more importantly, to *write* better than that. So the journal can also be a space of play that keeps alive the work of writing, a place for the writer within to indulge in the pleasures of words and sounds and images and storying without worrying yet about judgment and even without much thought – for now at least – of planning and revision'. Wylam, a journal-keeper 'for decades', keeps two different journals 'as a way of separating my own work as subject from, say, school, personal things, etc. A work journal and a personal journal, if you like'.

Since journals serve multiple purposes and take different forms, teachers might offer guidelines. A survey respondent wrote that she wants 'an artist's journal, not a diary', a journal 'that records their reading and writing and thinking about reading and writing'. Alyssa O'Brien's (2000) online syllabus for 'Introduction to Creative Writing: Fiction' notes that the writer's journal 'is a place where you jot down ideas for stories, make character sketches, record overheard dialogue, and list insights on form and craft that you gain from reading the work of others (both published work and that of your colleagues)'. Don Bogen (1981: 7–8) observes that the writer's notebook 'can be largely fragmented and freeform, geared toward exploration of the unconscious, like those of Roethke, or it can be more systematic, with daily entries involving a particular scene or idea, like those of William Stafford'. So he suggests that each approach 'could be imitated for a few weeks and the results compared'.

Students should also be told whether their journal will be private. If a main goal is to have a space for the personal, perhaps the teacher should not read it, but then how can the teacher know whether it's working – or whether some students are doing it at all? Franco (2004) requires a daily journal, but what's in it is the business of the writer. 'I check them, but I don't read them.' When I observed, she explained to students, 'I don't want to keep you from writing something you otherwise would write'.

She told me another teacher she knew 'required that all journal work be considered public and he'd give them time to show their journal to another student', but when she tried this, it didn't work. 'My women students said they were keeping two journals, one public and one private, which seemed to be self-defeating.' Some teachers who collect journals invite students to block out or sticky-note pages that are private.

A related issue is medium. The traditional journal is handwritten – and there's something to be said for forming words with gestures of the body as well as being able to add a drawing. The ubiquity of laptops makes a typed journal feasible. Many writers now keep something like a journal in the more public form of a blog, sometimes incorporating sketches and photos. Then the writer may also gather a limited audience that reads and responds.

Reading our places and remembering our lives

The journal is flexible enough to accommodate activities or exercises to help students recall past experiences and dreams or to pay attention to the world around them. Michelene Wandor (2008: 153) appears to believe that 'writing-as-therapy' is widespread in creative writing. She refers to 'the stress on memory, difficult emotional experiences, dreams, personal relationships' and insists that such things are for '[the students] to know and think about, not for teachers to coerce into public display'. I cannot say whether she is right about teachers in the UK, but my survey of mostly US teachers indicates little basis for her charge. Few of them indicated in my survey that they ask students 'to journal about highly personal, troubling, or traumatic experiences' – 73% gave such writing little or no emphasis. And if they do invite such writing, few if any would require 'public display'. However, some teachers do assign both observation and memory activities as means of invention.

Indicate the emphasis you give each of the following practices in your teaching of an introductory-level creative writing course (much emphasis = 5; some emphasis = 3; not used = 1):	5	4	3	2	1
Exercises to make students more attentive observers of the world around them, including language use	67, 42%	41, 26%	30, 19%	13, 8%	5, 3%
Exercises to help writers remember past experience for use in their main writing for the course	36, 23%	33, 21%	49, 31%	21, 13%	17, 11%

Exercises to help writers recall dreams or to use dreams, daydreaming or fantasies to find ideas for writing	8, 5%	12, 8%	34, 22%	49, 31%	53, 33%
Asking writers to journal about highly personal, troubling or traumatic experiences	5, 3%	12, 8%	21, 13%	37, 23%	79, 50%

Only 11% of responders said they give little or no emphasis in their course to 'exercises to make students more attentive observers of the world around them, including language use'. The rest give from some to much emphasis to such exercises. Chris Matthews (2005) described a 'studio exercise': 'I pass around intriguing objects and then set each in the center of the room and ask students to describe the object in as much detail as possible (as in an art class). No poems, nothing fancy; just observe and describe.' Phil Hey (2004) said he tells students, 'Go listen to people talk when you know they have nothing to gain by it'. As example, he mentions a conversation he overheard at a burger place between a couple of older guys: 'How's your dog?' 'Which one?' 'That yellow dog.' 'I haven't had that dog for 20 years!' Some teachers send students with their journals on a kind of scavenger hunt. My poetry students keep a 'bug journal' and their first assignment, early in the course, grounds the 'bug collection' metaphor:

> Go outside, snoop around for an hour, alone, with somebody else in the class, or with a nature lover, and find a real live bug. Spiders count, beetles, caterpillars, flocks of monarch butterflies now beginning to gather. Or go to Alton and see if the Great Blue Heron stalks the ponds or river. ('Bug' can include other wild animals, but not pets; pets give us what we want – like students taking tests – instead of saying what *they* have to say.) When you find your subject, describe appearance, actions, or both in rich detail that also suggests your attitude toward it. You might even play with making the structure or sound of the sentence somehow mimic or amplify the description.

I want them to see more and to see more carefully and thoughtfully, but I also want them to use the resources of language, including sounds, so that they begin to grasp the potential of poetry to name experience. I usually have students look or listen for language or image that illustrates current reading in the text so that they connect observation and reading.

Jill Baumgaertner (2004) said that she occasionally sends students on journeys into the landscape. 'Sit in a place and write down things they see people carrying. Sit by the road or take a little walk around campus. Write down combinations of people and vehicles.' In my poetry course, I've had students find a natural place of their own in September and revisit it at least once or twice more as the season changes, writing each time about what they observe and having with them a collection of poems that present experiences from nature, such as Mary Oliver's. Looking closely can uncover the strange and the wonderful within the too-familiar.

John Wylam (2004) wrote that a teacher ought to 'know the place well enough to be able to introduce it to them'. Most of his students 'were born and raised here; they don't see the poetry in it':

> As an example, on OH route 127 in a place called Darke County (a place I've been writing about off and on for a couple of years), there's a gravesite – for Annie Oakley. I kid you not. If you're a poet, and you pass a place like that, either you instinctually know that's a poem in the same way a shark knows what dinner smells like, or you've got work to do. I'd tell workshop students, and they'd look at me as though I'd suddenly broken into colloquial Venusian. They'd presumed she was buried somewhere out West... The point is just to open them up to what's already at hand. In one early exercise I love to do, their assignment is a draft set somewhere within the confines of the town of Bowling Green, paying strict attention to the borders (by itself that can yield results – what's it like across the border, down the interstate a few miles or states away? That sort of thing). They don't want to do this; they say, 'I don't know this place, it's so small, there's nothing here but the Tractor Pull and it's over already –' Which, of course, is exactly the point. They *don't* know this place, which can be an advantage if they allow it to be. That permission proves to be something they find difficult to give themselves.

Having students write about the familiar in order to defamiliarize it, 'to open them up to what's already at hand' so they see it as *material*, can be especially valuable in an introductory course. I teach in a small town of the kind most of my students think they know so well that they can stop paying attention. So I have written a guided tour that includes paths they usually miss – the alleys – and gives them different suggestions for writing:

> Along the way, stop here and there to write down observations. Listen to sounds, too, especially to their rhythms. Try to describe those sounds or their combination in words whose rhythm imitates the rhythm of those sounds. You may want to just describe them in prose first, listening to your sentences for a rhythm you can run with.

I also invite them to take different perspectives for analyzing what they observe:

> Think back about where you saw an interesting back yard while walking through the alley. Find your way back and then loop around to the front side of the property and compare the two. My hypothesis: people design front yards to make an impression, but their back yard reflects who they are for themselves. Think *stage*, then *backstage*. If you make any interesting discoveries, try writing about them, in a short witty verse form – perhaps ballad stanza, couplet or limerick.

The experience includes connecting the rhythms of writing to the rhythms of the body:

> On your return trip, taking whatever route you wish, try composing as you walk, not writing it down but composing and memorizing, reciting the words to the rhythm of footfall. When you get a good chunk of poem in your head, you can stop to put it on paper.

College students – mine at least – enjoy the novelty of being assigned to go out and do something other than the usual reading and writing, and they enjoy telling each other what they found or learned. And a writer's memo for the final portfolio frequently reports that a piece got its start on the alley walk or another observation activity.

Lee Ann Mortensen's (2004) syllabus for 'Creative Process and Imaginative Writing' suggests that if creativity can be learned it is learned through experiment, and one experiment is 'to *listen* – really listen – to the ideas, conversations, language, images, people, and situations that really call to me. What do you hear right now? What are your real obsessions? What are your fetishes in the world of language and being? If you think of something, write it down!' Once students have recorded a number of observations and ideas, they can read back through their journals to get a better idea of their fascinations and obsessions. That is, they are closer to identifying their subjects. Ann Frank Wake (2004) said, 'When we get to the middle of the term, I ask, What are your subjects? I tell them I've only written five poems that didn't have cornfields in them somewhere.'

Although much of what we write draws upon past experience, fewer teachers focus on helping writers actively remember – 24% gave this goal either little emphasis or none at all. Fewer yet include 'exercises to help writers recall dreams or to use dreams, daydreaming or fantasies to find ideas for writing', with 64% giving little or no emphasis to such activities or exercises. One who does is Connie Wachala (2000). Her 'Introduction to Creative Writing' syllabus says that during the first five weeks:

There will be an emphasis on journal writing and exploration of realistic and dream imagery and narrative movements in assigned readings, in-class reading, oral telling, in-class writing, and outside writing assignments. Readings that are heightened examples of the realistic and dream modes will be selected to be read in class. Students will write their dreams and journal entries with an emphasis on telling them as effectively and fully as possible.

My bug journal assignments often include bits of memory – or invitations to go from an observation to a memory that connects with it:

- **Overheard phrases.** From talk you hear between now and next class, write down words, phrases, even sentences, that are somehow *memorable*. Maybe it's the sound, maybe the freshness or oddness. Quote and then comment briefly on why you like the phrase or sentence: rhythm? sound pattern? euphony? cacophony? You may want to take a walk downtown or to a park or a garage sale to listen to older people talk.
- **Remembered phrases.** Dig back into your childhood to early memories of words and repeated phrases whose sounds somehow so appealed to you that they are still with you. Here's one example: when my father was angry and was telling someone, usually my mother, how wrong they were, he'd often follow a rhetorical question with 'Not by a jugful!' I puzzled over the phrase as a child, wondering what the jug could be full of.

The practice of solitude

Along with urging the daily practice of observing and writing, perhaps we should also teach busy and distracted college students to seek solitude. I've emphasized that we write for and among others, shaping our work through acts of reflection that also invite others' responses, but I acknowledge that we also write for ourselves and that our writing self needs the sanctity of solitude. We may be familiar with Rilke's (2000) advice to the young poet to 'Go within and scale the depths of your being from which your very life springs forth' (p. 12) and to descend 'into your inner self and into your secret place of solitude' (p. 13). Mary Oliver (1994: 116–7) is known for emphasizing solitude:

It is no use thinking, however, that the writing of poems – the actual writing – can accommodate itself to a social setting; even to the most sympathetic social setting of a workshop composed of loyal friends. It cannot. The work improves there and often the will to work gets valuable nourishment and ideas. But, for good reason, the poem requires of the writer not society or instruction, but a patch of profound and unbroken solitude.

This is the reason. The poem, as it starts to form in the writer's mind, and on paper, can't abide interruption. I don't mean that it *won't* but that it *can't*.

Student writers might be asked to locate their own writing sanctuary, free from interruption and distraction – including email, cell calls and texting – as well as times of day or night when they are at their best for writing.

They might also be asked to describe and perhaps discuss together the place or kind of place they find most suitable for writing.

Research practices

Most students assume that in a course called 'creative', they can forget about research. Bizzaro (2004: 294) argues that creative writing programs could go a long way toward equipping their students for the real work of writing by including 'the kind of research creative writers do'. He takes a broad view of research, highlighting 'skills that are equally useful in writing creatively and in reflecting upon what we do when we teach creative writing' (p. 301).

First, writers read differently from literary scholars – 'reading *as* writers and chiefly for technique'. Thus students might do 'author reports' that include what and how that author reads and how that reading has influenced the writing.

Second, writers must understand people and one means 'involves interviewing people about their experiences' (p. 301). He lists Robert Morgan and Tim Gautreaux as writers 'who speak to family members with the intention of finding subjects suited to their stories, listening to them closely to capture dialects appropriate to Appalachian and Cajun literatures' (p. 302). Introductory courses, especially in fiction and creative non-fiction, might teach such skills.

Third, students might investigate the *process* of learning to write:

> ... we believe in the writing process. We know that writing is a meaning-making activity and that, if we trust the process, it will lead us to the discovery of significance in much that we observe. And

as writers, we are better suited to reading, observing, and interrogating writing and writing instruction than most early composition theorists were to study composing methods and instruction, trained as they were as literary scholars. (pp. 302–3)

Such research also invites students to examine their own learning and thus to become more able to direct their own continued learning.

Fourth, writers know audiences. So it might be beneficial for students to find in the community people who are avid readers of the genre they are writing, perhaps even of the kind of work they want to do, and explore the variety of ways those readers actually respond to such work. We commonly invite practicing writers to class; what if we invited devoted readers and asked them who they read and how reading matters to them?

For a more personal research project, students might learn about the storytellers and poets in their family and write up, before they are lost, the stories from the family's oral tradition.

Identifying with and Imitating Writers and Writing

Recall that Rene Girard gives a central role in our becoming to imitation, arguing that people form even their desires by looking for those who seem to be what they might become and assuming that they could become like them if they could claim what that model possesses. We draw upon this tendency to identify with and imitate when we invite guest artists into our classrooms or ask students to find literary models to study and imitate.

Guest artists

Guest artists are usually generous, offering their work along with stories of their writing life and their reading practices and pleasures. Weeks later, students will cite the guest's words or say they've tried what he or she suggested.

One reason Joey Horstman (2005) brings in guest writers is to keep the course from being too much about his own ways of reading and writing. He also reads about 'writers talking about their own experiences' and passes along what he learns in order to help students imagine a writing life.

One male teacher said he brings in a poet around mid-course, preferring a female voice to balance his own. His guests usually also respond in conference to a few poems each of his students previously sent her, and he finds these conferences especially valuable. I've brought to campus the writer who has judged the entries for the campus literary magazine and arranged conferences with the best student writers. Usually they talk about the writing, but the best students have also learned about graduate programs the guest knows, and a few have kept in touch.

If bringing writers to class helps students identify with writers, so does getting students to attend readings. Some teachers make attending one or a few literary readings a part of course requirements. Elizabeth Swingrover (2004b) wrote that she encourages students to take the added step of buying books. She tells them:

> The best way to increase the 'market' for good literature is to buy it yourself, thus, effectively putting your money where your mouth is. 'How do I get my work published?' That's a fair question, but it should be rephrased to 'How much good literature have I actually bought (consumed) this year?' If I don't read and buy others' works, why should anyone buy mine?

Finding kindred spirits and models

Todd Davis (2005) talked about how his own becoming as a writer benefited from finding contemporary poets with whom he could feel a sense of kinship:

> The poetry my father had recited was Keats, Wordsworth, Longfellow, and the poetry I was studying as an English major – this isn't the language that would trip off my tongue. It wasn't until I came across Galway Kinnell, Mary Oliver, Wendell Berry that I thought, 'This is stuff I know as a son of a veterinarian.' I tell students, 'You'll try on a lot of voices before you get there, but eventually your voice will join with those of your mentors, your books.'

Thus some teachers assign students to find writers with whom they can identify. Richard Newhauser's (1999) 'Poetry Writing' syllabus calls for an oral presentation:

> A brief report (5–10 minutes) on one or two of your favorite poems in a book of poetry by one of your favorite poets in which you describe precisely what you find well-done in that person's book of poetry and in the poem(s) you are reporting on, and how your own work has been influenced by that poet or poem(s).

Students make copies of the poems available to the class.

Bill Davis (2004) has students turn in a poem of their own each week and at the same time turn in a poem by someone else. 'You might get Shakespeare, or you might get their friend.' They don't usually talk about the added poem 'unless one seems immediately relevant'. He said that he has been 'intrigued by the poems from someone else that they bring in'. Michael VanderWeele (2004) said he asks students to create anthologies for particular audiences and purposes – for example, better poems for the church bulletin than the ones that often appear there. One of his students created an anthology for homeschooling parents who were skeptical about modern poetry. Education majors created one for a class they imagined teaching. He said that thinking about audience is important. 'These are poems that have been helpful to me' is part of the idea. Students write an introduction to the anthology and perhaps a brief one to each poem, and sometimes they add one or two of their own poems. He said that these anthologies, when shared, also became 'important for building community'.

Memorizing

People who care about poems learn some 'by heart'. Paul Valery (1958: 72) writes that while the words of prose, once they have done their work, can be forgotten, the poem 'is expressly designed to be born again from its ashes and to become endlessly what it has just been'. Poetry 'stimulates us to reconstruct it identically'. *Assigning* learners to memorize poems has fallen out of favor. Yet Valery's observation suggests that memorizing could help students identify the qualities of a poem that help them to hold it in mind – and feel more like a poet because they possess poems. I did find one syllabus – for Jane Kuenz's (2004) 'Creative Writing' course – that called for memorization: 'Each student will memorize and recite to the class one of the poems from either of the class texts.' And Hunley (2007: 106) acknowledges, 'There are always a few groans at the start of every semester when my students learn that they will be expected to memorize forty or eighty lines of published poetry in addition to memorizing works of their own before a semester-ending class reading.' I urge students not just to memorize but to 'weigh each word', to experience the rhythm, and to 'feel how the lines partly move within that rhythm, partly break out'.

For reciting, I suggest that they visualize the images and actions of the poem so that not only its rhythms but also these images and actions guide their reading, especially its pacing. After reciting, they respond to questions, including 'Which aspects of the form of the poem make it easier to memorize than an equal quantity of prose?' and 'What of your present awareness of the poem became available to you only as you memorized it?' We also discuss this in class to consider ways that form and technique are experienced by readers.

The final move is imitation: 'try writing under the spell of the writer', perhaps imitating the rhythm and structure of the poem.

Imitation

Imitation isn't what it used to be. R. M. Berry (1994) writes, 'Prior to the nineteenth century the most widespread European model of the poet's education tended to de-emphasize individual creativity and to foreground the deliberate imitation of other poets' (p. 60). He adds, 'For ancient and Renaissance poets, literary practice was grounded on the encounter with other voices. Learning to write about a subject, character, desire, conflict, pain meant struggling to hear and be heard in a language always already speaking about these things' (p. 63). Probably because of the Romantic emphasis on individual expression and originality, imitation has fallen out of favor. However, the recent turn toward language and the social seems to be rescuing imitation, at least among teachers of creative writing. In response to a survey question about how much emphasis they gave 'imitation of selected aspects of published writers style or approach', only 26% said they gave it little or no emphasis, so about three-quarters of teachers appear to assign or at least encourage the practice. So does at least one textbook – Nicholas Delbanco's (2004) *The Sincerest Form: Writing Fiction by Imitation*.

Bogen (1981: 8) suggests we begin by having students imitate the processes of particular writers, beginning with their ways of getting started. He writes that

> ... as in the imitation of published texts, the artificiality – in some cases the very oddity – of the processes they imitate has a liberating effect. The goal is not great writing but varied experience, and the rationale for this kind of imitation is that this is the way writers actually start working, as distinguished from what the textbooks say.

He would also have students imitate different writers' revision process such as that of Louise Glück, who 'makes no corrections on a draft sheet but instead continually types and retypes the poem on which she is working, without looking at the earlier versions'. A method of some other writers that Bogen suggests trying on is perfecting a paragraph or page at a time before going on to the next (p. 11).

Teachers typically have students imitate style or structure. Jill Baumgaertner (2004) said she does 'a lot of exercises in class. Imitate style. Imitate grammar. Take a poem, figure out what the grammatical elements are, and write using those structures'. To this list, Todd Davis (2004), in his syllabus for 'Introduction to Creative Writing', adds attention to a writer's structuring:

> Here's what will make you a better writer: Reading good writing by those who have been tested by publication, by critics, by the passage of time. By paying close attention to how the writer has actually *constructed* or *built* the good story or poem that you are reading – and then imitating that good writing. And, after doing this for a time – two years, three years, 10 years – you will begin to develop your own style, likely composed of a wide variety of ingredients from the many authors you have read and admired. Hopefully, there will be something else in your style as well, something intangible of your own, mixed into the batter and baked into the story or poem that rises on the page before you.

Jim Heynen (2004) told me he also begins imitation by having students describe the piece of fiction:

> My first step is, *describe* this story without judgment. I push that until we fill the chart with description. Describe language, plot. Characters. That provides a firm foundation for extracting meaningful lessons for myself. The next question is, If you are attracted to it, does this story resonate for you? If so, assume in some way that you are getting a mirror: now, what is the equivalent in your own life? If the story is about fear of failure, what is your equivalent? If this story is about the pathos of compulsiveness, what's the equivalent in your own life. And then the question is, do you dare to let this become fiction, which means you will have to hyperbolize things you know about yourself. The weakness in you as much as the strength will reach out to the reader.

Although imitation may appear to be a turn away from originality, writers actually tend to take more risks when imitating – risks with language, form, point of view, structure, subject matter. They use the model to enter territory they haven't known how to enter on their own. As Bogen (1981: 6) writes, 'Imitation forces the student outside himself, freeing him, in effect, from the responsibility of being sincere', freeing him or her to 'experiment with techniques he would not otherwise have encountered' which 'might later be incorporated into a new sense of his own style'. Richard Robbins (2004) explained, 'Imitation requires the student writer to get inside an aspect of the imitated writer's style, or to start from a similar spatial, temporal, or conceptual point. So it immediately gets the young writer engaged with technique or content he or she might not otherwise be inclined to work with.' Tom Kealey (2004) said he especially values imitation as a way for students to try out additional voices:

> Our own voice is often a compilation of the voices of our favorite stories or novels or storytellers. The assignment itself is based on what story we are reading for that particular class. I've found that these assignments encourage students to think about voice. I haven't seen this happen in many other classes. Voice is easy to identify when we see it on the page, but it's difficult to explain or articulate in the abstract in discussion. I've found that if we concentrate part of the semester on imitations, then the idea of voice arises in workshop and in the individual stories.

Robbins emphasized letting writers find their own connection with the work imitated:

> I rarely direct the students as to what element to imitate. I simply put powerful poems in front of them and see what element of the poem they feel connected enough with to make a point of imitation. A student presented with Plath's 'Daddy', for instance, might write about a parent/child relationship, while the person next to her writes about something entirely different in nursery-rhyme verse, while the person next to him writes about something entirely different while consciously trying to make shocking metaphorical comparisons. If you target the element to imitate too directly, you eliminate that part of the assignment that forces students to bring something out of themselves based on pre-verbal, intuitive connections with the poem

Publication and performance

If 'publishing' means to 'make public', then simply reading to others in the class is a kind of publication. Cynthia Kuhn's (2004) syllabus for 'The Art and Craft of Writing' directs students, 'In a brief presentation (5–7 minutes), introduce a selection of your finished collection. Begin with a short discussion of your writing goals and processes'. Some teachers who end the course with such a reading make it more public by encouraging students to invite friends.

Sam Abrams (2004) suggests that students perform poetry in connection with other arts. His 'Creative Writing/Poetry' syllabus says, 'You are encouraged to explore other modes of performing your poetry: singing, antiphonal reading with small or large groups (draft the class as chorus!) or combining various media: poetry, visuals, recorded soundtracks, dance ...'.

Another way to 'publish' in written form is to write poems or stories as gifts for friends and relatives. Elizabeth Swingrover (2004b) wrote that she suggests to her students, 'You can give out chapbooks of your beloved poems to your friends for Christmas presents'. Paul Brooke (2004: 20) assigns his students to construct a book 'fashioned from their own creative pieces written over the course of two semesters of creative writing'. Students hand in two copies and he keeps one to display to students the following year.

Ways to reach wider audiences include a class publication on the web and the college literary magazine. Some teachers also urge writers to start trying to publish beyond campus. For their final project, as a way to help her advanced students 'think beyond the creative writing classroom', Nicole Mazzarella (2004) has students 'choose a literary journal where they would like to send their work, and then we have a mailing party'. In preparation, students look at three or four literary journals and then write up a proposal. 'I have them address them and write a cover letter. If they want to mail it they can.' She said that the activity 'gets them to think of a literary world outside their college experience'. In addition, they 'talk about self-motivation and what will keep you writing when no one is asking you to'. In addition, the experience 'makes them aware of where the criteria are coming from' and helps them begin to think of how they will resolve revision questions beyond the classroom setting.

Finally, 'publish' also means to solicit and select the work of others and make it available in a publication. A good reason for having a student literary publication is to give the most capable students a role in selecting the work of others – including the authority to articulate and defend their own judgments of it – and a role in presenting finished work in pleasing visual form.

Literary occasions

Good words should be celebrated, sometimes with occasions that include good food.

Some occasions can be brief and incidental. Foods that link to pieces just studied can make that experience more concrete, and connect the life-giving pleasures of eating to the life-giving pleasures of reading. My class reads Claudia Rankine's (2008) 'The man. His bowl. His raspberries', a richly suggestive poem in which a woman reads the way a man picks raspberries for signs of the kind of lover he is. The next class, I serve raspberry muffins made with raspberries I've picked.

As simple and profound an event as the passing of a season might be marked with a celebration, and the genres that have traditionally helped to create a sense of occasion can be composed by members of the class. Toasts are one obvious genre for such occasions. Literary dinners can be a source of inspiration. The internet makes examples readily available. The Robert Burns Dinner may be the best known, probably because its performance includes a variety of roles and because Burns gave us a richly oral poetry that is relatively easy to memorize and fun to recite – and that authorizes bawdiness.

Students might also write tributes or elegies to important people in their lives and then devote a class session to reading them.

Constructive Reflection

In Chapter 3, I emphasized ways reflection-in-action helps the writer to compose and revise a work-in-progress. It does more than that. As Yancey (1998) observes, when students reflect, they 'talk about writing, necessarily bringing to that talk their own experiences, their own assumptions, their own discourses' (p. 56). They 'can assign causality, they can see multiple perspectives, they can invoke multiple contexts' (p. 19). When teachers ask students to theorize about their writing in this way, then teachers 'begin to treat their students as writers – and, in turn, students begin acting the part' (p. 184). Such reflection thus becomes 'a primary means of inventing oneself as a writer' (p. 56).

Once students learn how to reflect upon their works-in-progress, they willingly respond to an invitation to write about their self-in-progress. This what Yancey calls *constructive reflection*, writing which advances 'the process of developing a cumulative, multi-selved, multi-voiced identity, which takes place between and among composing events, and the associated texts' (p. 14). Along any journey, it's good to pause from time to time to consider what we thought we wanted at the start, where we seem to have arrived at present, and where we want to go from here.

Opening dialogue and goal-setting

One immediate benefit of having students write their own goals is to put these in dialogue with the teacher's goals and to encourage an active role in composing that writer and person they seek to become. Here are opening-day guidelines to my fiction class:

> As teacher-protagonist, I take much of my motivation from the goals, desires, interests, and contributions of those in the course with me. So tell me what I don't already know about you: where and how did you really learn to read fiction? What, for you, are the qualities of a good story? Who are your favorite authors? Do you know good oral storytellers? What kinds of stories have you written or told at various times? Do you have story drafts that you want to turn into fiction? What experience have you had responding to others' writing?

Then I ask them, 'Say what mainly you have come for, perhaps in this way: by the end, what do you want to know, see, feel, be able to do, hold in your hands?' At the same time, I ask students to respond to and raise questions about the syllabus. This ensures that they read it (without my needing to take much class time to go over it) and lets them know that I want active collaborators, not compliant students. It also lets them sense how I think about the course and about the work we do together.

Expressing goals directly benefits some students too. If they're not sure what they want, expressing desire may begin to form desire. For those who do know what they want, declaring it may strengthen their resolve. Listen to Erica's voice:

> When I come out of this class, I would like to have a new energy about writing ... renewed confidence for taking risks and being creative, instead of constantly fighting the fear of failure. I want to have pulled out some stories that are swimming somewhere inside my head, and to have faced them, and straightened the kinks out of them, and made them something that can reach others.

She realizes also 'that writing will probably always have a degree of difficulty (and writers probably always have a bit of fear!). Still, pushing myself and working alongside others with new insights and ideas will undoubtedly force me to grow'. I notice that opening reflections often suggest a plot structure: a protagonist, with a desire, confronting known and unknown obstacles, feels apprehensive but dares to imagine triumph.

Hearing each writer's particular story is valuable for me too. I can begin to imagine how to accompany him or her on the journey toward becoming that better and more confident writer that they imagine becoming. I usually write a short response, identifying with their goals, offering encouragement, sometimes mentioning aspects of the course they have reason to anticipate.

An alternative is to ask for two episodes of goal setting. In the first, students tell briefly what brought them to the class and present their initial fears and hopes; in the second, written a couple of weeks later when they know more about the course, they say more specifically what they hope to accomplish in it.

Mid-course pulse checks

Periodically a teacher should learn how the course is working and invite students to ask that question for themselves. One means is to distribute a 'pulse check' with questions such as these: How is the class going? How is your group working? What has been difficult about asking for response? What has been difficult about responding to others' writing? What have you accomplished so far as a writer? What has surprised you? What's still getting in your way and what are you doing to overcome it? Another option is asking students to add a note about any of these to a writer's memo.

Also worth trying periodically is Brookfield's (1995) 'critical incident questionnaire', discussed in his *Becoming a Critically Reflective Teacher*. It asks students to respond briefly and anonymously toward the end of class to questions like these about the current class or past week of classes: When were you most engaged? When did you feel most distant from what was happening? What did anyone do that was helpful? What did anyone do that was confusing? and What in class surprised you the most? To those questions, one or two more specific ones can be added.

Brookfield recommends that teachers summarize the responses back to the class. This may be the most valuable part of the process because it takes seriously students' experience of learning and that lets them know that other students experience the class differently and have different expectations. Further benefits he mentions are discovering 'smoldering resentments' early, 'before they built to volcanic proportions' (p. 118), and helping the teacher to 'judge when radical changes are needed or when all that's called for is some clarification of purpose' (p. 124). This process is also a reminder that a good course is something that a teacher and students make together.

The constructive reflection at mid-course or end of course

A constructive reflection is a story of learning. Students' interest in telling this story is evident from their tendency to tell it in a writer's memo that accompanies a portfolio. Gabe's memo for his final portfolio begins with constructive reflection:

> I am very excited to present to you my Final Portfolio.
>
> Here is something I discovered. As I was picking my favorite poems throughout the semester, I realized that the subject matter of all of them is very near to me. They are pretty intimate things at some points and very silly at others. This portfolio reflects me in many ways. It is serious at times and humorous at times. It is about family and fantasy.
>
> Another thing I want to share with you is that I am celebrating something. I talk in my journey journal about my dry spell and how I did not really like my poetry from after break. I was choosing the poems for this portfolio and I saw poems from first half that I remember loving. I read them again and saw how bad they are. I realized that though I was going through a dry spell, I was still growing. I was still improving as a poet. And that makes me excited and thankful.

His pleasure in the telling is evident – he even capitalizes 'Final Portfolio'.

As Gabe's reference to his 'journey journal' indicates, I ask students for a separate constructive reflection focused on how they were able to use the course to develop as a writer in relation to goals they declared early in the course. In the syllabus, I state the question this way: 'As reader and writer of short fiction, how are you *different* than before (how have you changed in how you see or what you care about? what have you learned or what can you do?) and what course-related materials and events contributed in what ways to that change?' I usually ask for about 800 words. Most could write more, but then they might lose focus on the central themes of their journey.

Because I'm expected to turn in grades at midterm, I ask students for their first journey journal at that time; then the one they write at the end of the course can be simpler. Often I just give students several questions and invite them to use them as subheads, as Jeannine does:

> **How my poems have improved**
>
> After reviewing both my earlier work and the poems in my final portfolio, I have become aware of a significant difference. Giving a title to most of my poetry early in the course was a struggle; you said in Friday's journal that perhaps that was due to lack of focus in the poem. I can agree with this, as I do see a great deal more focus in my later poems, and suddenly coming up with titles became fun!

I also tried too hard to sound like 'a poet' earlier in the course. I was so worried that I wasn't a good enough poet, so I used obscure language and ideas in order to sound more like one. I think my breaking-through poems were my object poem and my Billy Collins imitation because they allowed me, for the first time, to stop worrying if my poetry sounded right. I found my own voice in these, and I believe they were better poems because of it.

Finding ideas for poems
You said early on that you wanted us to become 'great observers', and I think I have become, at least, a better observer during the course. I listen to what people say and how they say it, and am now in the habit of writing down phrases here and there and then finding time to come back to them and try to develop them into a poem. I suppose that's where most of my ideas come from – the people and words and conversations around me.

Getting response from groups
When getting response from my small group, I generally like to leave it wide open. I find that if I specify too much what I'm wondering about, they will pick at that piece, perhaps saying what they think I want to hear, and not commenting on other parts of the poem which may have more importance. Leaving the discussion open allows me to see my poem in a different way, through someone else's interpretation, or it helps me to focus on a part that I'd largely been ignoring.

Poetic challenges that best suited me
The first half of the course was really frustrating to me because of the regular verse we were assigned to compose. I am not good at writing regular verse, nor do I enjoy it. However, I now see that it was necessary to introduce us to those forms early on, then set us free during the second half of the course to pick and choose which ones we'd like to write. If you hadn't forced me to write a sonnet, Carl, I never would have done it. I hated every second of it – but now am glad to have accomplished it, and amazingly, it found its way into my final portfolio.

One kind of regular form I did enjoy was haiku. I like these poems because they are intended to describe a particular *moment* in nature, or in the world. Either way, it is one single moment that the poem is focused on. Because I'm not good at focusing on one moment myself,

I liked when the haiku forced me to. Like haiku, I generally like to center my poems around a particular image, rather than idea.

How my skills and attitude have improved as a reader of poetry
I've realized that there is wonderful poetry out there, and that it's not all that obscure, obtuse crap that we read in Intro to Lit. I realized my own personal tastes in poetry, and I found poets I enjoy and am eager to read more of.

Asking myself who the speaker is and to whom the poem is addressed has helped me, as well as asking myself whether certain objects or events in the poem are literal or figurative.

I've also realized that writing poetry is not an impossible feat, and can be done successfully without being a puffed-up pseudo-intellectual.

Class participation
I believe my class participation has always been strong, and my attendance is regular.

Small group participation
I have been pleased how my role has changed in my small group. Actually, how all of our roles have changed. No longer were we afraid to tell each other what we really think about poems, our real suggestions for it, or our real questions about ambiguities in the poem. It took a while, but we were finally comfortable with each other and with our own poetry and critiquing skills that we were able to make real improvements in each other's writing.

Jeannine illustrates how a constructive reflection involves looking back, re-reading goals, re-reading drafts as well as responses to them, exploring how not just the writing but also the writer has changed, and what enabled those changes.

Having students write constructive reflections intensifies the *time* of the course. One of my students told me that when she first attended a college where many older students attended, she noticed that while students her own age seemed to dwell outside of time, the older students brought the perspective of life experience to the course and projected the experiences of the course into their own future plans. Having traditional-age college students write about the goals they bring to the course and the plans they project beyond the course helps the course seem less like one assignment after another and more like a plot that is carrying them forward, getting them somewhere. Bruner (1993: 40–1) observes that 'we may properly suspect that the shape of a life as experienced is as much dependent upon the narrative skills of the autobiographer as is the story he or she tells about it'. In that case, teachers have a stake in helping students learn to narrate an experience of learning.

Constructive reflection as a story for teachers

Driven by the expectation to assess student learning, many colleges are asking students, especially those in writing and the arts, to create e-portfolios in which they collect representative work and use it to tell a story about their growth, discoveries and accomplishments. When such a story is constructed within a course, it can be easily adapted for those who assess the course and even the writing program. For instance, Dianne Donnelly (2010: 10) calls for careful scrutiny of the workshop, but then asks how, given the variances within our pedagogy, something as diverse as the workshop can even be properly scrutinized – 'how might we determine what happens in the workshop and why?' Well, one way to get multiple stories about what happened and why in a given workshop is to ask students to write stories about their learning.

As writers and teachers, we say that a profound experience has not fully happened until a good story is told about it. Thus it surprises me that only a minority of creative writing teachers ask students to write the story about what happened to them in the course. My survey asked teachers to indicate the emphasis they give to having students 'write about the ways they have grown or changed as readers or writers during the course or some portion of it'. Response tended to the extremes, with 26% saying they give the practice 'much emphasis' but 24% not asking for it at all. This division suggests two strikingly different ways of thinking about a course as an event. In the usual way of thinking, the teacher is the protagonist, and the course is successful to the degree that this teacher-hero's ways of seeing and thinking and reading become compelling for members of the classroom community.

In the countering image, the teacher accompanies students as much as he or she leads them, all the while helping students to view themselves as protagonists of their own stories of becoming, going where they need to go, sometimes into matters that are deeply personal.

I do want something to happen in a course; I want students to be changed, but I don't want to coerce this change, partly because the result is likely to be a false consciousness. As Parker Palmer (2007: 31) writes, 'what we teach will never "take" unless it connects with the inward, living core of our students' lives, with our students' inward teachers'. A strong 'inward teacher' both accepts and resists the teaching and advice of others – learns to engage with authority and talk back to authority, learns to imitate a model and then push back from the model.

In sum, then, to teach students to write and to compose themselves as writers and artists is to cause to flourish the give and take, the push and pull, of dialogue, between persons and within persons, an endeavor that always involves negotiating the personal.

References

Abrams, S. (2004) Creative writing/poetry syllabus. Rochester Institute of Technology.
Acosta, L.A. (2005) North Park University. Email to the author. 23 February 2005.
Anderson, C.M. and MacCurdy, M.M. (eds) (1999) *Writing and Healing: Toward an Informed Practice*. Urbana, IL: NCTE.
Apol, L. (2004) Michigan State University. Personal interview. 3 October 2004.
Bakhtin, M. (1981)*The Dialogic Imagination*. M. Holquist (ed.).C. Emerson and M. Holquist (trans.). Austin, TX: University of Texas Press.
Barker, J. (2004a) Northwestern College. Email to the author. 2–4 July 2004.
Barker, J. (2004b) Northwestern College. Personal interview. 7 June 2004.
Barker, K. (2004) Northwestern College. Personal interview. 7 June 2004.
Barreca, R. (1997) Contraband appetites: Wit, rage, and romance in the classroom. In R. Barreca and D. Denenholz Morse (eds) *The Erotics of Instruction* (pp. 1–11). Hanover, NH: University Press of New England.
Barreca, R. and Denenholz Morse, D. (1997) Preface. In R. Barreca and D. Denenzholz Morse (eds)*The Erotics of Instruction* (pp. vii–xvii). Hanover, NH: University Press of New England.
Barthelme, D. (1982) The school. In D. Barthelme *Sixty Stories* (pp. 304–7). New York, NY: Penguin.
Baumgaertner, J. (2004) Wheaton College. Personal interview. 28 September 2004.
Berlin, M. (2004) Knox College. Email to the author. 24 July 2004.
Berman, J. (2001) *Risky Writing: Self-Disclosure and Self-transformation in the Classroom*. Amherst, MA: University of Massachusetts Press.
Bernstein, C. (2006) Experiments. On WWW at http://writing.upenn.edu/bernstein/experiments.html. Last accessed 29 April 2008.
Berry, R.M. (1994) Theory, creative writing, and the impertinence of history. In W. Bishop and H. Ostrom (eds) *Colors of a Different Horse* (pp. 57–76). Urbana, IL: NCTE.
Biddinger, M. (2004a) Introduction to writing poetry syllabus. University of Illinois at Chicago.
Biddinger, M. (2004b) University of Akron. Email to the author. 23 September 2004.
Bishop, W. (1990) *Released into Language: Options for Teaching Creative Writing*. Urbana, IL: NCTE.
Bishop, W. (1994a) Afterword – Colors of a different horse: On learning to like teaching creative writing. In W. Bishop and H. Ostrom (eds) *Colors of a Different Horse* (pp. 280–95).Urbana, IL: NCTE.
Bishop, W. (1994b) Crossing the lines: On creative composition and composing creative writing. In W. Bishop and H. Ostrom (eds) *Colors of a Different Horse* (pp.181–97). Urbana, IL: NCTE, 1994.

Bishop, W. (1997) *Teaching Lives: Essays and Stories*. Logan: Utah State University Press.
Bishop, W. (1999) Places to stand: The reflective writer-teacher-writer in composition. *College Composition and Communication* 51 (1), 9–31.
Bizzaro, P. (1993) *Responding to Student Poems: Applications of Critical Theory*. Urbana, IL: NCTE.
Bizzaro, P. (1994) Reading the creative writing course: The teacher's many selves. In W. Bishop & H. Ostrom (eds) *Colors of a Different Horse* (pp. 234–47).Urbana, IL: NCTE.
Bizzaro, P. (2001) Comment: Kostelanetz's rhetoric of isolation: Or, sometimes I feel lonely too. *College English* 64 (2), 237–42.
Bizzaro, P. (2004) Research and reflection in English studies: The special case of creative writing. *College English* 66 (3), 294–309.
Bizzaro, P. and McClanahan, M. (2007) Putting wings on the invisible: Voice, authorship, and the authentic self. In K. Ritter and S. Vanderslice (eds) *Can It Really Be Taught: Resisting Lore in Creative Writing Pedagogy* (pp. 77–90). Portsmouth, NH: Heinemann.
Black, L.J. (1998) *Between Talk and Teaching: Reconsidering the Writing Conference*. Logan, UT: Utah State University Press.
Bly, C. (2001) *Beyond the Writer's Workshop: New Ways to Write Creative Nonfiction*. New York, NY: Anchor.
Bogen, D. (1981) Beyond the workshop: Some alternatives for the undergraduate creative writing course. ERIC document 233 342 CS 207 548. On WWW at http://www.eric.ed.gov/PDFS/ED233342.pdf. Last accessed 15 February 2011.
Bogue, B. (2004a) Ball State University. Email to the author. 5 August 2004.
Bogue, B. (2004b) Ball State University. Personal interview. 1 October 2004.
Booth, W. (1988) *The Company We Keep: An Ethics of Fiction*. Berkeley, CA: University of California Press.
Boulter, A. (2004) Assessing the criteria: An argument for creative writing theory. *New Writing: The International Journal for the Practice and Theory of Creative Writing* 1 (2), 134–40.
Bracher, M. (1999) *The Writing Cure: Psychoanalysis, Composition, and the Aims of Education*. Carbondale, IL: Southern Illinois University Press.
Brooke, P. (2004) Travelling theory: Exploring the deep rainforest of the creative writing classroom. *New Writing: The International Journal for the Practice and Theory of Creative Writing* 1 (1), 15–22.
Brooke, R. (1987) Truth and resistance: Teaching as a form of analysis. *College English* 49 (6), 679–91)
Brooke, R. (1991) *Writing and Sense of Self: Identity Negotiation in Writing Workshops*. Urbana, IL: NCTE.
Brooke, R., Mirtz, R. and Evans, R. (1994) *Small Groups in Writing Workshops: Invitations to a Writer's Life*. Urbana, IL: NCTE.
Brookfield, S.D. (1995) *Becoming a Critically Reflective Teacher*. San Francisco, CA: Jossey Bass.
Bruner, J. (1993) The autobiographical process. In R. Folkenflik (ed.) *The Culture of Autobiography: Constructions of Self-Representation* (pp. 38–56). Stanford, CA: Stanford University Press.
Burke, K. (1966) *Language as Symbolic Action: Essays on Life, Literature, and Method*. Berkeley, CA: University of California Press.

Burroway, J. (2003) *Writing Fiction: A Guide to Narrative Craft*. New York, NY: Longman.
Catrone, L.E. (1984) *Writing, Producing, and Selling Your Play*. Englewood Cliffs, NJ: Prentice-Hall.
Cockroft, M. (2005) Waynesburg University. Personal interview. 29 November 2005.
Coggins, M. (2011) The singer affair: How a crush on a teacher landed me a role in her novel. *The Huffington Post*, 12 March 2010. On WWW at http://www.huffingtonpost.com/mark-coggins/the-singer-affair-how-a-c_b_495291.html. Last accessed 11 February 2011.
Cook, H. (2004) Redeemer College, Ontario. Email to the author. 13 September 2004.
Coyne, S. (2002/2008) Morningside College. Emails to the author. 3 January 2002 and 28 May 2008.
Davis, A.B. (2004) Truman State University. Email to the author. 14 September 2004.
Davis, T. (2004) English 50: Introduction to creative writing. Pennsylvania State University, Altoona.
Davis, T. (2005) Pennsylvania State University, Altoona. Personal interview. 29 November 2005.
Davis, W. (2004) Baylor University. Personal interview. 25 March 2004.
Dawson, P. (2005) *Creative Writing and the New Humanities*. New York, NY: Routledge.
Day, C. (2005) Creative writing syllabus. The College of New Jersey. On WWW at http://dayc.faculty.tcnj.edu/creative_writing_course.htm. Last accessed 16 April 2007.
Delbanco, N. (2004) *The Sincerest Form: Writing Fiction by Imitation*. Boston, MA: McGraw Hill.
Desjardins, S. (2004) Creative writing syllabus. Maricopa Community College. Online, no longer available.
Donnelly, D. (2010) Introduction: If it ain't broke, don't fix it; or change is inevitable except from a vending machine. In D. Donnelly (ed.) *Does The Writing Workshop Still Work?* (pp. 1–27). Bristol: Multilingual Matters.
Dunphy, M. (2004) Oakland University. Email to the author. 31 July 2004.
Eagleton, T. (1983) *Literary Theory: An Introduction*. Minneapolis, MN: University of Minnesota Press.
Elbow, P. (1973) *Writing Without Teachers*. New York, NY: Oxford University Press.
Elbow, P. (1986) *Embracing Contraries: Explorations in Learning and Teaching*. New York, NY: Oxford University Press.
Elbow, P. (1990) *What is English?* New York, New York, NY: Modern Language Association.
Elbow, P. (1991) Reflections on academic discourse: How it relates to freshmen and colleagues. *College English* 53 (2), 135–55.
Elbow, P. (1993) Ranking, evaluating, and liking: Sorting out three forms of judgment. *College English* 55 (2). 187–206.
Elbow, P. and Belanoff, P. (2000) *A Community of Writers: A Workshop Course in Writing*. Boston, MA: McGraw Hill.
Elliot, G. (1994) Pedagogy in penumbra: Teaching, writing, and feminism in the fiction workshop. In W. Bishop and H. Ostrom (eds) *Colors of a Different Horse* (pp. 100–26). Urbana, IL: NCTE.

Emile, P. (2004a) University of Nebraska. Email to the author. 17 July 2004.
Emile, P. (2004b) University of Nebraska. Personal interview. 16 July 2004.
Farber, J. (1990) Learning how to teach: A progress report. *College English* 52, 135–41.
Farquhar, J. (2004) Purdue University. Email to author. 9 September 04.
Felman, S. (1989) Psychoanalysis and education: Teaching terminable and interminable. In R.C. Davis and R. Schleifer (eds) *Contemporary Literary Criticism: Literary and Cultural Studies* (pp. 596–614). New York, NY: Longman.
Franco, G. (2004) Knox College. Personal interview. 15 September 2004.
Frase, B. and McAsey, M. (1998) Peer visits: How to start productive conversations on teaching. *National Teaching and Learning Forum* 7 (3). On WWW at http://www.ntlf.com/html/pi/9803/peer_1.htm. Last accessed 8 April 2006.
Frizell, M. (2004) Southwest Minnesota State University. Email to the author. 25 August 2004.
Futrell, R. (2004) Cedarville University. Email to the author. 1 October 2004.
Geisel, S. (2004) Wright State University. Email to the author. 23 September 2004.
Gere, A.R. (1987) *Writing Groups: History, Theory, and Implications*. Carbondale, IL: Southern Illinois University Press.
Gere A.R. (1999) Whose voice is it anyway? In C.M. Anderson and M.M. MacCurdy (eds) Writing and Healing: Toward an Informed Practice (pp. 25–33). Urbana, IL: NCTE.
Girard, R. (1972) *Violence and the Sacred*. Patrick Gregory (trans.). Baltimore, MD: John Hopkins University Press.
Girard, R. (1978) *Things Hidden Since the Foundation of the World*. Michael Metteerand Stephan Bann (trans.) Stanford, CA: Stanford University Press.
Glavin, J. (1997) The intimacies of instruction. In R. Barreca and D. Denenholz Morse (eds) *The Erotics of Instruction* (pp. 12–27). Hanover, NH: University Press of New England.
Grimm M. (2004) Case Western Reserve University. Email to the author. 24 October 2004.
Gross, P. (2010) Small worlds: What works in workshops if and when they do? In D. Donnelly (ed.) *Does the Writing Workshop Still Work?* (pp. 52–62). Bristol: Multilingual Matters.
Guenette, M. (2004) Madison Technical College. Email to the author. 26 August 2004.
Guenette, M. (2007) Engl 266–30022 Writing fiction and poetry syllabus. Madison Technical College.
Haake, K. (1994) Teaching creative writing if the shoe fits. In W. Bishop and H. Ostrom (eds) *Colors of a Different Horse* (pp. 77–99).Urbana, IL: NCTE.
Haake, K. (2000) *What Our Speech Disrupts: Feminism and Creative Writing Studies.* Urbana, IL: NCTE.
Hagstrom, A. (2004) Beyond tolerance: The Biblical notion of hospitality as the model of a Christian university. *Christianity and the Soul of the University*. Conference. Baylor University, Texas, 25–27 March.
Hall, A.C. (2004) Ohio Dominican University. Email to the author. 23 September 2004.
Hall, R. (2005) The pregnant muse: Assumptions, authority, and accessibility. In A. Leahy (ed.) *Power and Identity in the Creative Writing Classroom: The Authority Project* (pp. 87–97). Clevedon: Multilingual Matters.

Heaney, S. (1996) Lecture at the Guthrie Theater, Minneapolis, MN. 19 September.
Hedeen, P. (2002) Wartburg College. Email to the author. 5 January 2002.
Hey, P. (2004) Briar Cliff University. Personal interview. 12 July 2004.
Heynen, J. (2004) St Olaf College. Personal interview. 2 April 2004.
Heynen, J. (2005) St Olaf College. Email to the author. 29 November 2005.
Hicks, P. (2004a) Augustana College, Sioux Falls. Email to the author. 7 September 2004.
Hicks, P. (2004b) Augustana College, Sioux Falls. Personal interview. 25 August 2004
Holbrook, C. (2004a) Hamline University. Email to the author. 11 and 20 August 2004.
Holbrook, C. (2004b/2005) Hamline University. Personal interview. 23 June 2004 and 21 July 2005.
Holquist, M. (1991) *Dialogism: Bakhtin and His World*. New York, NY: Routledge.
Horstman, J. (2005) Bethel University. Personal interview. 29 November 2005.
Hugo, R. (1979) *The Triggering Town: Lectures and Essays on Poetry and Writing*. New York, NY: WW Norton and Co.
Hunley, T.C. (2007) *Teaching Poetry Writing: A Five-Canon Approach*. Clevedon: Multilingual Matters.
Huot, B. (2002) Toward a new discourse of assessment for the college writing classroom. *College English* 65 (2), 163–180.
Indiana University Creative Writing Program (2006). Admissions. On WWW at http://iub.edu/~mfawrite/admissions/. Last accessed 19 June 2011.
Jarrett, M. (2004) Pennsylvania State University, York. Email to the author. 29 August 2004.
Kealey, T. (2004) Stanford University. Email to the author. 13 September 2004.
Keats, J. (1899) *The Complete Poetical Works and Letters of John Keats*. New York, NY: Houghton, Mifflin.
Konkle, L. (2004) The College of New Jersey. Email to the author. 5 August 2004.
Kroll, J. (2004) The resurrected author: Creative writers in 21st-century higher education. *New Writing: The International Journal for the Practice & Theory of Creative Writing* 1 (2), 89–102.
Kuenz, J. (2004) Creative writing syllabus. University of Southern Maine.
Kuhl, N.(2005) Personal therapeutic writing vs. literary writing. In A. Leahy (ed.) *Power and Identity in the Creative Writing Classroom: The Authority Project* (pp. 3–12). Clevedon: Multilingual Matters.
Kuhn, C. (2004) The art and craft of writing syllabus. Metropolitan State College of Denver.
Laaveg J. (2004/2005) Mt Pleasant Community School, Iowa. Email to the author. 9 September 2004 and 29 January 2005.
Leahy, A. (2004) Chapman University. Personal interview. 29 September 2004.
Leahy, A. (ed.) (2005) *Power and Identity in the Creative Writing Classroom: The Authority Project*. Clevedon: Multilingual Matters.
Leahy, A. (2010) Teaching as a creative act: Why the workshop works in creative writing. In D. Donnelly (ed.) *Does The Writing Workshop Still Work?* (pp. 63–77). Bristol: Multilingual Matters.
Lerman, L. (2003) Toward a process for critical response. *Community Arts Network*. On WWW at http://www.communityarts.net/readingroom/archivefiles/2003/10/toward_a_proces.php. Last accessed 28 May 2007.

Lindner, V. (2004) The tale of two Bethanies: Trauma in the creative Writing class. *International Journal for the Practice and Theory of Creative Writing* 1(1), 6–14.
MacDiarmid, L. (2004) St Norbert College. Email to the author. 9 July 2004.
Maier, C. (2004) University of Illinois at Urbana-Champaign. Email to the author. 30 July 2004.
Malone, D. (2005) Union University. Email to the author. 4–5 January 2005.
Matthews, C. (2005) Washington and Lee University. Email to the author. 11 February 2005.
May, R. (1939) *The Art of Counseling*. New York, NY: Abingdon Press.
Mayers, T. (2005) *(Re)writing Craft: Composition, Creative Writing, and the Future of English Studies*. Pittsburgh, PA: University of Pittsburgh Press.
Mazzarella, N. (2004) Wheaton College. Personal interview. 29 September 2004.
McCann, A. (2004/2005) Northwestern College, St Paul. Personal interview and conversations. 2004–5.
Morson, G.S. and Emerson, C. (1990) *Mikhail Bakhtin: Creation of a Prosaics*. Stanford, CA: Stanford University Press.
Mortensen, L.A. (2004) Creative process and imaginative writing syllabus. Utah Valley University.
Mozina, A. (2004) Kalamazoo College. Personal interview. 6 October 2004.
Muench, S. (2004) Lewis University. Email to the author. 20 July 2004.
Murphy, A. (1989) Transference and resistance in the basic writing classroom: Problematics and practice. *College Composition and Communication* 40, 175–87.
Murray, D.M. (1985) *A Writer Teaches Writing*. Boston, MA: Houghton Mifflin.
Murray, D.M. (1989) Unlearning to Write. In J.M. Moxley (ed.) *Creative Writing in America* (pp. 103–113). Urbana, IL: NCTE.
Myers, D.G. (1996) *The Elephants Teach: Creative Writing Since 1880*. Englewood Cliffs, NJ: Prentice Hall.
Newhauser, R. (1999) English 3303 – Poetry writing. Trinity University, San Antonio, TX.
O'Brien, A.J. (2000) ENG 117: Introduction to creative writing: Fiction syllabus. Stanford University, Stanford, CA.
O'Connor, F. (1969) *Mystery and Manners*. New York, NY: Farrar, Straus & Giroux.
Oliver, M.(1994) *A Poetry Handbook*. San Diego, CA: Harcourt Brace.
Oliver, M. (1995) *Blue Pastures*. New York: Harcourt Brace.
O'Reilley, M.R. (1993) *The Peaceable Classroom*. Portsmouth, NH: Boynton/Cook.
O'Reilley, M.R. (1998) *Radical Presence: Teaching as Contemplative Practice*. Portsmouth, NH: Boynton/Cook.
Ostrom, H. (1994) Introduction: Of radishes and shadows, theory and pedagogy. In W. Bishop and H. Ostrom (eds) *Colors of a Different Horse* (pp. xi–xxiii). Urbana: NCTE.
Palmer, P. (2007) *The Courage to Teach: Exploring the Inner Landscape of a Teacher's Life*. San Francisco, CA: Jossey-Bass.
Payne, M. (2000) *Bodily Discourses: When Students Write About Abuse and Eating Disorders*. Portsmouth, NH: Boynton/Cook.
Percy, L. (2004) Email to the author. 21 September 2004.
Perry, G. (2007) Art & trauma: Danger and dynamics in the creative writing workshop. *Educational Insights* 11 (1). On WWW at http://www.ccfi.educ.ubc.ca/publication/insights/v11n01/articles/perry.html. Last accessed 22 February 2001.

Perry, G. (2010) Potentially dangerous: Vulnerabilities and risks in the writing workshop. In D. Donnelly (ed.) *Does the Writing Workshop Still Work?* (pp. 117–129). Bristol: Multilingual Matters.
Peterson, K. (2004) Bethel College. Email to the author. 29 September 2004.
Petty, A. (2005). Who's the teacher?: From student to mentor. In A. Leahy (ed.) *Power and Identity in the Creative Writing Classroom: The Authority Project* (pp. 77–86). Clevedon: Multilingual Matters.
Pfefferle, W.T. (2004) Georgetown College. Email to the author. 20 August 2004.
Pfefferle, W.T. (2006) Poetry syllabus #2. Georgetown College. On WWW at http://wtp62.com/syllab5.htm. Last accessed 11 April 2007.
Phelps, L.W. (1989) Images of student writing: The deep structure of teacher response. In C.M. Anson (ed.) *Writing and Response: Theory, Practice, and Research* (pp. 37–67). Urbana, IL: NCTE.
Piirto, J. (2002) *'My Teeming Brain': Understanding Creative Writers*. Cresskill, NJ: Hampton.
Pipher, M. (2003) *Letters To a Young Therapist*. New York, NY: Basic Books.
Plath, J. (2004a) Illinois Wesleyan University. Email to the author. 23–26 July 2004.
Plath, J. (2004b) Illinois Wesleyan University. Personal interview. 16 September 2004.
Platt, D. (2004) Purdue University. Email to the author. 21 September 2004.
Rankine, C. (2008) The man. His bowl. His raspberries. In M. Boisseau, R. Wallace and R. Mann *Writing Poems* (p. 255). New York, NY: Pearson/Longman.
Rate My Professors (2011). On WWW at http://www.ratemyprofessors.com/.
Ratzlaff, K. (2004) Central College. Email to the author. 26 August 2004.
Reddy, S. (2004) University of Chicago. Email to the author. 27 July 2004.
Ridl, J. (2004) Hope College. Personal interview. 7 October 2004.
Ridl, J. (2008) Degrading the grade. On WWW at *Ridl.com* http://ridl.wordpress.com/2008/02/19/degrading-the-grade/. Last accessed 27 April 2008.
Rienstra, D. (2005) Calvin College. Email to the author. 6 January 2005.
Rilke, R.M. (2000) *Letters to a Young Poet* &ûe Possibility of Being. New York: MJF Books.
Ritchie, J. and Ronald, K. (1998) Riding long coattails, subverting tradition: The tricky business of feminists teaching rhetoric(s). In S. C. Jarratt and L. Worsham (eds) *Feminism and Composition Studies: In Other Words* (pp. 217–38). New York, NY: Modern Language Association.
Ritter, K. (2001) Professional Writers/writing professionals: Revamping teacher training in creative writing PhD programs. *College English* 64 (2), 205–227.
Ritter, K. and Vanderslice, S. (2006) *Can It Really Be Taught? Resisting Lore in Creative Writing Pedagogy*. Portsmouth, NH: Boynton/Cook.
Rivard, T.J. (2004) Indiana University East. Email to the author. 10 September 2004.
Robbins, R. (2004) Minnesota State University, Mankato. Email to the author. 14 September 2004.
Roberson, M. (2004) Central Michigan University. Email to the author. 26 August 2004.
Sajé, N. (2004a) The politics of literary evaluation. *The Writer's Chronicle* 36(6), 24–32.
Sajé, N. (2004b) Westminster College. Personal interview. 11 September 2004.
Sajé, N. (2005) Westminster College. Email to the author. 22 January 2005.

Scholes, R. (1985) *Textual Power: Literary Theory and the Teaching of English*. New Haven, CT: Yale University Press.
Scott, A. (2004) Ball State University. Email to the author. 18 August 2004.
Seitz, J.E. (1999) *Motives for Metaphor: Literacy, Curriculum Reform, and the Teaching of English*. Pittsburgh: University of Pittsburgh Press.
Shelnutt, E. (1989) Notes from a cell: Creative writing programs in isolation. In J.M. Moxley (ed.) *Creative Writing in America* (pp. 3–24). Urbana, IL: NCTE.
Skorczewski, D.M. (2005) *Teaching One Moment at a Time: Disruption and Repair in the Classroom*. Amherst, MA: University of Massachusetts Press.
Slattery, E. (2004) Indiana University East. Email to the author. 10 August 2004.
Sofer, A. (2002) Intro to creative writing syllabus. Online, no longer available.
Sommers, J. (1989) The writer's memo: Collaboration, response, and development. In Chris Anson (ed.) *Writing and Response: Theory, Practice, and Research* (pp. 174–186). Urbana, Ill: NCTE.
Sommers, N. (2006) Across the drafts. *College Composition and Communication* 58 (2), 248–57.
Spahr, J. (2004) Mills College. Email to the author. 9 September 2004.
Spear, K. (1988) *Sharing Writing: Peer Response Groups in English Classes*. Portsmouth, NH: Boynton/Cook.
Stafford, W. (1978) *Writing the Australian Crawl: Views on the Writer's Vocation*. Ann Arbor, MI: University of Michigan Press.
Stafford, W. (1986) *You Must Revise Your Life*. Ann Arbor, MI: University of Michigan Press.
Starkey, D. (2010) The creative writing workshop in the two-year college: Who cares? In D. Donnelly (ed.) *Does The Writing Workshop Still Work?* (pp. 148–59). Bristol: Multilingual Matters.
Swander, M. (2004) Iowa State University. Personal interview. 27 September 2004.
Swander, M. (2005) Duck, duck, turkey: Using encouragement to structure workshop assignments. In A. Leahy (ed.) *Power and Identity in the Creative Writing Classroom: The Authority Project* (pp. 167–79). Clevedon: Multilingual Matters.
Swingrover, E. (2004a) English 205 syllabus, spring. University of Nevada, Reno. Online, no longer available.
Swingrover, E. (2004b) University of Nevada, Reno. Email to the author. 10 August 2004.
Tammaro, T. (2004) Minnesota State University, Moorhead. Email to the author. 26 August 2004.
Tobin, L. (1991) Reading students, reading ourselves: Revising the teacher's role in the writing class. *College English* 53 (3), 333–48.
Tobin, L. (1993) *Writing Relationships: What Really Happens in the Composition Class*. Portsmouth, NH: Boynton/Cook Heinemann.
Tobin, L. (2004) *Reading Student Writing: Confessions, Meditations, and Rants*. Portsmouth, NH: Heinemann.
Townsend, A. (2005) Denison University. Email to the author. 17 January 2005.
Trapp, J. (2005) Waynesburg University. Personal interview. 20 September 2005.
Valery, P. (1958) *The Art of Poetry*. D. Folliot (trans.). New York, NY: Pantheon.
Vandenberg, P. (2004) Integrated writing programmes in American universities: Whither creative writing? *International Journal for the Practice and Theory of Creative Writing* 1 (1), 6–13.

Vandermeulen, C. (2005) The double bind and stumbling blocks: A case study as an argument for authority-conscious pedagogy. In A. Leahy (ed.) *Power and Identity in the Creative Writing Classroom: The Authority Project* (pp. 49–62). Clevedon: Multilingual Matters.

VanderMey, R. (2004) Westmont College. Email to the author. 13 July 2004.

Vanderslice, S. (2008) Sleeping with Proust vs. tinkering under the bonnet: The origins and consequences of the American and British approaches to creative writing in higher education. In G. Harper and J. Kroll (eds) *Creative Writing Studies: Practice, Research and Pedagogy* (pp. 66–74). Clevedon: Multilingual Matters.

VanderWeele, M. (2004) Trinity Christian College. Personal interview. 27 March 2004.

Vivian, R. (2004) Alma College. Email to the author. 9 July 2004.

Wachala, C. (2000) Syllabus for introduction to creative writing – Summer. Calumet College of St Joseph. Online, no longer available.

Wake, A.F. (2004) Elmhurst College. Personal interview. 9 September 2004.

Wandor, M. (2008) *The Author is Not Dead, Merely Somewhere Else*. London: Palgrave.

Webb, J. (2003) Depression and creative writing students. *Text7* (1). On WWW at http://www.textjournal.com.au/april03/webb.htm. Last accessed 13 February 2011.

Welch, N. (1997) *Getting Restless: Rethinking Revision in Writing Instruction*. Portsmouth, NH: Boynton-Cook.

Westbrook, S. (2004) Just do it: Creative writing exercises and the ideology of American handbooks. *New Writing: The International Journal for the Practice & Theory of Creative Writing* 1 (2), 141–48.

Wiley C. (2004) Introduction to creative writing. University of Colorado Denver.

Wiley, C. (2005) University of Colorado, Denver. Email to the author. 7 January 2005.

Williams, B.T. (2004) Syllabus for creative nonfiction. University of Louisville.

Williams, T. (2004) Bowling Green State University. Email to the author. 24 August 2004.

Willis, P. (2004) Westmont College. Email to the author. 4 and 10 October 2004.

Wilson, E.K. (2004) University of Colorado, Denver. Personal interview. 18 September 2004.

Wylam, J. (2004) Bowling Green State University. Email to the author. 19 August 2004.

Yagoda, B. (2003) What shall we call the professor? *The Swarthmore College Bulletin*. September. Online, no longer available.

Yancey, K. (1998) *Reflection in the Writing Classroom*. Logan, UT: Utah State University Press.

Note: Web addresses listed in references were active as of March 2011.

For Product Safety Concerns and Information please contact our EU Authorised Representative:

Easy Access System Europe

Mustamäe tee 50

10621 Tallinn

Estonia

gpsr.requests@easproject.com